Kicking Off the Bootstraps   Environment, Development,

and Community Power in Puerto Rico

Society, Environment, and Place

Series Editors: Andrew Kirby and Janice Monk

Kicking Off the Bootstraps

Environment, Development, and Community Power
in Puerto Rico

Déborah Berman Santana

The University of Arizona Press   Tucson

The University of Arizona Press
© 1996 Arizona Board of Regents

∞ This book is printed on acid-free, archival-quality paper.
Manufactured in the United States of America

04 03 02 01 00   6 5 4 3 2

Library of Congress Cataloging-in-Publication Data
Berman Santana, Déborah, 1952–
Kicking off the bootstraps : environment, development, and
community power in Puerto Rico / Déborah Berman Santana.
p. cm. — (Society, environment, and place series)
Includes bibliographical references (p.   ) and index.
ISBN 0-8165-1590-5 (cloth : acid-free paper)
ISBN 0-8165-1591-3 (pbk. : acid-free paper)
1. Economic development—Environmental aspects —Puerto Rico—
Salinas. 2. Environmental degradation—Puerto Rico—Salinas.
3. Community organization—Puerto Rico—Salinas. I. Title.
II. Series.
HC154.5.Z7S347   1996
338.97295—dc20 96-10096
CIP

British Library Cataloguing-in-Publication Data
A catalogue record for this book is available from the British Library.

Contents

List of Illustrations

Figures

Maps

Table

Acknowledgments

As is true with most books, so many people helped me in so many different ways that it would be impossible to list them all without inadvertently omitting someone. I write here to acknowledge my sincere appreciation and gratitude to all.

First, I wish to thank the editors and staff at the University of Arizona Press for their encouragement, support, expert revisions, and general helpfulness throughout this long process. I also am grateful for the Ciriacy-Wantrup Postdoctoral Fellowship in Natural Resources (University of California, Berkeley) and the Faculty Research Award Program (State University of New York, Albany); both provided research and financial assistance that enabled me to write this book. I greatly appreciate the time and effort that several friends and colleagues spent critiquing my initial writings and offering suggestions for improvement; in particular, I thank Laura Pulido, Hal Barton, Diane Rocheleau, and Beth Dickinson.

So many people helped me in Puerto Rico that any specific thank-you list will almost certainly be incomplete. However, I owe my deepest debt of gratitude to the people of Salinas. Their generosity of spirit and willingness to share their stories and concerns with me not only made this study possible, but also filled me with love and appreciation for their beautiful home. I hope that this book may prove useful to them in some way. I especially wish to thank Tata Santiago for taking the time to review an earlier draft; her specific criticisms and suggestions are reflected in the finished product.

Much of the credit for this study goes to my collaborators, critics, supporters, and friends. Any blame for errors, of course, rests with me alone.

List of Abbreviations

ADT	Autoridad de Derecho al Trabajo (Right to Work Authority)
AEE	Autoridad de Energía Eléctrica (Electric Energy Authority)
AES	Applied Energy Service
AFofL	American Federation of Labor
ARPE	Autoridad de Reglamentos y Permisos(Regulations and Permit Authority)
ATP	Asociación de Trabajadores Puertorriqueños (Puerto Rico Workers' Association)
BFI	Browning Ferris Industry
CCPP	Comité Comunal Playa y Playita (La Playa/Playita Communal Committee)
CGT	Confederación General de Trabajadores (General Confederation of Workers)
CIO	Congress of Industrial Organizations
COINTELPRO	Counterintelligence and propaganda
CRUV	Corporación para Renovación Urbana y Vivienda (Corporation for Urban Renewal and Housing)
ECLA	United Nations Economic Commission on Latin America
EIS	Environmental Impact Statement
EQB	Environmental Quality Board
FEPI	Federación Estudiantil Pro-Independencia (Pro-Independence Student Federation)
FLT	Federación Libre de Trabajadores (Free Federation of Labor)
FUPI	Frente Universitaria Pro-Independencia (University Pro-Independence Front)
GDP	Gross Domestic Product
GNP	Gross National Product
JTPA	Job Training Partnership Act
MAREA	Movimiento al Rescate Ecológico Ambiental (Movement for Environmental and Ecological Defense)

MPI	Movimiento Pro-Independentista (Pro-Independence Movement)
NOAA	U.S. National Oceanic and Atmospheric Administration
OSHA	Federal Occupational Safety and Health Act
PCP	Partido Comunista Puertorriqeño (Puerto Rican Communist Party)
PIP	Partido Independentista Puertorriqueño (Puerto Rico Independence Party)
PNP	Partido Nuevo Progresista (New Progressive Party)
PPD	Partido Popular Democrático (Popular Democratic Party, or *populares*)
PRIDCO	Puerto Rico Industrial Development Corporation
PSP	Partido Socialista Puertorriqueño (Puerto Rican Socialist Party)
PT	Propriedad Trabajadores (Worker-owned enterprise)
PUEDES	Pueblo Unido en Desarollo de Salinas (People United in Salinas's Development)
RICO	Racketeer-Influenced Corrupt Organizations
SARA	Superfund Amendments and Reauthorization Act
SCT	Servicios Científicos y Técnicos (Scientific and Technical Services)
SOUS	Sindicato de Obreros Unidos del Sur (United Southern Workers Syndicate)
SURCCO	Sur Contra la Contaminación (South Against Contamination)
UITA	Union Independiente Trabajadores de Aeropuertos(Independent Airport Workers' Union)
UNEP	United Nations Environmental Program
USAID	United States Agency for International Development
UTIER	Union de Trabajadores Independiente de Electricídad y Riego (Independent electrical and water workers' union)

Kicking Off the Bootstraps   Environment, Development,

and Community Power in Puerto Rico

Introduction   Why Salinas? Why This Book?

A Personal Account

My first visit to Salinas took place in October 1990, while accompanying an environmental educator on a speaking trip. He had been invited to lecture to junior high school students on the dangers of hazardous waste dumping and incineration, as well as to educate them about recycling. His visit was part of a local campaign to unite Salinas against the proposed siting there of a regional toxic waste landfill. Driving south from San Juan on a sunny, hot morning, we ascended and crossed the island divide between the humid north and more arid south in less than an hour. As we began our descent we could see the vegetation change to less vividly green, more drought tolerant plants. We rounded one bend and suddenly the calm Caribbean Sea spread out before us, sparkling like a jewel. To the east, only smoke pouring from an industrial complex along the coast marred the perfect blue of the sky. We soon left the highway and the rocky, mostly brown hills behind for the coastal plain. Passing the entrance to an army base located in the hills, as well as a nearly dry river, we then entered the *pueblo* of Salinas, a compact, typically Puerto Rican town made up of one- and two-story, mostly older concrete or wooden buildings, many painted in pastel colors, and clustered around a tree-shaded plaza.

We arrived at the school and were greeted by teachers and two "thirty-something" men from the local community newspaper. They took us to the first class, where the students were very interactive, asking questions, laughing, and otherwise reacting to the information presented. Everyone in the room seemed to know about and oppose the proposed landfill. The students also had very definite ideas about action; to the speaker's question of what they could do to stop the landfill, several called out, "Strike!" The students clearly enjoyed this break from their normal routine. At the same time they were curious about the stranger who was engaging them in an entertaining matter about serious and potentially frightening issues. At one point a girl leaned over and whispered to me, "Is he a politician?" I asked her in turn if he sounded like a politician to her, to which she replied, "Yes!"

At the end of class the mayor of Salinas and one of the municipal assembly members took my friend and me to lunch at a large seaside restaurant. Our table was one of many on an expansive porch overlooking Rincón Bay, not far from a pier where dozens of pleasure boats were docked. At the time I thought that the delicious fresh fish we ate had been locally caught. (Later I learned that only the smaller restaurants regularly used the local catch; the bigger establishments, which were often not locally owned, bought their fish elsewhere.) I noted the strong show of unity against the regional landfill displayed by the two politicians despite their belonging to rival parties. The assembly member explained that this particular restaurant was located close to the neighborhood where she had grown up, a poor *barrio* of fishermen and ex-sugarcane workers like her father. I was impressed with the beauty of the bay and said as much, whereupon both politicians expounded on Salinas's barely tapped potential for the fishing and tourist industries.

After lunch the assembly member brought us to the local newspaper, housed in a modest wooden building not far from the plaza; there I again saw the two men whom we had met at the school, along with several other people. Through informal conversation I learned that these were some of the local community activists who were responsible for organizing opposition to the landfill. They were Salinas natives who had dedicated themselves to looking for alternatives to Salinas's problems of poverty, unemployment, and environmental degradation. Their newspaper, put together on a Macintosh Plus computer, contained local news, stories, poetry, and other features. It was also full of information about the dangers of regional landfills, as well as the political intrigue involved in its proposed siting in Salinas. The assembly member was treated with great camaraderie by the others, even though she did not share the same ideological background. The activists spoke of their successful campaign some ten years earlier against construction of a Monsanto Corporation herbicides plant, not far from where I had eaten lunch; ironically, I was familiar with the story, because a college friend of mine had mentioned it in her dissertation about the politics of environmental regulation. I further learned that these activists and I had friends in common among the Puerto Rican community in New York: people with many connections among leftist, feminist, and progressive circles around the island. We left Salinas late that afternoon and began the ascent to the mountains and towards San Juan. But the visit sparked my interest in Salinas and the people there, and I felt that I would return.

Why do academics become interested in particular projects? Part of it, of course, has to do with the learning experience of taking what you've studied from books and measuring it against real life. There is also the opportunity to visit places and meet people whom you might otherwise not have an opportunity to know. You hope that they will also benefit in some way from the interaction. For example, you might be able to make certain resources and information available to them, or at least lend a helping hand to whatever they need done. Perhaps your outsider's perspective might even trigger new ideas for resolving problems that are sometimes too close to be seen clearly by those most involved.

What academics often do not admit is that they also get involved in particular research projects for very personal reasons. In my own case this was clear: as a Puerto Rican reared mainly in New York City but from the same class background as most *salinenses*, I found I had much in common with many of the people whom I got to know. As often happens in "outside/insider" situations, the commonalities sometimes masked or confused the differences among us. Though at times painful, this experience later allowed some insights into the dynamics and difficulties of the work in Salinas. I also learned that my personal struggle to define, determine, accept, and empower myself—to decolonize myself, so to speak—was very common among Puerto Ricans, both on the island and in the United States. Nor is this struggle limited to Puerto Ricans; the need and desire to see and define ourselves, and to gain the power to determine our own lives, is at the heart of all struggles for self-determination, for independence (political or otherwise), and for a more ecologically and socially sustainable development alternative.

My doctoral dissertation provided a detailed description and analysis of how the Salinas initiatives came to be. Yet, I was more interested in understanding the lessons to be learned from the experience, particularly how "sustainable development" might practically be approached. This book is therefore a product of life experience, academic knowledge, and the desire to learn from both in order to help bring about positive and lasting change.

The book's organization is as follows: the first chapter recognizes the fact that while everyone seems to support "sustainable development," it is at present conceived of too vaguely to be of much practical use in actually guiding real strategies. I begin by breaking down the concept into its components of development and sustainability; I review the traditional understandings of them, explore their roots, and discuss some of the weaknesses that (among other things) make sustainable development so problematic. I also begin to address the problems of scale, the meaning of "community," and the idea of participation. Chapter 1 ends by introducing the Salinas story as appropriate and useful towards achieving a clearer idea of what sustainable development should mean.

After I describe and discuss the geographical setting in chapter 2, I provide in the next two chapters a historical background for the failures of "development" that have inspired present-day activism in search of locally based alternatives.[1] In chapter 3 I tell a story of economic, social and environmental exploitation, within the context of colonial domination and development strategies. Then, because people individually and collectively respond to forces acting on them, I recount, in chapter 4, a history of resistance that leads directly into present-day activism in Salinas.

Recognizing that, as one local put it, "resistance is not enough," I go, in chapter 5, beyond resistance to look at the present efforts to develop positive alternatives. Who are the activists? What are their motivations and influences? What kind of projects have they started, and how have they fared? How do they attempt to mobilize their community, and how successful have they been? How have they worked with government, non-profit organizations, and others? Have they formed coalitions with other like-minded groups throughout the island? In sum, what have they accomplished so far? Because the present activism is engaged in a long-term, uphill struggle, I discuss and analyze, in chapter 6, the obstacles the alternatives face within Salinas (and among the activists), as well as the most serious roadblocks posed by factors outside of Salinas. The chapter also details what would be necessary (if not sufficient) for successful implementation of the proposed alternative.

With the Salinas experience in mind I return in chapter 7 to "sustainable development," and attempt to rethink both development and sustainability in a clearer and less contradictory manner. I also consider and reject the idea that local sustainable development is not possible as I explain why I believe the only way out of our present destructive path is to figure out how to make alternatives like that of Salinas possible. After going beyond "participation" to talk about power, I consider the lessons of the Salinas experience in offering a working definition of sustainable development. Finally, I ask in this closing chapter where we go from here: what can we do? I address the issue of appropriate and necessary roles of various sectors and interests in achieving alternatives. For example, what are the roles of community leaders? Nongovernmental organizations and other outside activists? Local business? Local and central government? My feeling grows that there may be an appropriate (and in some cases necessary) role for each; however, one problem is that even when these roles are acknowledged they are not often well understood. As a woman whose roots have informed her chosen career, I also discuss the role that concerned academics might play in promoting real alternatives, for real people, in real places. My sincerest hope is that this book will contribute in some small way to this great endeavor.

1 Searching for Alternatives

This is a story of a beautiful place with serious problems. Although Salinas, Puerto Rico, is rich in resources, it is plagued by poverty and dependence. Its people and environment have suffered from the effects of modern colonialism and "development." But Salinas also is home to a group of activists who are looking for alternatives. They have dedicated themselves to working to develop programs based upon community-directed, environmentally and socially responsible use of local resources. By doing so they seek ways to empower their community to make the key decisions concerning local economic planning. In this, Salinas is hardly unique, for stories abound of similar efforts throughout the world among the least powerful and most marginalized people. Examples of "grassroots" groups — as distinguished from nongovernmental organizations from outside the target population (Bebbington and Thiele 1993, 7) — range from community development cooperatives in depressed industrial towns of eastern Canada (Cossey 1990) to locally initiated economic projects in rural Mexico as part of a wider demand for community control of needed natural resources (Blauert and Guidi 1992). They are as well known as the "base communities" associated with Latin American "liberation theology"; they are also as obscure as local efforts to develop economic alternatives for an ex-logging town in California's Sierra Nevada.

These stories, spanning continents and crossing borders between the so-called First and Third Worlds (or North and South), point to the widely recognized need for something radically different from the status quo. This is a fairly recent phenomenon, since a generation ago strong criticism of development theory and practice was rejected by mainstream policymakers; moreover, talk of environmental limits to economic growth was relegated to the intellectual and activist fringes. Scarcely twenty years have passed since the publication of *Limits to Growth* (Meadows 1972) first attracted widespread attention to development's ecological costs. Subsequent reports and international conferences, aided by the creation of the United Nations Environment Program (UNEP) in 1972, began increasingly to insist that the world agenda include the environment. But it was not until the World Commission on Environment and Development published a report in 1987 that the issue took center stage (Stokke 1991).

This widely heralded and much quoted document, titled *Our Common Future* but commonly known as the Bruntland Report, called for a reordering of the world's priorities to include a commitment to "sustainable development," defined as "development that meets the needs of the present without compromising the ability of future generations to meet their own needs" (United Nations. WCED 1987, 8). The Report's condemnation of the practice of borrowing "environmental capital from future generations," as well as its call for an "international sustainable economic order," seemed to finally gain the ears of global leaders during the 1992 World Conference on Environment and Development in Río de Janeiro, Brazil.

Since the Bruntland Report's publication sustainable development has become increasingly acceptable in the centers of political and economic power, from national governments and international organizations to corporate boardrooms. It has even become part of the U.S. government's war on drugs: as part of this campaign the United States Agency for International Development (USAID) has been enlisted to teach "sustainable development," which, according to the agency's semiannual report "includes local participation, democratic institution building, and social programs for the poor," as an alternative to the cultivation of coca in Andean countries (USAID 1993, 5).

And herein lies the problem with sustainable development: if everyone can be for it — activists, intellectuals, bureaucrats, corporations — regardless of the obvious conflicts of interest among them, then how useful can the definition be when concrete strategies are actually attempted? Critics charge that the concept is being packaged in terms as vaguely defined and broadly acceptable as possible, that neither challenge the notion of development as growth nor speak clearly of the need for political and economic restructuring. Moreover, concern for equity or social justice often appears to be quietly de-emphasized, and replaced with a call for an undefined "local participation" (Lélé 1991). Others observe that "we frequently encounter moral convictions as substitutes for thought" in the literature (Redclift 1992, 2), instead of the much needed application of intellectual rigor to the inherent contradiction between our traditional understanding of development and the desirability of sustainability. By critically reviewing how both development and sustainability have been conceptualized, we should be better able to appreciate the problems posed by defining and applying the concept of sustainable development.

Development

Traditional development economics arose after World War II to answer the question Why are some countries wealthy, powerful, and ever advancing, while others seem mired in poverty and backwardness? Experts in this new field asserted that the right mixture of savings, investment, and foreign aid would enable "underdeveloped" countries to follow the same historical path the developed countries had traveled (Rostow 1960). Economic development was to be measured by the ability of a "backward" nation to expand its output at a rate faster than the growth rate of its population, and to sustain annual increases over 5 percent in its gross national product (Todaro 1985, 83). Development economists took the Keynesian prescription for government intervention in stagnant economies from the First to the Third World. Although it differed from neoclassical economics regarding market intervention and comparative advantage (discussed below), development economics shared the neoclassical preoccupation with market supply and demand in analyzing economic activity and determining policy, to the near total exclusion of political, historical, social, or environmental factors.

Racism and Colonialism:
Roots of Development and Modernization

Analyses of traditional development theory and policy form a voluminous and impressive body of literature. The underlying role of racism and colonialism in the formulation of "development" and "modernization," however, represents a virtually unexplored avenue of inquiry. Knowledge of this role is needed, first, to understand our prevailing and faulty notions of progress, and then, to open ourselves to real alternatives.

Racism may be defined as beliefs and practices that are based on assumptions of inherent superiority or inferiority of specific peoples, and that are used to justify and reproduce structural inequality (Jackson 1987). Like all practice, racism is rationalized and justified by theory, or a systematic explanation of the world around us. Since racist practice "from personal abuse to colonial oppression" (Blaut 1992, 289) is a cornerstone of the world political and economic order, it should not be surprising that the theory that supports it might change somewhat through time, according to the intellectual environment.

Blaut (1992) has noted three different theories used to rationalize racist practice since the rise of Europeans to world domination. The first, "religious racism," holding sway until the nineteenth century, claimed that the conquest by white European Christians of nonwhite heathens was part of a divine plan. The Darwinian revolution effectively put an end to biblically rationalized theories among academics; accordingly, scientific justifications for racist practice, namely, "biological racism" superseded religious racism. Here evolutionary theory was extended to human beings; genetic superiority was said to explain the so-called white race's political and economic domination of the nonwhite races of humanity. Additionally, some prominent geographers[1] advanced a theory of "environmental determinism" to help explain, among other things, the natural superiority of Europeans and the natural inferiority of Africans. They claimed that the "temperate" climate of Europe was most conducive to developing superior human populations in nearly every important respect; by contrast the "torrid" tropics retarded development and allowed inferior genetic qualities to reproduce themselves. Such thinking predominated in both academic and policy circles at the dawn of the twentieth century; it was repeatedly used to justify the United States' conquest of much of North America and colonialist expansion overseas, including that to Puerto Rico (Hofstadter 1955; Healy 1988).[2]

Complementary to the prevailing biological racism and environmental determinism was the thinking by mainstream economists about global economic differentiation. They considered the disparity in roles played by the colonizer and colonized countries in the growing world economic system a perfectly natural consequence of "comparative advantage." In other words, the mostly tropical and colonized regions were naturally disposed toward extracting raw materials such as mahogany and producing agricultural goods such as sugar, which were either impossible or unprofitable for the "advanced" countries to produce for themselves. By the same token, the temperate colonizer countries had the invigorating climate and "advanced" human qualities needed to specialize in manufactured goods — which was considered impossible or unprofitable to duplicate in the colonies.

By the mid twentieth century biological racism had lost its respectability, partly due to theoretical critiques (Peet 1985; Blaut 1992), but primarily as a result of the horrific consequences of Nazi Germany's racist policies.[3] Geographers, in particular, took great pains to distance themselves from environmental determinism, even to the point of virtually splitting human geography from physical geography (Peet 1985). Academics, however, still continued to justify racist practices, this time using a cultural argument: while acknowledging that all peoples were innately equal as far as potential, they argued that European culture supposedly contained some special qualities that allowed societies there to advance intellectually, technologically, and so on. By this same reasoning, the "backward" societies lacked those special qualities or contained special cultural features that inhibited development. It was therefore necessary for underdeveloped societies to follow the example and tutelage of western Europeans (and North Americans), if they hoped to solve their crushing problems of poverty and backwardness. Economically, the acceptance of "comparative advantage" for the colonized countries began to be replaced by calls for Western-style development (with a particular emphasis upon export-led, colonizer country–financed manufacturing).

This last argument, known as "cultural racism," granted non-Europeans the possibility of perfectibility;[4] however, its assertion that backward nonwhite societies needed to move away from their own cultures, still contained the racist message of Europe's "inherent" superiority. Cultural racism underlay the dominant thinking in theories of development and modernization; moreover, it provided an explanation for inequality among nations without placing responsibility on colonialist exploitation — thus allowing it to continue. There was no acknowledged connection between the wealth and power achieved by the colonizer countries and the poverty and weakness suffered by the colonies. Instead, the twentieth century's underdeveloped countries were considered to be simply at an earlier development stage; they therefore must go through the same stages that northwestern Europe and the United States had passed through in order to become "developed" and "modern."

Cultural Indicators of (Under)Development and (Pre)Modernization

Although development economists believed that development could be measured by the growth of Western-style production and consumption, modernization theorists — whether sociologists (Lerner 1958), anthropologists (Redfield 1941), or political scientists (Almond 1960) — added that noneconomic factors, such as cultural characteristics, were also responsible for the economic backwardness of the Third World. They thus added features characteristic of modern "Western" societies to the definition of development. Some went so far as to equate development itself with modernization (Scott 1973).

Cultural factors that were thought to encourage development could be found in the developed countries, including: industrialization, urbanization, and a completed demographic transition; weakening of traditional beliefs and community structures; a consumer society with pervasive commodification of land, labor, capital, values, recreation, and so on, along with powerful mass media and communications; nationalism replacing regionalism, including more cultural homogenization (along with marginalization or destruction of unassimilable minorities); more social mobility; a utilitarian and separatist view of the (human-dominated) environment; and more emphasis on competition and individualism.

Following this same line of reasoning, one could find those factors impeding development in the cultural characteristics of "underdeveloped" countries, and they were generally the opposite of those of the developed countries, including: agricultural, rural societies, where traditional beliefs and community structures were still powerful; a nonexistent or incomplete demographic transition and commodification process; significant regionalism, cultural diversity, and social stability; a tendency to view communities as part of the natural environment (or at least to view humans as unable to control nature); and greater approval of collective values than of individualistic ones.

Theorists and planners looked on industrialization as key to development and modernization. They favored export-led industrialization, in particular, for accelerated incorporation into the global economic order; it became one of the most popular strategies for pushing backward countries along the path to development and modernity. Puerto Rico's Operation Bootstrap was the world's first program of Third World development through export-led industrialization. This post–World War II strategy inspired W. Arthur Lewis's "dual-labor sector" theory of development (1950, 1955) and formed part of the blueprint for development programs such as the United Nations' Point Four, the Alliance for Progress (Levinson and de Onís 1972), the maquiladoras and "twin plants" of the Mexico-U.S. border, and the Caribbean Basin Initiative (Dietz 1986; Pantojas García 1990). Bootstrap's influence is also felt in the United States, for it contributed to the proposed model for inner city economic development known as "Urban Enterprise Zones." We can briefly describe the strategy as one offering incentives (such as tax breaks, cheap nonunionized labor, and low-cost infrastructure) to attract capital, materials, and knowledge from developed to developing countries, to be transformed by local labor into products for export to the developed countries. Its supporters have argued that it would lead to increased industrialization, urbanization, and corresponding cultural change of the developing country so that it would more closely resemble the developed countries. However, its disarticulated nature — that is, separation of economic processes from the available resources and production for consumption needs elsewhere — accelerated the modern process of human alienation from the natural environment, thus increasing the chances of both environmental and social degradation as a "cost" of development. Certainly, this appears to have been the case in Salinas.

Although development theory (and its underlying cultural racism) rejected genetic determinism, it could nevertheless be accused of encouraging a form of social Darwinism, through its outlining of a unilinear evolutionary model for all human societies. Moreover, the presumed necessity for political tutelage of "backward," "underdeveloped," or even "developing" (this last term being widely used today) nations recalls nineteenth-century notions of the "white man's burden," or in other words, the duty of Europeans to act as fathers to the "childlike" nonwhite peoples.[5]

Critiques of Development

In sum, mainstream developmentalists during the 1940s and 1950s defined development both as measurable economic growth and as a social evolutionary process by which a primitive society (by Western industrial standards) became modern economically, socially, and politically. Nonetheless, almost from the beginning it was apparent to some observers that economic growth alone did not eliminate poverty, and frequently made it worse. Marxists were among the early critics of development, seeing it as an outgrowth of imperialism (Baran 1957). Economic planners of the United Nations Economic Commission on Latin America (ECLA) advocated import-substitution industrialization and regional trading blocs as strategies to help that region "catch up" to the United States (Rodríguez 1980). By the 1960s, however, writers associated with the "dependency school" criticized ECLA for failing to take colonialist exploitation into account to explain Latin America's problems. By this they meant that colonialist exploitation had fueled First World development, at the same time that it resulted in underdevelopment in the Third World. They therefore saw the solution to underdevelopment in terms, not of catching up, but rather of ending First World exploitation of the Third World (see, for example, Frank 1966).

By the 1970s feminist researchers were adding their voices to the rising chorus of criticism. They documented the crucial economic role played by women in the Third World (more recently called the "South") and warned that by ignoring this role development was condemning the majority of the world's population to greater poverty (Boserup 1970). During the next twenty years feminist criticism both documented the fundamentally flawed nature of development thinking (Deere 1990) and proposed alternatives conceived of by Southern women (Antrobus 1989). Although considered closer to the mainstream, "development with equity" theorists rejected the narrow equation of development with economic growth, in favor of an approach that also stressed meeting people's basic needs (see, for example, Chenery 1979; Streeten 1981).

Criticism was also directed at the tendency of mainstream economics to base policy recommendations on an idealized view of "rational economic man," with his perfect (or equal) access to choice, as well as on the capacity of the "invisible hand" of market supply and demand to regulate itself and supply material needs. Unfortunately, none of these ideals had much basis in observed reality, particularly in colonized settings. Among the shortcomings of mainstream economics was its failure to take into account compelling nonrational explanations for human behavior, such as ethical concerns or the desire for community. Critics also took it to task for emphasizing competitiveness over security and dignity and for promoting disarticulated economic strategies such as export-led industrialization (Landsberg 1979).[6] Additionally, the mainstream tendency either to ignore the environment or to treat it as an unlimited source of resources and waste absorption, plus the failure to factor in environmental or social costs, greatly exacerbated the prevailing practice of destructive and unsustainable development (O'Connor 1989).

Other critics sought to examine more closely the moral and ethical bases for determining development strategies. For example, political economist Denis Goulet tried to emphasize more universal social, political, and philosophical concerns in defining development as "the entire gamut of changes by which a social system . . . moves away from a condition widely perceived as unsatisfactory in some way toward some condition regarded as "humanly' better" (1975, 333). His collaborations with leading liberation theologians such as Paolo Freire (Goulet 1974) and Gustavo Gutiérrez manifested their influence in Goulet's suggestion that "liberation" more accurately expressed people's real aspirations than "development" (1971, 480). The influence of liberation theology can also be clearly discerned in writings on developmental ethics (see, for example, Kruijer 1987).

In fact, some critics of development have gone so far as to say that the term *development* itself is not useful for those wishing to promote concrete improvements in the material well-being of the world's poor. For example,

Lakshmann Yapa contends that modern poverty is caused by "efforts to improve 'standards of living' through ever-higher levels of production and consumption of material goods and services — that is, through an accelerated growth in GNP" (1993, 254). In other words, poverty is created by the very process of development itself. It has become increasingly apparent that development as it is traditionally conceived of is not the solution, but rather is part of the problem. Clearly, in order to have any success at constructing a clear and effective concept of sustainable development that can lead to social and ecological improvement — rather than the reverse — development itself must be redefined.

Sustainability

Most of the discussion of sustainability deals with ecological (as opposed to social) sustainability, and as such is referred to extensively in ecology and natural resource management. For ecologists it is fundamentally concerned with maintaining biodiversity at the genetic, species, and ecosystem levels. We should not misunderstand sustainability as a blanket call to preserve so-called natural environments without any change or interference, as we might infer from the pronouncements of some eco-activists. On the contrary, "a physically active world has given rise to a biologically dynamic world. One interpretation of the concept of sustainability is thus, perhaps surprisingly, the retention of global abilities to adapt to change" (Palmer 1991, 7–8). In other words, because nature is dynamic rather than static, maintenance of the widest possible genetic, species, and ecosystemic diversity is a critical feature of ecological sustainability. Moreover, since it is both natural and necessary for humans to identify parts of their natural environment for use as resources, the question is therefore not whether it should be done, but how.

Natural resource management is responsible for overseeing human use of renewable resources such as forests and fisheries. Such activity is considered to be sustainable when it does not threaten the integrity — that is, the innate capacity to maintain overall complexity and diversity, their very health and viability, over time — of the ecosystems that provide the context for such activity (Iverson and Corbett 1994). The newly emerging literature on "ecological economics" emphasizes that "sustainability requires at least a constant stock of natural capital, construed as the set of all environmental assets" (Pearce 1992, 69).

As for "intergenerational equity" — taking into consideration the needs of future generations for an undiminished natural resource base — some writers refer to it as the "backbone of sustainability" (Meyer and Helfman 1993, 569). Since, as J. R. Palmer argues (1991), we cannot know what future generations may require, nor what environmental changes might occur, it makes sense to leave as much diversity as possible in order to leave the maximum number of options open for the future. Over fifty years ago Aldo Leopold emphasized this logic: "If the land mechanism as a whole is good, then every part is good, whether we understand it or not. If the biota in the course of eons, has built something we like but do not understand, then who but a fool would discard seemingly useless parts? To keep every cog and wheel is the first precaution of intelligent tinkering" (1978, 190).

Yet, although some writers have stressed the ultimate inseparability of ecological and social sustainability in asserting that "nature and humanity will be liberated together or not at all" (Gudynas 1990, 146), the sustainable development literature has to date paid far too little attention to the social component of sustainability, or to the importance of "preserving the social basis of human life" (Lélé 1991, 609). This neglect should not be surprising, given that the traditional separation of the natural and social sciences tends to work against interdisciplinary cooperation (Norgaard 1994). This separation follows along the lines of Western thought, which, in its typical divisions of reality into opposing dualisms, tends to separate humans ("culture") from "nature." Ironically, although mainstream proponents of economic growth and environmental activists are often seen as adversaries, they both tend to share this same nature/culture dichotomy; indeed, "some ecological work has a distinct air of viewing human society as an intruder and despoiler of the ecologist's central object of value, a natural or natural-looking ecosystem" (Simmons 1993, 185).[7] Then, too, environmental organizations with predominantly middle- and upper-class constituencies have often been accused of an elitism that may be antigrowth out of a (perhaps unconscious) desire to "kick the ladder down behind them" (cited in Anderson 1991, 6); it is frequently alleged that their "selective" environmental concern extends only to "threats to rural peace and wildlife" and is "little concerned with the far more desperate problem of the urban environment"(ibid.).

But perhaps the most important reason behind the nearly exclusive focus on the ecological component of sustainability rests with the powerful economic and political interests (and their institutions) who profit from inequitable distribution of resource benefits; they are thus likely to be more comfortable with so-called objective, nonpolitical work associated with much of the natural sciences, precisely because of political considerations. For an elite minority of countries—as well as for elite minorities within each state—such inequality is the source of their power. Although it has become increasingly apparent that resource overuse and pollution by the rich are largely responsible for the growing global environmental crisis, even well-regarded work such as the Bruntland Report "chose to point at poverty itself as [the] main cause of environmental disruption and could not identify its own position in this context. It is therefore logical that the dominant powers in the world embraced the Report as one of the most progressive and important of the decade" (de la Court 1990, 135). Accordingly, "there is a political attempt to move the ecological agenda away from the issues of [resource use and degradation] by the wealthy. Thus, in the wake of the Bruntland Report, the study of poverty as a cause of environmental degradation has become more fashionable—and richly funded—than the study of wealth as the main human threat to the environment" (Martínez-Alier 1991, 123).

It seems clear that conceptualizing and applying successful alternatives to the present destructive course requires, among other things, an interdisciplinary approach that is as inclusive as possible. I. G. Simmons observed that "though we associate the natural sciences with analysis and the breaking down of phenomena into their constituents (reductionism) for study" (1993, 185), ecology's concern with interrelatedness allows it to "emphasize links rather than differences" (ibid.). Nonetheless, some contributions by ecology to the "sustainable development" literature must also be criticized for tendencies to encourage "evolutionist and biologically grounded theories of human society" (Redclift 1992, 194)—what often amounts to an updated social Darwinism influencing some ecological perspectives in rich countries (Martínez-Alier 1991).

Human Carrying Capacity:
Ecology without Politics?

Indeed, it has become fashionable to attempt wholesale application of concepts and techniques meant for the study of plants and animals to what are largely social and political problems. One example is the use of "carrying capacity" to determine optimal human population size. Victor Anderson explains that "in ecology, the paradigm case of growth is growth in the population of a species. The normal pattern is that populations grow until some feature of their environment, perhaps a predator or a limited food supply, brings that growth to a halt, or pushes it into reverse . . . but clearly the size of the human population doesn't by itself determine the degree of environmental impact, because human beings consume different goods and services, use different technologies to produce them, and are organized in different sorts of societies" (1991, 14).

In the case of Puerto Rico, the "doctrine of nonviability" justified the disarticulated "Bootstrap" economic strategy and its dependent political status — that is, the island was not viable because it was too small, too poor in resources, and too overpopulated (Berman Santana 1996). Policies such as mass emigration and sterilization of more than 35 percent of the island's women were supposed to keep Puerto Rico from exceeding its "carrying capacity," thus enabling its people to escape poverty (Maas 1976). In fact, places such as Salinas have suffered more economic, social, and environmental degradation since they began to experience development — and would probably be even more destitute were it not for dependence upon government aid. Among other things this state of affairs indicates that more attention needs to be paid to social sustainability; an issue of this importance should not be forced to depend upon faulty understandings of population, resources, and development for resolution.

There are more reasons for questioning the applicability of the concept of carrying capacity to human societies, among them the fact that it cannot fairly be applied unless ecological territory and political boundaries coincide — which is hardly the case anywhere. Additionally, Martínez-Alier (1991) observes that the question of whether densely populated developed countries exceed their carrying capacities is rarely considered, while at the same time it is constantly asked of poor states. The inherent contradictions are sharply underscored even among some experts on human carrying capacity; for example, population biologist Gretchen Daily (Hurwitt 1994) admits that disproportionate use of resources in rich countries (she estimates that the average baby born in the United States will grow up to have thirty times the impact on the environment of a baby born in Bangladesh) indicates that poor countries are not really at the center of global population issues. Apparently political variables, such as unequal resource-benefit distribution and resource transfers from poor to rich countries, are not being significantly factored into the carrying capacity equation. That this clearly problematic concept is still so popular should at least raise some questions as to whose interests it ultimately serves.

We certainly need to make use of the best and most rigorous research in both the natural and social sciences to determine what constitutes sustainable human use of natural resources; however, little of real value will be accomplished as long as we maintain the fiction of scientific objectivity and avoid difficult political issues. At best, such attempts are merely inadequate; at worst, the biological determinism implicit (sometimes explicit) in narrowly based and reductionist calculations of carrying capacity — to name just one example — may encourage a revival of nineteenth-century scientific racism. Not only could this be used to justify a new wave of global exploitation and oppression; at this late date, it could also perhaps threaten our very survival.

In view of all the enormous challenges facing our own and coming generations, it is time to address social sustainability with the same attention and urgency we are bringing to ecological sustainability. Thankfully, we are beginning to acknowledge that the loss of genetic, species, and ecosystem diversity caused by developmentalism may perhaps threaten our own existence; but we also need to start asking what kinds of dangers are posed by the devaluation and destruction of human experience and knowledge, in all its rich diversity.

Other Questions

Questions about the usefulness of sustainable development do not stop with defining and reconciling development and sustainability. There is the question of scale: local, regional, or global? Are local strategies feasible if they run counter to more powerful interests? Must sustainable planning be accomplished at the regional or even global level, in order to make a difference where people actually live and work? Who is ultimately responsible for preserving the basis of our survival?

Neither advocates nor critics of sustainable development seem to agree among themselves about the appropriate scale for conceptualizing, planning, and implementing policies that embody the concept. Many have pointed out that efforts to achieve localized, small-scale development at odds with the prevailing interests of the state and of global capital often appear naïve and seem doomed to failure. Although there is little doubt of the corporate profitability of globalization — at least in the short-term — some writers are beginning to recognize the importance of actors at the local level in successful long-term economic development and environmental protection. For example, Ignacy Sachs observed that development is ultimately measured at the local level:

> In spite of the internationalization of the economy and the transformation of our planet into a "global village," development or misdevelopment manifests itself in the final analysis where there are people. In this sense, then, there can be no development other than local development. . . . [W]e can identify latent resources, waste that can be eliminated, production capacities that can be converted for a moderate financial layout, and numerous opportunities for saving energy and raw materials, only if we call on local initiative. Finally, it is at this level too that the choice of priorities and the identification of society's needs must to a large extent be made. (1987, 105–9)

Local groups often prove to be the most knowledgeable and committed stewards of local resources (Goodman and Redclift 1991); "consequently, the goal of sustainable development will be furthered when local groups have more influence over . . . the way the environment is used" (Bebbington and Thiele 1993, 14). Please note that in arguing for a local focus I am not minimizing the importance of the state, the power of capital, nor the need for planning global sustainability. In fact, the role of each in turn — and how each relates to one another as well as to local sustainable development — must be addressed. However, the case study presented here argues that "top-down" approaches are part of the problem, not part of the solution.

Another question is: What is meant when we talk about "the community." This could be understood as referring to so-called communities of affinity, such as political parties or the workplace, which have traditionally served as bases to organize for change. Or perhaps the term could be identified with "new social movements" such as environmentalism or feminism, which have attracted much attention recently, particularly in Latin America (Slater 1985; Escobar and Alvarez 1992). We shall see that the Salinas story acknowledges an important role for all of these various groups. Nonetheless, because building local foundations for global sustainability requires (among other things) reconnecting people to their environment, I believe we should be focusing on more territorially based communities: barrios, towns, regions, those communities that share a strong element of place-based identity. In saying this I am not minimizing the importance of affinity- or issue-based activism; neither do I dismiss the importance of organizing at the workplace. But we need to recognize that in this "new world order" of industrial downsizing, high unemployment, migrating labor forces, and expanding informal economic sectors, "the relative numbers of blue collar workers . . . are so small that no significant action for structural change can be expected by organizing labor only at its place of work. . . . [T]his near majority of the population cannot be effectively organized except at their place of residence which is increasingly becoming a place of production as well" (Friedmann 1987, 28–29). Moreover, issue-oriented activism tends to generate broad but shallow coalitions, which can form invaluable paths for networking but are not appropriate for building and sustaining deeply rooted, permanent projects in specific places. The experience of Salinas indicates that it is at home where we are most likely to find the long-term interest necessary for long-term change.

Even when we restrict "community" geographically, its meaning is far from clear. Are all the people who live in a particular location considered part of the community — rich as well as poor, young as well as old, newcomers as well as indigenous? What degree of power should each have in their particular locale's development planning and environmental protection? What about those who are intimately connected with the place through a variety of ways, yet live elsewhere? What happens if plans that benefit some locals harm the interests of others? And what is meant by "benefit"? Advocates of "community empowerment" and "local benefits" will need to clarify exactly what they mean.

Questions about the community are important, since many proponents of sustainable development, from community activists to institutional theorists, emphasize "community participation" in their proposals. One international panel of experts defined community participation as "the creation of opportunities to enable all members of a community and the larger society to actively contribute to and influence the development process and to share equitably in the fruits of development" (United Nations 1981, 5). As is typical of much mainstream work, such a definition is too vague to be of much value to us. As one observer put it, "clearly, much more information is needed if we are to know who participates, what participation entails, and how it can be promoted" (Midgely 1986, 24).

Many projects that claim to feature "community participation" are planned at the state or even international level by "experts" who are unfamiliar with the historic and day-to-day reality of the people and the environment in the particular community. They rely upon professional organizers, whom they in turn expect to mobilize local leaders to bring about community participation. Such participation often consists of nothing more than attending public hearings, or perhaps working at some jobs (usually temporary) created by the program; rarely are the least powerful community members invited from the very start to become a determining part of planning, decision making, and implementation processes. They are excluded because development strategies are not merely "theoretical models of opposing rationalities among which a varied assortment of policymakers have to choose" (Pantojas García 1990, 1), but actually represent ideological constructs of a dominant class that are set in motion primarily for its own benefit. In short, within "top-down" or "outside-in" strategies for local development (often clearly influenced by the same cultural racism that informed modernization) efforts to ensure community participation can become merely attempts to coerce local acquiescence to plans that were created by and primarily benefit elites (who may or may not be local residents). When one expert admittedly wrote a well-regarded review article to assist the policymakers "in the decision as to when it is or is not appropriate to include community participation as a component" (Moser 1989, 79), it becomes obvious who really is in control.

If that is the case, what alternatives are left? If those who have primary decision-making powers for any program will also most likely be its chief beneficiaries, then "community participation" should involve increasing the ability of all people in a community to determine their needs, identify and utilize their individual and collective resources, and plan and implement their own development strategies. What about defining the community itself — to whom does this term refer? If we take a place-based view of community, in terms of the people who "belong" there (growing up, living, working, raising a family, dying), then we must accept that these communities are likely to contain people of a variety of social, economic, and ideological backgrounds. However, in most of the literature advocating some form of "grassroots development," "community empowerment," "participatory democracy," and so on, the indicators of success seem to be whether the poorest, most marginalized, and least powerful people and groups are benefiting the most and are increasingly able to participate in making the decisions that affect themselves, their families, and their environment. This criterion should make sense because, after all, any program that ends up enriching the privileged few without improving the lot of the poor majority (or even worsening it) would not represent an alternative to the development that places like Salinas have already experienced.

Finally, I do not wish to minimize the difficulties involved in achieving sustainable development, or to ignore the formidable obstacles to locally based alternatives. Not the least of these is the challenge of community mobilization: that is, convincing historically powerless people that they have the ability to take charge of their own future, and then to work together to do so. Another obstacle is the relationship of the activists or their plans to the state, regardless of whether cooperation is sought or an adversarial posture is adopted. Clearly, the state has the power to make or break most community initiatives; moreover, it is never likely to relinquish its accumulated centralized power without a fight. And we must recognize that community-directed plans will face nearly overwhelming competition if they require control of resources that are coveted by private interests, whether they be local businesses or transnational capital. I will address such concerns later, in light of the Salinas experience. Nevertheless, I do not see such obstacles as arguments against a community-directed, local focus; rather, they indicate a challenge that must somehow be met in order to bring about truly sustainable development. It is my hope that this book will provide some assistance toward meeting that challenge.

With these issues in mind we now turn to the case study, to ground theory in real-life experience. This is a story of local activism in Salinas, Puerto Rico, which is searching for a "sustainable" alternative to its previous development experience. In that experience powerful outsiders determined the strategies, reaped the benefits, and left it environmentally, economically, and socially degraded. The story of Salinas provides an interesting and important study of efforts within a community to determine its own development. Puerto Rico offers an excellent geographical and historical background for such a study, because its post–World War II "Operation Bootstrap" was the first Third-World, export-led industrialization development program and was used as a blueprint for similar programs throughout the world.

2 The Geographical Setting

The first step in discussing community control of resources for development in any location is to learn what the physical environment is like. How have natural resources been identified and used over time, and why? What have been the economic, social, environmental, and political effects of such use? Once we have this information we can begin to understand current problems and evaluate the proposed alternatives.

Salinas: A Geographic Panorama

The *municipio*[1] of Salinas is located on Puerto Rico's south (Caribbean) coast some twenty-three miles (38 km) east of Ponce, Puerto Rico's second largest city. Salinas is bound by the municipios of Santa Isabel to the west, Coamo to the northwest, Aibonito to the north, Cayey to the northeast and Guayama to the east, while the southern boundary is marked by the Caribbean Sea. It covers an area of sixty-nine square miles (179 km²), or 45,760 *cuerdas*,[2] making it Puerto Rico's fourth largest municipio. Salinas lies some fifty miles (80 km) southwest of San Juan, the capital of Puerto Rico. According to the 1990 U.S. Census Salinas's population is 28,335 (see Map 2.1).

The municipio of Salinas extends southward from the steep volcanic slopes of the Cayey Range,[3] through rolling uplands (see fig. 2.1), to the southern coastal plains comprising half of its territory. Along the coast can be found sandy beaches, mangrove forests, swamps, salt flats, offshore islets, and coral reefs. Soils are characterized as deep and well-drained, except in the "swamp-marsh association" of the immediate coastal area (U.S. Dept. of Agriculture. Soil Conservation Service 1977). Salinas is located in the center of an extensive, interconnected blanket of alluvium several miles wide and more than forty miles long, which runs along

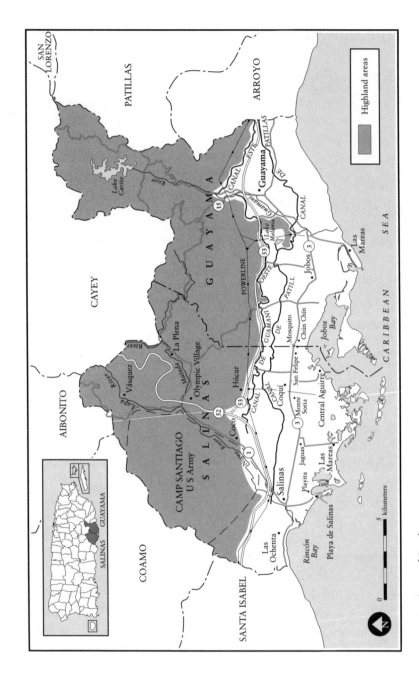

Map 2.1 Area of Study

Figure 2.1   Salinas uplands

Puerto Rico's south coast east of Ponce. Just north of the town of Salinas a three-mile-wide belt of Altura-type soils runs from east to west throughout the municipio; Altura soils are considered to be the island's best agricultural lands (Haines et al. 1968, A77). The soils and level topography are thus especially well-suited for commercial agriculture.

Water

The Nigua River (also known as the Salinas River) rises in the Cayey Range and flows eighteen miles (29 km) toward the southwest before emptying into the Caribbean just west of the town of Salinas. The Lapa and Majada Rivers, which drain the northeastern portion of the municipio, are the Nigua River's principal tributaries. The Jueyes River forms the boundary between Salinas and Santa Isabel.

As is true of all other rivers flowing south from the *Cordillera Central,* surface flow of the Nigua River is intermittent once it reaches the coastal plain. The drainage basin of the Nigua River covers some fifty-three square miles (137 km²) and drains three-quarters of the municipio. The

Nigua River's alluvial fan covers twelve square miles (31 km^2) and extends one mile west of the river's present course, while its eastern boundary is at the base of low hills as far as four miles (6 km) from the river. The fan is important because it stores and transmits large quantities of water; during 1961 an average of 23 million gallons per day (26,000 acre-feet/year) was extracted from the alluvial fan without apparent negative effects (McClymonds and Ward 1966,C231). At present some wells in the area are capable of producing from 125–1,463 gallons of water per minute (Jobanes 1989).

Groundwater associated with the south coast's interconnected blanket of alluvium has been the primary water source for the region's irrigated acreage, industrial development, and residential population. In addition, the system of canals and tunnels connected to the Carite and Patillas reservoirs, located in the Cayey Range northeast of Guayama supplies some 25 percent of Salinas's water needs; this water has traditionally been earmarked for agricultural irrigation (U.S. Army Corps of Engineers 1977).

The larger streams of Puerto Rico's southern slope rise in the Cordillera Central, which is the island's primary drainage divide. The peaks and main escarpment of the Cordillera Central range between 2,500 and 4,500 feet (750–1,200 meters) above sea level, while the coastal plain has a slope of 30–80 feet per mile (19–50 m/km). In general river channels are very steep in the mountains and become progressively less steep in the foothills and on the coastal plain. Such steepness is significant on Puerto Rico's south coast because at no place east of Ponce is the island divide more than fifteen miles (28 km) from the Caribbean Sea; stream velocities are therefore high on the coastal plain during floods (Haire 1971).

The *pueblo* of Salinas is located entirely within the flood plain of the Nigua River. A law prohibiting construction in flood zones went into effect in Salinas after much of the coastal area was designated as a flood zone following a flood in 1981, which has had the effect of inhibiting the economic development of the pueblo. The authorities inconsistently enforce the regulation, however; local residents allege that it constrains small local businesses and less affluent community members, whereas it rarely hinders projects undertaken by wealthier and outside interests. Again, extensive damage caused by flooding of the Nigua River on January 6, 1992, has added a sense of urgency to local calls for flood control.

Climate and Vegetation

The southeastern regional coastal area averages fifty inches (1,129 milli-meters) of rainfall annually (Puerto Rico Department of Natural Re-sources and U.S. Department of Commerce 1983, 8). The nearly constant easterly trade winds, however, combine with high temperatures to cause annual evaporation rates averaging sixty-two inches (1,575 mm), thus reducing the effect of the rainfall and contributing to a dry climate not commonly associated with a humid tropical island (U.S. Army Corps of Engineers 1977, 8).

Besides coastal mangroves, the predominant natural ecological forest community is Coastal Dry Forest (Picó 1974). A remnant of the original forest and shrub cover is maintained and administered as the Aguirre State Forest, located in the coastal area just east of the Salinas-Guayama border. Another small plot is conserved in an uplands park in Guayama imme-diately south of the Patillas irrigation canal, and adjoining the new ICI Pharmaceuticals complex; isolated stands also survive throughout the area. Grasslands form a nearly complete natural ground cover in non-forested areas and are maintained by fire on the southern slopes of the Cordillera Central.

The Coastal Area

At the eastern end of the Salinas coastline is Jobos Bay, which is shared with the municipio of Guayama. The bay is a semi-enclosed estuary[4] whose fresh water is provided by underground springs. In and around Jobos Bay are mangrove forests, coral reefs, and marine meadows — three highly productive biological communities. Some eighty-eight species of birds have been identified, including the endangered brown pelican (*Peli-canus occidentalis occidentalis*). Jobos Bay is home to 240 species of inver-tebrates and 263 species of fish. The bay also provides a habitat for a num-ber of marine animals on the U.S. endangered species list, among them the sea turtle (*Eretmochelys imbrincata*) and the manatee (*Trichechus mana-tus*). Jobos Bay's importance as a protected breeding and feeding ground, in relation to the potential for developing a commercial fishing industry along Puerto Rico's south coast, has been recognized for some time.[5]

Figure 2.2 Natural canals through the Mar Negro Forest

The mangrove forests and coral reefs protect the coast from the destructive effects of high-energy surf, such as that generated by hurricanes. The mangroves, in particular, have prevented nearby coastal areas from flooding, a notable resource in a region considered susceptible to high water. The Jobos Bay area contains Puerto Rico's second largest and most diverse remaining mangrove community. Its main component is the 1,200-cuerda (490 ha) Mar Negro (Black Sea) Forest, located just west of the bay. The Mar Negro Forest contains lagoons,[6] tidelands, and canals providing interchange with the Caribbean Sea (see fig. 2.2). It derives its name from the dark color of the lagoons, caused by the decay of large quantities of organic material, as well as from resin from the mangroves. In addition to being a rich hunting and fishing location, the forest has traditionally provided materials for fishing implements.

In 1981 the Jobos Bay National Estuarine Research Reserve (also known as Jobanes) was established, under the joint administration of the Puerto Rico Department of Natural Resources and the U.S. National Oceanic and Atmospheric Administration (NOAA). The reserve is comprised of 2,883 cuerdas (1,140 ha) of sandy beaches, dry and mangrove forests (including the Mar Negro Forest), coral reefs, submarine meadows, territorial waters, and seventeen islets known as the Cayos Caribes comprising 155 cuerdas (67 ha). Jobos Bay is Puerto Rico's second largest bay and is one of the best-protected harbors along the island's south coast; it has thus been attractive not only for its natural environment, but also for the development of heavy industry (Puerto Rico Department of Natural Resources and U.S. Department of Commerce 1983, 5). In 1994 the nature reserve opened its new headquarters on the grounds of Central Aguirre, next to the old American Hotel. Although some look upon the move as a commitment by the government to ecotourist development, others think it more likely that this reserve merely represents one of many competing interests for control of the valuable sugar mill property.

The village of Las Mareas de Salinas[7] (pop. 700) lies at the western end of the Mar Negro Forest. An abandoned salt-mining operation lies southwest of the community. North of Las Mareas, along the north side of Highway PR 3 and across from the settlement of La Jagua, is the Salinas International Speedway, a popular attraction built on the site of a former military airport. A German-owned company specializing in the recycling of tin is located immediately west of the Speedway. The land just east and west of the Speedway is dedicated to agriculture; the land south of the highway is planted mainly in sugar cane, whereas plantains, bananas, squash, and beans predominate on the land along the north side. One can observe a considerable amount of weed-filled fallow acreage as well. Villa Abey, a family-style resort and campground, is located north of the highway and just over a mile east of the Speedway. Three miles east of the Speedway one finds the town of El Coquí (pop. 3,000). The Puerto Rico Industrial Development Corporation (PRIDCO) built two factories located immediately west of El Coquí and leased them to a succession of firms; the most recent occupants are a fruit drink producer and a manufacturer of polyester resin for electrical circuit breakers.[8]

Along the northwest coast of Jobos Bay is the 250-cuerda (101 ha) Central Aguirre sugarmill complex and company town (pop. 1,000), surrounded by prime sugar-growing lands; the mill, which closed in 1990, has docking facilities on Jobos Bay. The Aguirre electric power complex borders Central Aguirre to the southwest and also adjoins Jobos Bay. The mile-square complex consists of four units, which began operations

Figure 2.3   Jobos area pharmaceutical cluster

between 1974 and 1977 and use residual fuel oil as combustible material. A view by night of the complex from a boat in Jobos Bay reveals what appears to be a giant infernal city of fire, noise, and smoke. Behind the plant, adjoining the Jobanes nature reserve, are wetlands belonging to the power plant complex. Officially the wetlands are part of a buffer area; however, in 1989 the government's Electric Energy Authority (known as AEE) admitted to having dumped used transformers containing PCBs and asbestos in those lands, as well as within the municipal solid waste landfill.[9] This landfill is located right next door, as is the settlement of Monte Soria, established in 1976 as an overflow from Central Aguirre. The facility's operating problems were evident during a visit in January 1991, as when I observed scores of violations, including mounds of rotting garbage piled up outside the entrance and burning wastes within. In addition to the municipal landfill numerous clandestine dumps are located throughout Salinas, and burning garbage is a common sight.

Moving eastward along Jobos Bay along Highway PR 3, we see the village of San Felipe, located three-quarters of a mile (1 km) east of El Coquí; it was founded after the devastating Hurricane San Felipe of 1928. The settlement of Mosquito straddles the Salinas-Guayama border, and the Guayama settlement of Chun Chin adjoins Mosquito; the latter two arose during the 1940s as extensions of San Felipe. The three contiguous communities have a combined population of roughly two thousand. A factory manufacturing plastic containers is located immediately east of Chun Chin. The town of Jobos (pop. 3,000) is located two and a half miles (4 km) east of the Salinas-Guayama border, as is the original office of the Jobanes Nature Reserve and Aguirre State Forest.

Between one and three miles east of Jobos one finds the Guayama regional prison, surrounded by five pharmaceutical plants which were established between 1978 and 1992 (see fig. 2.3). The newest and northernmost plant, British-owned ICI Pharmaceuticals, is located only a few hundred meters from the new toll highway PR 53, which runs along the foothills. The ICI complex was developed on a 129-cuerda parcel of farmland on alluvial soil; the site had been rezoned in 1978 to allow industrial development. Meanwhile, SmithKline Beecham, the area's first pharmaceutical plant, is located on the 25 cuerda (10.12 ha) former site of sugarcane-growing Hacienda Josefa, just over one mile southeast of Jobos. Once known as SmithKline French (and still referred to locally as "la SKF"), the plant opened in 1978 (see Map 2.2).

The Phillips Puerto Rico Core petroleum refining complex is located just five hundred meters east of SmithKline Beecham; the refinery is located directly east of Jobos Bay and sprawls along the west side of Highway 710. Built in 1965 on 150 cuerdas of former agricultural land, it has a refining capacity of 20,600 barrels per day. Also located here is Phillips Paraxylene, Inc., a petrochemical subsidiary that opened in 1977 and produces 590 million pounds of paraxylene annually. The Phillips complex takes up the area between the former Laguna Las Mareas de Guayama and the Caribbean Sea. In addition to providing Puerto Rico with gasoline the refinery produces toluene, naphtha paraffin, butane, paraxylene, orthoxylene, mixed xylenes, and benzene (which is used to produce petrochemically based synthetics, especially nylons). During the 1960s Laguna Las Mareas was opened up to the sea to provide a port for

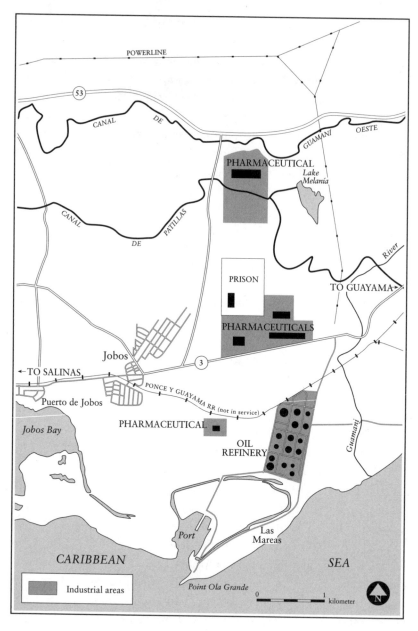

Map 2.2 Jobos Industrial Areas

the refinery; unfortunately, the destruction of this lagoon disrupted drainage in the area, causing serious flooding and forcing most of the residents of Las Mareas de Guayama to abandon their community.

Back in Salinas, to the west along the coast from Jobos Bay and the Mar Negro Forest are Point Arenas — a nearly inaccessible mile-wide triangle of white-sand beach, coconut palm trees, and mangroves — and Rincón Bay. Point Arenas separates the Mar Negro from Rincón Bay. Access to its lush mangroves, palm trees, and white-sand beach (Salinas' best beach, according to many residents) is via boat, an often flooded footpath, and an unpaved road (usually closed) that passes through privately owned land. Rincón Bay is home to the villages of Playita and La Playa de Salinas, as well as to a dozen seafood restaurants and a rapidly expanding luxury marina owned by a San Juan architect. Rincón Bay itself is protected by coral reefs, offshore cays, and mangroves.

Highway PR 701 leads north from the community of La Playa about a mile and a half to the pueblo of Salinas. Along the east side of PR 701 lies a cluster of ten factory buildings built and owned by PRIDCO. As of 1994 three sites were vacant. The other buildings are leased by seven firms which provide a total of 425 jobs. Four of the firms are Puerto Rican–owned businesses, two are United States-owned, and the last is French-owned. Products made here include disposable industrial safety clothing, plastic injection molds, women's clothing, men's shoes, electrical instruments, military boots, and eyeglasses.

Two residential communities built during the 1970s are located across the highway from the factories: Brisas del Mar, a public housing project, and La Margarita, a middle-class *urbanización* (one-story tract homes built by the Puerto Rican government). The two settlements occupy the former site of Hacienda Margarita and are located entirely within the flood plain of the Nigua River. Longtime residents have described the occasional flooding that used to envelop the cane fields in a shallow lake, where "you could sometimes catch fish with your hands." This nostalgic memory is of little comfort to today's residents, who on January 6, 1992 — Three Kings' Day — were shocked by a sudden flood that filled many homes with a layer of thick mud.

The coastal lands west of Salinas Pueblo were devoted entirely to sugarcane throughout most of the twentieth century; squash, chayote, beans, and peppers are now planted as well. Las Ochenta (pop. 2,000) is the largest rural settlement west of the Pueblo; it was established during the 1940s and 1950s through a government rural development program that parceled out the land.

The Uplands Area

Six miles (9 km) northeast of the town of Salinas, and just over one mile (2 km) east of the San Juan–Ponce toll highway (PR 52), one finds the Puerto Rico government–owned Olympic Village, the island's center for sports training and development. Although the Village currently makes use of eighty cuerdas of hilly terrain, it has acquired a total of fifteen hundred cuerdas for future development. Construction began in 1984, and the first phase was inaugurated in 1986. The facilities were designed to provide for world-class training and competitions in a wide range of sports. The center plans to offer complete educational (from secondary through university graduate studies), conference, and recreational facilities.[10] Although administration of the Village alone provides 150 jobs (not including the school and various concessions), it has been described by a local resident as "in Salinas, but not of Salinas."

The hilly uplands were traditionally dedicated to agriculture, including tobacco, mixed tropical region crops such as plantains, and the raising of animals such as pigs and chickens, in addition to cattle ranching. As in the rest of Puerto Rico, agriculture there has suffered a drastic decline since World War II. In recent years, however, the aviculture industry has grown enormously on the island. In 1976 the Rural Development Corporation of the Puerto Rico Department of Agriculture sponsored a project of family farms at the former site of Hacienda Húcar, located just east of toll highway PR 52 and four miles (7 km) northeast of the Pueblo. The twenty-eight project families raise chickens for the broiler industry of the neighboring municipio of Coamo. "Project Húcar" provides direct permanent employment for fifty-six people. A new toll highway that opened in 1994 (PR 53), which runs through the Salinas highlands from Highway PR 52 to Guayama (and is planned eventually to circle the east coast) passes immediately to the south of the project. Before construction began the Rural Development Corporation expressed fears that the noise and dust it generated would force relocation of at least some of the Húcar farmers (Puerto Rico Highway Authority 1986).

North of the town of Salinas, and west and north of PR 52 is the extensive U.S. Army training camp known as Camp Santiago. Its establishment during World War II and expansion during the 1950s displaced at least seven communities of small-scale, subsistence farmers. The owner of the largest estate, Los Ausubos—a member of Salinas's largest land-owning family, the González—was compensated for the military expropriation. Los Ausubos had also been home to many poor *campesinos*, who for generations had worked on the land and had informal use rights; they were not compensated. The displaced families settled in nearby uplands communities such as Vásquez (pop. 2,000), Coco (pop. 2,500), and La Plena (pop. 1,500). Beginning in the 1940s, the Puerto Rican government acquired large tracts of rural land and parceled them out to displaced rural inhabitants, who built their own homes with the aid of neighbors and with materials provided by the government's "mutual aid" program.[11] Long-time residents claim that rainfall has decreased during the fifty years since agricultural land use ceased in the northwestern third of Salinas municipio, in effect, since the establishment of Camp Santiago.[12]

Camp Santiago covers more than a third of the territory of the municipio of Salinas. Immediately adjacent to the camp's northwestern flank, along the border with the municipio of Coamo, is a sector known as Las Piedras Chiquitas (Little Stones), which is a critical habitat for *Zanthoxylum tomasianum*, an endangered plant species. At present serving primarily the Puerto Rico National Guard, Camp Santiago is used for arid region combat training—most recently for the Persian Gulf war. The presence of the base means that neither the municipio nor the Commonwealth has control over use of a third of Salinas's territory, yet they must deal with the environmental, economic, and social impacts of Camp Santiago on the area. (Indeed, in an interview during October 1991 the mayor of Salinas mentioned the base as one of the factors limiting economic development, because it occupies such a large percentage of the municipio's territory.) Environmental problems include the dumping of toxic and other substances in landfills located within the camp that are not subject to inspections by civilian government agencies. Several wells in surrounding communities have been contaminated, possibly from leaching of contaminants from the military landfills into the underground aquifer. The camp is also blamed for much of the deforestation of the Nigua River watershed and for the clogging up of the channel with debris, which is believed to have worsened flooding downstream. Numerous cases have been documented of injuries and deaths to residents, especially to children who find explosives and other training munitions. The camp generates a maximum of only sixty civilian jobs, including summer employment during the National Guard summer camps; nor do military personnel contribute much to the local economy, since the camp has its own well-equipped stores.[13]

In 1989 the U.S. Army Corps of Engineers began trying to gain access to 105,000 additional acres in Puerto Rico for military training; the plan became public knowledge in Puerto Rico during fall 1990. Of sixteen proposed sites twelve were located within or near the municipio of Salinas, including the aforementioned Piedras Chiquitas and Jobos Bay. If the army's plan was fully carried out, the pueblo of Salinas would effectively become surrounded by army land; one could characterize such an eventuality as the "Viequesization" of Salinas (recalling Puerto Rico's island municipio which has lost over 70 percent of its territory to the U.S. Navy, and which is a focal point for anti-U.S. sentiment). Nearly all proposed locations were environmentally or culturally sensitive, since they contained the natural habitats of endangered species or sites of archaeological and historical interest; the proposal thus prompted stiff opposition from both environmentalists and the Puerto Rico Department of Natural Resources. Faced with such strong opposition, the army announced in 1991 that it would revise its proposal and request fewer sites.[14]

Salinas: The Possibilities

What type of economic strategy might appear to be appropriate for Salinas, given its geographical setting? To begin with, identifiable natural resources include a sunny year-round climate. The municipio contains extensive level land with fertile alluvial soil, which is good for commercial agriculture. There is also extensive underground water, plus infrastructure for irrigated water fed by mountain reservoirs. Salinas enjoys a large, well-protected bay and long coastline, containing the three richest marine environments for sustaining sea life: mangrove forests, coral reefs, and underwater marine meadows. Just offshore are islands and protected areas, with sandy beaches and often calm waters. There are documented prehistoric sites as well as sites representing every stage of local history, including a well-preserved sugar colony.

Salinas also is rich in human resources, particularly in agricultural and farm skills for a wide range of crops and domesticated animals. The coastal population possesses a wide variety of fishing and sea-foraging skills, including diving, implement making, navigation and coastal ecology, boat care, and the processing and elaboration of fish and seafood products. Salinas is known throughout Puerto Rico for its fish and seafood cookery. Many locals are extremely knowledgeable about the area's natural and cultural history. Finally, Salinas has a long tradition of community cooperation in economic and other areas.

What should an economic strategy that wisely uses Salinas's existing natural and human resources, first to satisfy local needs, but also to connect and trade with others, look like? As far as specific industries are concerned, they should emphasize the obvious choices, such as mixed agriculture. Family farmers could "lease-to-own" and cultivate their own land, with cooperatives managing larger-scale crops and marketing. The fishing industry is another obvious choice. Worker-owned enterprises could organize fishing, equipment care and operation, product elaboration and marketing.

A place with Salinas's natural beauty and cultural interest has considerable tourism potential. To reduce dependence on large-scale outside capital investment, a plan to build up the tourist industry should support local ownership and management of tourism businesses. It should therefore emphasize smaller-scale projects, such as guest house–type hotels and campgrounds, smaller restaurants using the local catch, development and care of beaches, and local tour guides; it may also be easier to limit the negative environmental impact of smaller-scale projects than that of big Cancún-style resorts. Boating should encourage low-impact craft such as kayaks, canoes, rowboats, and sailboats. Larger vessels could be chartered and locally captained for group excursions, including ones to other Caribbean islands. In order to protect endangered marine mammals and reduce injury to humans, the "jet ski" or water-skimobile should be limited to areas where its use does not conflict with other uses. Appropriate development would discourage proliferation of highly polluting craft, particularly gas-guzzling luxury yachts, while sport fishing would not be allowed to interfere with the local fishing industry. The local area could be a paradise for snorkeling and scuba diving. Tourism could also emphasize cultural and historical interest; prehistoric and historical sites could be restored and visited, and bicycling and hiking tours could also be promoted, including tours in the uplands area.

The plan should encourage local artistry and artisanship, both for tourist-oriented work and for local needs. Carpentry, for example, is in great demand in Puerto Rico; in Salinas there already exist considerable skills in related areas that could be developed. Careful planning could help create businesses that fill specific niches in the needs for clothing and related products, while existing local expertise in this field could be further developed. As for manufacturing, it should emphasize processing agricultural and sea products to meet local and islandwide demand, and possibly to export. Other types of manufacturing could be established and supported as well, so long as they do not destroy more jobs for the local work force than they create, and providing that they do not destroy or constrain the natural resources that sustain the other industries. Finally, a strategy that promotes worker-owned local businesses would give people a stake in their success, reduce government dependence, and help achieve the community's economic, cultural, social, and political integration.

Salinas: The Reality

The geographic panorama reveals among other things, however, that over a third of the land is sealed off for military use, and that the base has contributed to deforestation and contamination of the main drainage basin, soils, and underground water; it was also one of the forces that pushed people off productive lands and into crowded villages. We see that housing for poor and working people was subsequently built in the floodplain of an ecologically stressed river. Heavily polluting industries, we will learn, compete for land and water with agriculture and residents, and they use the sea, soil, ground water, and human lungs as refuse bins. And we notice that the beautiful coastline is in many cases being auctioned off to the highest bidder. These human features on the landscape of Salinas indicate that what has occurred here is very different from what we might assume to be appropriate development. What did happen, and why, helps explain why Salinas, so rich in natural resources, has been plagued by poverty and dependence. In particular, Salinas's development experience — where the state and outside capital determined the strategy, reaped the benefits, and left the area environmentally, economically, and socially degraded — also forms the historical context for today's activism.

During the final century of Spanish rule land grants were used to attract European immigrants to Puerto Rico, although in many cases the land was already occupied by rural peasants. In general the latter maintained informal use rights to the land and its resources in exchange for their labor. However, soon after Puerto Rico became a U.S. colony in 1898 extensive North American investment transformed Salinas and other coastal areas into a highly commercialized agricultural enclave, based primarily on the production of sugarcane for export. The best land was taken to grow the profitable crop; only the least accessible upland areas were left relatively untouched by the transformation. Much of the landless rural population was forced to migrate to the sugar areas and compete for wage labor. The promise of jobs in Salinas's rapidly expanding sugar industry attracted landless peasants from throughout southern Puerto Rico; as a result Salinas's population more than doubled within ten years of the U.S. takeover and continued to grow steadily through the first half of this century. They began to crowd into workers' shantytowns, and spent all the money they earned to buy imported food. This pattern was repeated throughout Puerto Rico.

Interestingly, at the time of the U.S. invasion the island was nearly self-sufficient in food, and in fact exported produce to nearby islands (Hill 1899). Within a few short years, however, Puerto Rico became a country that could not feed itself, and where there were not enough jobs to go around. This new state of affairs contributed to what became the dominant doctrine of the island's "nonviability": that is, Puerto Rico was seen as too small, too overpopulated, and too lacking in natural resources to survive as an independent country. It followed, therefore, that there was no option but to continue economic and political dependence upon the United States. This assumption helped shape Puerto Rico's pioneer program of development through export-led industrialization, known throughout the world as Operation Bootstrap.

Operation Bootstrap emphasized using tax and other incentives to attract to the island outside resources that cheap labor would transform into export goods at a tremendous profit for foreign investors. The program aimed to increase foreign capital investment, industrial production, and per capita income as quickly as possible; it did not aim for balanced development of agriculture and industry, the equitable distribution of income, or the achievement of an integrated national Puerto Rican economy. It was a disarticulated strategy that called for using primarily outside resources, not those of the island, to produce goods to meet foreign needs, not those at home.

Key to understanding this strategy was the contention that the island was virtually devoid of natural resources (García Martínez 1978). This contention betrayed a lack of understanding about the subjectivity involved in defining natural resources, which are simply parts of nature that humans have identified and appropriated for their economic benefit; in fact, what may be considered a natural resource by one society or era may not be so defined by another (Spoehr 1956). More important is the question of who has the power to identify, control, exploit, and benefit from particular resources; this issue was all but ignored by those who justified Operation Bootstrap by pointing to Puerto Rico's "lack of natural resources" (Hanson 1962, 10).[15]

Notwithstanding the ideology of scarcity, Salinas is clearly endowed with considerable natural resources; however, the power to define and exploit them has belonged to capital and to the state (both U.S. rulers and their colonial allies), not to the people of Salinas. First, the sugar industry took advantage of Salinas's favorable climate, extensive level topography, fertile soils, abundant water, and an excellent natural harbor. Next, industrialization exploited the same natural resources (except soil fertility), plus the ready availability of cheap electric energy. Then, during the last twenty years the incipient tourist industry has been emphasizing the attractions of a tropical coastal environment. Each successive economic phase has generated successively fewer jobs, thus effectively institutionalizing the unemployment problem and forcing more people to depend upon government assistance or to leave; in fact, the municipio lost more than 7 percent of its population during the first twenty years following Operation Bootstrap. Moreover, places such as Salinas are paying a heavy environmental price for their so-called development; they have thus lost out on both sides of the "jobs versus environment" debate. This cost is hardly surprising, in part because the process of separating people from their resources (and from an understanding of their uses, benefits, and limitations) cannot help but increase unsustainable resource use, and even destruction. Moreover, it is also likely that wherever environmental disarticulation is promoted, social dislocation is sure to follow.

Operation Bootstrap also widened inequality between the consumer-oriented middle and upper classes, located mainly near San Juan, and the poor majority, particularly those "out on the island." Increased regional and class inequality has contributed to the recent phenomenon of privatizing coastal areas to provide well-to-do San Juan residents with vacation homes and tourist businesses. Among other things it has increased coastal ecological degradation, restricted traditional local access to now private resources, and created widespread resentment over the "invasion of the rich." Finally, the "Puerto Rico model" succeeded in deepening (and perhaps making permanent) Puerto Rico's near total economic and political dependence on the United States. It is against this backdrop of failure of the dominant strategy to benefit the average Salinas resident that local activists are trying to create a less dependent and destructive alternative.

3 Exploitation

To begin to understand the origins of Salinas's current activism in search of alternatives, one must first go back to the formation of the municipio of Salinas, its conversion into a sugar colony, and the changes triggered by Operation Bootstrap over the last forty years. The general pattern of land and resources primarily benefiting the privileged few has its roots in the period of Spanish rule. Then, following the U.S. invasion of Puerto Rico in 1898, the landscape was transformed at a stroke from a region of mixed agricultural and pasture land to one dominated by sugarcane. Cane filled the entire plain and was extended into dryer areas by means of an extensive irrigation system fed by underground water and mountain reservoirs. Human settlement patterns characterized by haciendas and isolated peasants' settlements virtually disappeared, as thousands of dispossessed peasants migrating to Salinas to work in the sugar industry formed densely settled workers' villages. At the center of the local economy and the spatial order was Central Aguirre, Puerto Rico's second largest sugar refinery.

During the late 1960s Central Aguirre began losing money and was taken over by the Puerto Rican government, which kept it open for twenty more years. Its final closure in 1990 was sudden and without any provision for economic transition; the effect of the closure has thus been disastrous for the local economy. This is in part because, although Puerto Rico's famous development program known as Operation Bootstrap transformed the island into a modern industrialized society, it also marginalized Salinas economically and politically and produced environmental and social degradation. More jobs were lost than were created, and welfare dependence and circular migration became a way of life for many. Moreover, the exacerbated class and regional inequalities were expressed locally by the increasing privatization of coastal resources for the benefit of well-heeled San Juan residents, a source of great resentment in Salinas.

Before the U.S. Invasion

The coastal region of what is today the municipio of Salinas was known in pre-Columbian times as the domain of the indigenous Taíno *cacique* (chief) Abey, who took part in the 1511 war against the Spanish. Abey was captured and exiled to Santo Domingo, and his community was destroyed by the victorious invaders.[1] During the seventeenth century Spanish settlers began mining the rich salt deposits that extended along the coast from the Nigua River east as far as Jobos Bay (the word *salinas* means salt works). Tobacco, bananas, and coffee were all grown commercially, and cattle ranching and horse breeding became important toward the end of the eighteenth century. The pueblo of Salinas was first mentioned in the geography of Puerto Rico written by Frau Iñigo Abbad y LaSierra, published in 1776; at that time Salinas was a *barrio* of the municipio of Coamo. Sugarcane was first planted in Salinas in 1810.

During the early nineteenth century Spain attempted to fill revolutionary Haiti's place in the world sugar market through modernizing and stimulating the sugar industry in its two remaining American colonies, Cuba and Puerto Rico. To facilitate the change, Spain offered all potential European colonists immigration incentives, particularly if they possessed investment capital or knowledge and skills related to sugar production and marketing (Cruz Baez 1977, 32; Morales Carrión 1983, 96–98). In Puerto Rico Spain awarded settlers generous land grants in return for commitments to develop agriculture. The land often was already occupied by subsistence farmers, who — under harsh new forced-labor laws — suddenly found themselves obligated to contribute their labor to the new owners' cash crops in return for the privilege of living on the land. There was also a dramatic increase in the slave trade from Africa to Puerto Rico and Cuba, primarily to meet growing labor demand in the sugar industry.[2]

Land ownership in sugar-growing areas such as Salinas was concentrated among a small number of privileged men, especially recent immigrants; in fact, the municipio of Salinas was established in 1841 under their control. Small-scale ownership, although still accounting for over 90 percent of the island's farms in 1899, made up only 28 percent of the agricultural land.[3] Owners conceded informal land-use rights to poor residents, who grew subsistence crops, raised hogs and chickens, and fished in

rivers and along the coast (Morales Carrión 1983, 102). By 1897 the
island census registered four thousand residents of Salinas, of whom 98
percent had been born in Puerto Rico; more than 75 percent could neither
read nor write. Some 21,500 of Salinas's nearly 46,000 cuerdas were
dedicated to pasture land, while nearly 1,000 cuerdas were planted in
sugar cane, 232 cuerdas in coffee, and nearly 700 cuerdas in minor fruits
and other crops (Martínez de la Jara 1975).

The pattern of formal land and resource use rights for the privileged few
was already firmly established in Salinas well before the twentieth century.
The region was sparsely populated and rich in natural resources, however,
and exploitation for profit was not well organized. For example, the low
percentage of sugarcane acreage reflected the difficulties experienced by
the industry on the island during the second half of the nineteenth century,
primarily due to a lack of investment capital. Although there were some
pockets of modernization, the industry as a whole stagnated until it was
revitalized by the flood of North American capital that followed the U.S.
invasion and occupation of Puerto Rico during the Spanish-American War
of 1898 (Dietz 1986: 60–61).

Sweet Gold: The Rise and Fall of Sugar

Early Sugar Era, 1898–1930

Between 1898 and 1930 Puerto Rico was converted into an agricultural
economic enclave, based primarily on one crop: sugarcane; by the 1930s
the industry constituted 70 percent of the island's exports (see fig. 3.1).
During this period sugar acreage on the island climbed from 15 percent to
44 percent of all cultivated land, and represented most of the best agricultural land on the island (Perloff 1950, 84–85). The first twenty years
of U.S. rule saw expansion of the island's infrastructure, particularly of
harbors, roads, and irrigation facilities, all to facilitate the expansion of
the sugar industry (Morales Carrión 1983, 173). As of 1928 four North
American corporations controlled 50 percent of all land planted to sugarcane and produced half of the island's sugar, all of which was destined
exclusively for the U.S. market (Diffie and Diffie 1931). They owned ten of
the island's forty operating sugar mills; more important, seven of the ten

Figure 3.1   Sugar cane in Salinas

most productive mills belonged to the "Big Four." Those segments of the local elite who had benefited from their North American economic connections since before the invasion controlled the balance of sugar production, commerce, and finance (Picó 1988, 198).

One of the most important of the "sugar colonies" was Salinas's Central Aguirre sugar mill complex and company town, located along the northwest coast of Jobos Bay, complete with docking facilities and a railroad. Its design was strongly reminiscent of plantations of the southern United States in that in both its architecture and its spatial layout it reflected the hierarchy that ruled its inhabitants. The lowest area was home to the factories, warehouses, and bungalows for central workers, including cooks, maids, and gardeners. The company town boasted its own hospital, schools, and stores. The areas with higher elevation and a view of the Caribbean contained a golf course, two hotels (a wooden building for Puerto Ricans and a stone mansion for North Americans), a theater, a swimming pool, and two segregated social clubs, as well as the spacious residences of the North American company executives.[4] The story of Central Aguirre's rise and fall offers a microcosm of Puerto Rico's sugar era, the island's first modern era of intensive exploitation for the economic benefit of the privileged few.

Shortly after the Spanish-American War's end four North American businessmen bought Salinas's Hacienda El Nuevo Aguirre, which contained a sugar mill and other machinery and some two thousand cuerdas of prime sugar-growing land; they also acquired twelve miles of railroad and corresponding equipment, as well as two smaller mills in Guayama.[5] Their efforts were facilitated by the 40 percent devaluation of the Puerto Rican *peso* and its quick conversion to the U.S. dollar, a policy that ruined many *hacendados* and forced them to sell their property (Picó 1988, 231–32; Morales Carrión 1983, 144).[6] During the first four decades of the twentieth century the Aguirre Corporation proceeded to strangle surrounding sugar operations and to acquire their land and equipment until the company owned more than twenty thousand acres of cane fields, milled over nine thousand tons of sugar per day, and virtually controlled the sugar industry between Ponce and Patillas. The tremendous expansion of production required a corresponding development of the region's water resources. This development not only resulted in increased exploitation of the local aquifer, but also impelled the construction of extensive irrigation systems fed by canals connected to upland reservoirs.

Anthropologist Sidney Mintz offered this moving description of the southern coastal region's sugar-dominated landscape:

One stands on a vast alluvial plain . . . an immense, well-developed sugar-cane-producing region, a place where . . . North Americans had penetrated most deeply into the vitals of pre-1898 Puerto Rican life. . . . [T]he road, the villages stretched along it, and such occasional barren fields were the only interruptions to the eye between mountains and sea; all else was sugar cane. It grew to the very edge of the road and right up to the stoops of the houses. When fully grown, it can tower fifteen feet above the ground. At its mature glory, it turned the plain into a special kind of hot, impenetrable jungle, broken only by special pathways . . . and irrigation ditches. (1985, xvii–xviii)

Locations such as Salinas provided the physical environment (soils, water, climate) and social environment (landless rural population providing abundant cheap labor) for centering the island's economy overwhelmingly on sugar production, to which the United States contributed heavy private capital investment, modern techniques and equipment, and free access to an almost unlimited market for the product. In turn, Puerto Rico provided a captive market for U.S. agricultural and industrial surpluses. The conversion of agricultural land from food to sugar production necessitated importation of food from the United States to the island. In Salinas, the Aguirre Company also owned and operated the southern region's dominant commercial businesses. The main stores were located within Central Aguirre, whereas smaller branches could be found on other sugarcane plantations in the area. The shopping system for the stores was as follows: each worker or employee received a ticket every Monday. Each day of work was perforated on the ticket, which employees used to shop at the stores; they also used it to pay for electricity. At the end of the week, the company deducted total purchases from wages and paid the remainder — if there was any — in cash. The average wage in 1932 was $.075 per hour, and a twelve-hour workday was the rule.[7] The average adult male cane worker spent $.74 per week more on food and other necessities than he earned, making it necessary for the women and children of the household to seek wage work as well (Gil-Bermejo García 1970, 284–5). Some women and children also worked in the cane fields, earning 25–50 percent less than the men.

Aguirre was known for its willingness to put into practice innovations in growing and processing sugarcane and was considered to be a model agro-industrial enterprise. At its height of prosperity Aguirre generated eight thousand jobs during the busy season, as well as thousands of indirect jobs.[8] Workers traveled to Aguirre-owned lands from all over Salinas and neighboring municipios. They worked as cane cutters and transporters, irrigation pipe carriers, railroad personnel and mechanics, as well as mill operators. Although some jobs were year-round, most were provided by the zafra, or cane-harvesting season, roughly from January to July. During summer and autumn (el tiempo muerto, the "dead time," between planting and harvesting of sugarcane) the average cane worker had little or no work.[9] Many women also earned a living cooking and washing laundry for the workers, who — if their families had not moved to Salinas — resided in former slave barracks or with local families during the week. Within Salinas, workers established communities such as El Coquí as a direct result of the expansion of the sugar industry.[10] Residents were predominantly landless rural peasants from both coastal and uplands areas throughout southern Puerto Rico.[11] They crowded into areas not suited for cane; often they used *bagasse* (cane residue) to fill up wetlands, over which they hastily constructed crude wooden shacks. These instant workers' colonies did not have running water or sanitation, which exacerbated health problems such as hookworm and dysentery, especially among children.

Salinas thus exemplified the fundamental agrarian and social changes in Puerto Rico produced by the U.S. occupation during the early twentieth century. High-value export crops — above all, sugar — replaced food crops, peasants became rural wage laborers, land was consolidated in large agricultural units, and the hacienda-style agriculture and seigniorial social structure virtually disappeared, except in more isolated mountain regions (Wessman 1977, 173–77). The economy was increasingly centralized, where decisions concerning investment and production were controlled from without, production was completely oriented toward the U.S. market, and profits benefited primarily North American investors. The old pattern of elite control of land and resources was intensified, resulting in less availability of local resources to meet the needs of Salinas's rapidly growing poor majority.

The development of an impersonal, absentee corporate capitalist sugar industry, however, plus the creation for the first time of wage workers' communities — comprised of formerly isolated rural peasants now obliged to seek work and housing together — fomented among the sugarcane workers a class consciousness configured around elements of alternative culture based upon the need for collective struggle and "combative solidarity" (Quintero Rivera and García 1982, 67). Popular resistance therefore found a major avenue of expression through the labor movement.

Although Puerto Rican workers had participated in strikes during Spanish rule, the first major labor organization was founded in 1899, soon after the U.S. takeover. Sugar and tobacco workers dominated the

Free Federation of Labor (known as the FLT), and in 1915 the Socialist Party was created to allow union leaders to run for political office under the banner of a "worker's party" (Quintero Rivera and García 1982, 146). Central Aguirre experienced major strikes in 1905, 1915, and 1920. Workers' demands included wage increases, a reduction in the working day from fourteen to eight hours, the prohibition of child labor, and abolition of the *agrego* system (Silén 1978, 66).[12] Increasing militancy among workers and a wave of government repression characterized the strike of 1920, with the sugar growers calling for military intervention to break the strike (Taller de Formación Política 1982a, 122). This strike is still remembered in Salinas, because police murdered two unarmed workers and imprisoned twenty-five in Salinas Pueblo, triggering a march of angry residents through the streets.[13]

Sugar and Politics During the Turbulent 1930s and 1940s

The Great Depression halted the expansion of the sugar economy of the island. New North American investment in Puerto Rican sugar virtually disappeared during the 1930s, due primarily to the Depression, but also to the quotas on production and the often violent labor unrest on the island, which was centered upon the sugar industry. The price of sugar dropped from $.05 per pound in 1923 to $.02 per pound in 1929, and plunged further to $.009 per pound in 1932 (Pantojas García 1979, 84). That the sugar corporations managed to maintain a margin of profit during the first half of the 1930s was due to extraordinary protectionist measures on the part of the U.S. government, as well as to a dramatic decline in wages: for the fiscal year 1928–29 the average wage for laborers in the cane fields was $.96 per day, whereas by 1933–34 the average daily wage of $.62 represented a 35 percent reduction. Then in 1934 Congress reduced the quota for Puerto Rican sugar exports to the U.S. by 25 percent, resulting in a 300,000-ton excess production of cane, a reduction in the grinding season from 150 to 80 days, and a loss of twenty-five thousand jobs (Gil-Bermejo García 1970, 274). By paying growers not to plant sugarcane, the government reduced the proportion of land actually planted to sugarcane by 20 percent, which particularly affected the smaller, locally owned farms. If one adds to this the contraction suffered by other sectors such as tobacco and fruit (and the already declining coffee industry), a clear picture emerges of the collapse of export agriculture, the basis of the Puerto Rican economy (Pantojas García 1979, 85–86). By 1935 some 50 percent of heads of families were estimated to be unemployed, creating a desperate situation.

In 1933 the FLT signed a labor contract that many sugar industry workers considered grossly unfair.[14] Wildcat strikes broke out all over the island during the winter of 1933–34. Workers in Guayama and Salinas were the first to call upon Nationalist leader Pedro Albizu Campos for help[15] and formed the first chapter of the Puerto Rico Workers' Association (ATP) to challenge the FLT. Washington, which feared any possibility of popular unification of socialist and nationalist sentiments, viewed these events with alarm.[16] Almost immediately U.S. General Blanton Winship, director of the military repression of the Philippines anticolonial rebellion, was named governor of Puerto Rico; in addition, Army intelligence agent Colonel Francis Riggs was sent to head the island's police force. In 1936 Riggs was assassinated by two Nationalist Party members, triggering a wave of repression that (among other things) resulted in the massacre of unarmed protesters in Ponce and put Nationalist leaders in U.S. prisons for up to ten years.

The year 1934 also saw the creation of two additional organizations. The first was Afirmación Socialista, formed with the intention of renovating the Socialist Party from within. Other members left the party altogether to form the Partido Comunista Puertorriqueño (PCP). Seeing their mission as one "to sow the seeds of revolution within the base" (Quintero Rivera and García 1982, 110), the PCP did not attempt to create new unions to rival the FLT, nor did they openly repudiate the Socialist Party until 1940. Both Afirmación Socialista and the PCP had active chapters in Salinas.

Then, in 1939 the Popular Democratic Party (PPD or *populares*) was formed as a loose coalition composed of former members of the pro-autonomy Liberal Party's left wing, socialists, New Deal technocrats, urban and rural laborers, small farmers, and commercial sectors not allied with the sugar interests. Led by Luís Muñoz Marín and promising "Bread, Land, and Liberty," the new party managed to win control of the Senate in

1940. The populares instituted some rural land reform, promoted state-owned industrialization, and greatly expanded government institutions dealing with economic planning and social welfare.[17]

At the same time dissident sugar workers, rebelling against the thoroughly discredited FLT, joined with unions from a wide variety of industries to form the General Confederation of Workers (CGT), which supported the PPD.[18] In 1942 the sugar industry sector of the CGT was organized into the Sugar Syndicate of Puerto Rico, under the leadership of PPD leaders and former sugar workers Armando Sánchez and José "Chepo" Caraballo, both based in Salinas. Rejecting a contract signed by the FLT and the growers, the Sugar Syndicate waged a paralyzing and sometimes violent strike that was supported by workers in other CGT-organized industries. The action led to creation of the PPD-dominated Puerto Rico Wage Board, which would set and enforce minimum wages for all economic sectors (Quintero Rivera and García 1982, 121–24).

From the beginning the populares had managed to appeal to both nationalist and socialist sentiment on the island without seriously antagonizing Washington. Once in control they also proved themselves capable of ensuring that U.S. interests were best served by the PPD's remaining in power, while utilizing the powerful tools of government to retain the support of most Puerto Ricans.[19] After the party's overwhelming electoral victory in 1944 the PPD set out to control the Puerto Rican labor movement, a step party strategists considered necessary to promote the island's industrialization. They succeeded in dividing the CGT in 1945 into the "Authentic CGT" and the "Government CGT." Leaders of the "Authentic CGT" — many of whom were *independentistas* or Communist Party members — were frequently jailed, exiled, and otherwise persecuted (Quintero Rivera and García 1982, 125; 135–36; Silén 1978, 117–18).[20]

By contrast, "Government CGT" leaders were offered government posts. For example, Salinas's José "Chepo" Caraballo was named to government posts during the 1940s and helped organize labor on the island for the AFofL during the 1950s.[21] In 1961 he left that position to form a new union of sugar industry workers, the United Southern Workers' Syndicate (SOUS for its initials in Spanish). Enjoying strong support from the PPD central government and ruled with an iron hand by the charismatic Chepo, SOUS managed to become the leading representative of the sugar workers within a few short years.[22] The union stressed community service and demanded loyalty of its members. Its 1964 constitution prohibited membership in the Communist Party, and members openly critical of the leadership were threatened with expulsion.[23] In addition to representing its members and fighting to keep Central Aguirre open, sous ran a union pharmacy and constructed a "workers' temple" in Salinas, the union's headquarters.

The Decline of Sugar in Puerto Rico, 1952–1990

Labor and fertilizer shortages and the disruption of ocean transportation during World War II resulted in a slight decline of sugarcane production. The immediate postwar period, in contrast, saw a rapid increase both in land planted in sugarcane and in production, so that in 1952 a record 1,359,481 tons of raw sugar was produced in Puerto Rico, the fifth consecutive year that Puerto Rican sugar production exceeded its quota allowance. To address this situation, in 1953 the U.S. Department of Agriculture imposed restrictive proportional shares on the island's production quota amounting to a 15 percent reduction on all except small farmers. Sugar growers responded by curtailing many practices that entailed short-term expenses (such as the type of cane planted) but that over the long term would have increased productivity (Pringle 1969, 28). At the same time, the industrialization of Puerto Rico was gathering momentum and would soon overtake agriculture as the island's leading productive sector. The sugar industry would shortly face increasing competition for land use and other resources from industrialization, urbanization, and growing agricultural sectors such as the dairy industry. Since the record year 1952, sugar has undergone a pronounced and steady decline. By 1992 the Puerto Rican sugar industry teetered on the edge of extinction; it was no longer able to meet all of the island's needs, let alone constitute an export product.[24]

In spite of the irreversible decline of the island's sugar industry, the Aguirre Sugar Corporation continued to be a profitable enterprise until 1967. That year the corporation was acquired by a group of French businessmen, who quickly replaced the largely Puerto Rican management with Cuban émigrés and explored ways to sell off some of the company's land, then valued at thirty million dollars. The firm printed brochures extolling the potential for converting Central Aguirre's Jobos Bay port into one suitable for heavy industry. The nearby presence of the newly opened Phillips Puerto Rico Core petroleum refinery, just east of Jobos Bay, was a prime recruitment factor. Also attractive was the AEE's plan to build a major power plant complex next door to Aguirre, in order to offer cheap energy for industry.[25]

Between 1967 and 1970 the Aguirre sugar operation lost some fourteen million dollars; in 1969 alone it lost six million. The losses were attributed to a variety of reasons, among them a drought, a strike, serious management problems stemming from the change of ownership and staff, and the new owners' interest in real estate speculation. Then, in July 1970 the company abruptly announced the closure of Central Aguirre, and more than three thousand workers suddenly found themselves on the unemployment lines. The move also threatened the municipal tax base, since in 1970 half of Salinas's income from tax revenues came from Aguirre. In the face of this disaster, and after months of futile negotiations with the company, the Puerto Rican government decided to expropriate all the properties and assets owned by the corporation. The move was virtually unprecedented in Puerto Rican history; it was vehemently attacked as reminiscent of actions taken by the most nationalist or "Communistic" Latin American governments and was considered to be a bad signal to outside investors. Within a month Central Aguirre had reopened, now as part of the government-owned Puerto Rico Sugar Corporation. The Aguirre Corporation owners took the government to court, and in 1976 the government was ordered to pay more than twenty-three million dollars for the expropriation.[26]

Central Aguirre passed through another crisis in 1978, as a result of Governor Carlos Romero Barceló's announced policy of eventually closing all of the sugar mills, one by one. Union leaders, environmentalists, and agricultural experts questioned various government policy decisions. Among the most controversial issues were the failure of the government to allocate three million dollars to bring Central Aguirre into compliance with EPA pollution standards by 1980, the practice of sending the Aguirre land's best crop to Central Mercedita in Ponce for milling, and the decrease of sugar planted and workers employed, despite the government's promise to maintain thirty-six hundred jobs.[27] Here there was no problem of lack of sugarcane forcing the closure, as there had been elsewhere, and Aguirre's losses seemed to be consistently out of proportion to those of the other mills. "There were strange unknown factors" involved, contended the sugar workers' union, hinting at plans for land speculation.[28] The union leadership went as far as to suggest that the refinery and government-owned sugar lands be sold to the workers if the Sugar Corporation could not properly administer them. Finally, the government kept the mill open and promised to improve management.

As the sugar mill employing the greatest number of workers, Central Aguirre was projected to be the last of Puerto Rico's sugar mills to close; accordingly, sugar cultivation — the area's principal economic activity and employment source — was expected to continue with equal or greater intensity for the immediate future (Padín, Torres Rodríguez, and Maysonet Negrón 1981, 101). Nonetheless, only half of Aguirre's more than twenty thousand acres were being planted in sugarcane; since the 1960s much good land had been leased or sold to petrochemical and other capital- and energy-intensive enterprises, with consequent ecological damage. In 1981 the Secretary of Agriculture implemented a plan to reduce Aguirre's operating losses through leasing the fields to private growers. Unfortunately, these growers were not properly screened on the basis of their financial and agricultural suitability, according to the president of the Puerto Rico Sugar Corporation; moreover, many selections were apparently made for political reasons and amounted to de facto gifts of valuable land.[29]

Because Aguirre was the sugar mill consistently reporting the biggest losses, its possible closure became a subject of constant discussion in 1989; however, Secretary of Agriculture Félix Rodríguez assured the public in August that no decision would be taken until studies were carried out to determine how to reemploy the workers, as stated in House of Representatives Resolution 571.[30] In an exclusive interview with Salinas's community newspaper on August 22, 1989, SOUS President José "Chepito" Caraballo, Jr. (son of "Chepo," who died in 1978) lamented the lack of participation by workers or the local community in any study, but admitted that the union had not prepared an independent assessment of the sugar operation. However, the union did have a strategy for combating the closure of the sugar refinery that included marches, picketing, publicity, meetings with government officials and politicians, and above all, effective communication with the workers.[31]

When the time came, however, the union leaders displayed an uncharacteristic lack of initiative. On December 8, 1989, the Aguirre management and the leadership of SOUS jointly convened a meeting in which 1,007 workers were informed of the mill's possible closure in April 1990. Central Aguirre's operating losses were cited as the reason. A 1989 study by Price Waterhouse concluded that Aguirre's cost of producing sugar reached $55.79 per quintal, making it the most expensive of the Puerto Rico Sugar Corporation's five mills to operate; Aguirre alone was responsible for 47 percent of the Corporation's thirty million dollars in losses, the study added. Although the closure would be a serious economic blow to Salinas, at the union's urging Aguirre's workers voted in favor of the government's proposal for retraining or reemployment and more than six million dollars in termination compensation.[32]

Not everyone accepted the economic rationale for the closing. One local accountant found that the study had included in Aguirre's' losses nearly eight million dollars in retroactive benefits awarded in court to workers, as well as a million dollars in attorney's fees. Upon subtracting those amounts, the accountant figured the cost of producing Aguirre's sugar was actually $33.83 per quintal, which was lower than Central Mercedita's cost of $36.41.[33] Moreover, the employment study promised by the Secretary of Agriculture was never carried out, indicating that there were no plans to provide jobs for the workers. In answer to the question, "Why not close Mercedita instead of Aguirre?" some locals wryly observed that the family of Governor Rafael Hernández Colón's wife had interests in Mercedita. Salinas's local newspaper reported that the mill was being closed to make way for an expansion of the Aguirre power plant complex next door, as part of a long-term plan to greatly expand the generating capacity of the complex in order to attract more energy-intensive industries to the area. Others cited plans by PRIDCO to convert the Aguirre grounds into an industrial park. Still others charged that the sugar operation was being shut down as punishment by the ruling PPD, because in 1988 the traditionally PPD municipio had elected a mayor from the pro-statehood opposition party, the Partido Nuevo Progresista (PNP). Everyone agreed on

Figure 3.2 Central Aguirre: Neglected monument to the sugar era

at least one point, however: the closing of Central Aguirre was disastrous for Salinas. Some 62 percent of the sugar mill's workers were Salinas residents; moreover, the municipio lost 13 percent of its operating budget due to the closure and loss of tax revenues and had to cut back services.[34]

To make matters worse, in 1990 Caraballo became enmeshed in allegations of corruption that threatened to put an end to what little power sous still had left. Millions of dollars in claims awarded to sugar workers had been handed over to the union leader by the Sugar Corporation for distribution between 1986 and 1990. Complaints by workers about not receiving the money due them prompted public hearings in San Juan, in which some officials concluded that Caraballo had not made proper accounting for all of the funds received. In 1991 Caraballo was given a court order to produce sous records for an audit by the Office of the Comptroller; however, claiming that the Comptroller lacked the authority to audit sous, the union leader vowed to go to jail rather than hand over the records. Public allegations and legal battles dragged on through the next general election, and forced Chepito to put his oft-stated political ambitions on hold.[35]

The Aguirre sugar mill, now quiet for the first time in more than a century, still looms over the landscape (see fig. 3.2). In some ways Salinas is still a sugar town, clinging to the nearly moribund sugar industry, as each year less acreage is planted in cane. In poor workers' villages — still partly shantytowns — many working-age males are skilled in agricultural work but in little else. Circular migration between Salinas and the United States, whether as migrant agricultural workers or to the urban ghettoes, is a fact of life for many.

The organization and struggles of Puerto Rican workers in the early part of the twentieth century could be considered the spark that propelled popular resistance to the exploitation posed by the sugar industry. Their very success in altering political and economic structures also led to their demise as a political force, however. The PPD's co-option, regimentation, patronage, and control of the sugar workers' labor organization (along with other labor sectors) compromised labor's ability to organize resistance and agitate for change, whereas the substitution of industrialization for agriculture led to a steady numerical decline in organized agricultural labor. The proud earlier history of the sugar workers is still mentioned in Salinas as providing a historical background for present-day popular struggles.

Unfulfilled Promises:
The Legacy of Operation Bootstrap

Looking south from the mountains toward the panorama of Salinas's coastal plain and the shimmering Caribbean beyond, one is struck first of all by open spaces. From far away it appears to be an idyllic and still rural area; the first-time visitor might well expect to see diverse agricultural pursuits, leading to fleets of fishing and tourist vessels at sea. As one descends closer, however, it becomes apparent that all is not well. The rosy haze hanging somewhat incongruously in the otherwise cloudless blue sky emanates from a giant energy complex along the bay to the east. The uplands area just east of the highway is fenced off, the land scarred and eroded almost down to bare rock in places; soon a sign announces the presence of a military training camp.

Along the coastal plain much fallow, weed-filled land extends among the agricultural plots. Here and there are abandoned factory buildings, stores, houses. Along one small bay an expanding marina and tourist complex threatens to eat up neighboring coastal mangroves and modest homes; its yacht-filled docks seem to be squeezing out the small boats filled with fishing nets and lobster traps. To the east, mangrove forests have been cut down and waterways have been filled to make room for fenced-off summer homes. Piles of garbage choke up some wetland areas, empty lots, and roadsides. Secluded beaches are stained with oil. Residents, especially children, suffer from strange skin, respiratory, and nervous ailments. Families and communities are increasingly torn apart by the ills of modern poverty and the need to migrate in search of work. This is also part of the modern Salinas landscape, after a generation of development under Operation Bootstrap.

After World War II the Puerto Rican government initiated Puerto Rico's renowned Operation Bootstrap, which gave rise to the phrase "industrialization through invitation." The island's industrialization experience has passed through three phases: first, labor-intensive, relatively low capital investment manufacturing, such as clothing and shoes; second, heavy industrialization related to the petroleum refining and petrochemical industries; and finally, capital-intensive, mostly high-tech industries, typified above all by pharmaceuticals.[36]

The First Phase:
Labor-Intensive Manufacturing

From the beginning of Operation Bootstrap mainland firms took advantage of the traditional exemption from federal taxes for businesses operating in U.S. territorial possessions, plus ten- to fifteen-year exemptions from Puerto Rican taxes under the Puerto Rico Industrial Incentives Act of 1947. They also benefited from the island government's provision of buildings with low rental fees, roads, and cheap water and electricity. Add to these benefits wages that averaged only one-quarter of those on the mainland, and profits were up to four times what they would have been at home (Chase 1951). By the mid-1960s, however, gradual extension of federal labor and wage regulations to Puerto Rico, combined with increased union organizing, resulted in higher wage standards. Meanwhile, international trade agreements reduced some obstacles to foreign access to U.S. markets, facilitating relocation of labor-intensive firms to countries with even cheaper labor. Tax exemptions granted at the beginning of Operation Bootstrap began to expire, and their extension proved not to be a sufficient incentive for many companies to remain on the island.[37]

Relatively few manufacturers were directed by PRIDCO to Salinas during the first phase of Operation Bootstrap. Sugar remained at Salinas's economic center, while most U.S. industries preferred to locate in the San Juan area. Those that did open included firms producing pens, boots, pantyhose, and women's clothing.[38] By 1980 the first three had used up their tax exemptions and were gone, taking with them some one thousand jobs. The women's clothing firm, known as Salinas Manufacturing, went through several changes of ownership and exemption renewals before finally shutting its doors in 1990, sending 150 mostly female workers to the unemployment lines.

The Second Phase:
Petroleum-Based Industrialization

At the same time that Puerto Rico was losing its competitive advantage in labor-intensive manufacturing, changes in U.S. oil-import policy made it possible for the island to import large quantities of cheap oil and feedstocks (Puerto Rico. Office of Energy 1979). Until 1974 foreign crude oil and naphtha were cheaper than U.S. domestic supplies. Since Puerto Rico was exempted from U.S. import quotas it could obtain foreign crude oil at $1.00–$1.50 per barrel less than the mainland price, a considerable cost advantage. Attracted as well by tax and other incentives, the refining and petrochemical industries expanded rapidly on the island, particularly on the south coast. The Puerto Rican government also embarked on an ambitious construction program of petroleum-fired power plants during the 1960s and early 1970s, the largest of which was the Aguirre energy complex, located on Jobos Bay next to Central Aguirre. As an additional incentive to locate on the island, Public Law 82 of 1967 allowed the sale of electricity to industrial plants at lower prices than to commercial and residential consumers. So although Puerto Rico was declining as a destination for labor-intensive manufacturers, it was becoming increasingly attractive to capital-intensive heavy industries. In fact, during the 1970s factories located in Puerto Rico supplied between 20 and 30 percent of U.S. demand for petrochemical materials (Morales Cardona 1979, 214).

Unfortunately, this strategy failed to generate the hoped-for direct and indirect employment in sufficient numbers to solve Puerto Rico's chronic problem of high unemployment. At its height the petroleum refining and petrochemical industries consumed 35 percent of Puerto Rico's energy-generating capacity, but provided only 5 percent of the island's income and 1 percent of employment (Morales Cardona, Sánchez Cardona, and Caldari 1975, 35). Then, the drastic increases in foreign oil prices after 1973 dealt the island's petroleum industry a blow from which it never recovered. During the late 1970s and early 1980s the island sank deep into a recession so severe that in both 1982 and 1983 its real gross domestic product actually declined. Dragged down by the U.S. recession and the continuing rise of oil prices worldwide, Puerto Rico's official unemployment rate reached 25.3 percent in January, 1983 — the highest figure since the Great Depression. Meanwhile, the construction of massive power plant complexes left Puerto Rico with an enormous generating surplus after two giants of the island's petrochemical industry shut down between 1978 and 1982. The AEE invested little in preventive maintenance, with the result that the island's energy system is capable of operating at only 58 percent of its capacity (Misión Industrial de Puerto Rico 1991, 13).

The second phase of Operation Bootstrap had brought heavy industry and a massive power plant complex to the area around Jobos Bay. According to the Puerto Rico Economic Development Administration (known in Spanish as *Fomento*) the Phillips oil refinery, which opened in 1965, was supposed to provide thirty thousand direct and indirect jobs for that region (Centro de Estudios Puertorriqueños 1980). In reality it never generated more than two thousand jobs, many of which were filled by workers from other regions on the island. The only truly downstream industry established as a result of the refinery was Phillips subsidiary Fibers International, "the petrochemical industry's principal existing linkage to textiles and apparel" (Puerto Rico Economic Development Administration 1975, 2). The firm began operations in 1966, was bought by the Chevron Corporation in 1976, and closed in 1981. Of its eighteen hundred employees in 1981 some three hundred were Salinas residents.[39] As late as 1981

Fomento was still talking of downstream industries from Phillips. However, as of 1992 the refinery employed three hundred workers and generated an additional 30 jobs at its on-site subsidiary Phillips Paraxylene — a grand total of 330 jobs.

The Third Phase: "936" and Pharmaceuticals

Faced with the collapse of the petrochemical industry, Puerto Rican economic planners searched desperately for new ways to attract and benefit from U.S. firms. The passage in 1976 of Federal Tax Law Section 936 provided a powerful recruitment tool, particularly of pharmaceutical firms. Although tax exemptions for North American firms operating in U.S. possessions have existed since the 1920s, profits had traditionally been taxed once they were repatriated to the mainland home company; section 936 allowed such profits to be repatriated tax-free.[40] Puerto Rico also changed two aspects of its traditional tax-exemption incentives. First, billions of dollars of profits made in Puerto Rico operations would be deposited in financial institutions located on the island, rather than circulating elsewhere in the world, thus providing a gigantic boost to Puerto Rico's banking industry. Second, the commonwealth government would now charge a 10 percent "tollgate tax" on profits leaving the island for the mainland; in this way the Puerto Rican treasury would benefit from the transfer of profits from the island to the mainland.[41]

The measure has proved to be extremely profitable for participating U.S. corporations. Among other things it is in large part responsible for making Puerto Rico the pharmaceutical capital of the world (Puerto Rico. Planning Board 1990, 4:3).[42] In 1990 the pharmaceutical firms alone accounted for 30 percent of Puerto Rico's exports but for only twenty thousand jobs, or about 2 percent of total island employment.[43] Nevertheless, "la 936" has not been without its share of controversy; although intense and skillful lobbying efforts have helped the measure survive numerous attempts by U.S. legislators and the Internal Revenue Service to eliminate it, its future is at best uncertain.[44]

Since the late 1970s an increasing percentage of the agricultural lands of the Jobos area of Guayama has been developed into an industrial park, following a plan dating back to the "cheap oil" era (Puerto Rico. Planning

Board 1974, 1991). A new superhighway was completed in 1994 in the foothills between Salinas and Guayama, along with highways connecting it to PR 3 at El Coquí and the Phillips refinery; these were considered vital to extensive new industrial development of adjacent lands (Puerto Rico. Highway Authority 1986). The industrial potential of Central Aguirre has not gone unnoticed; even before the closing of the sugar mill PRIDCO had announced plans for an industrial park to take advantage of Aguirre's attractions: a harbor, geographic proximity to South America and the Caribbean, extensive level land, abundant underground fresh water, and electric power generating capacity at the Aguirre electric energy complex next door. As of 1994, however, the Aguirre industrial park had not yet materialized.

Fomento directed its recruitment efforts almost exclusively at U.S. and foreign firms; it made little attempt to encourage locally owned ventures. For example, Salinas Convert, Inc., a Puerto Rican–owned plastics recycling operation, was established during the summer of 1991 in one of Fomento's buildings just south of Salinas Pueblo. When the firm was fully operational its president hoped to generate 140 jobs. The recycling project was slow to expand for two reasons, however; first, because the Regulation and Permits Administration (ARPE, after its initials in Spanish) delayed issuing the required permits, reportedly because it was located within a flood zone. Second, the recycling process to be used was technologically sophisticated and required considerable capital outlay for equipment; the firm had not been able to secure a large loan, and its PRIDCO tax exemption was delayed. Salinas Convert, Inc., was thus limited in its operation; as of 1992 it employed only eighteen workers. Without the extra support or incentives commonly granted to outside ventures, by 1994 Salinas Convert had gone out of business.[45]

In 1992 residents of Salinas held 80 percent of the 524 jobs generated by the eleven manufacturing plants located in Salinas. The firms received twenty years of tax exemption, and the average hourly wage was $4.69. Firms that were typical of Operation Bootstrap's early "labor intensive" phase generated more than 60 percent of the jobs. Manufacturing within Salinas provided barely 6 percent of the municipio's jobs; this was one-third of the percentage of jobs generated by manufacturing in Puerto Rico as a whole.[46] So we see that after more than forty years of Operation

Bootstrap sugar had ceased to be the backbone of Salinas's economy, yet manufacturing had not managed to replace it.

Effects of Operation Bootstrap

According to its architects Operation Bootstrap was intended to accomplish the economic development and modernization of Puerto Rico. As expected, the substitution of higher-wage manufacturing jobs for extremely low-wage agricultural employment — which had provided most of the island's jobs during the first half of the twentieth century — provided a crucial building block for constructing a "modern" society. Operation Bootstrap succeeded brilliantly in rapidly transforming the island into a modern, industrialized, and largely urbanized society. This transformation also effected or deepened a number of disturbing trends, however. First, the "Puerto Rico development model" has provoked severe environmental degradation, which threatens the health of the island's citizens and the natural environment. Second, it did not solve the island's unemployment problem, but rather served to further institutionalize it. Finally, the development strategy widened inequality between the consumer-oriented middle and upper classes and the poor majority; moreover, it aggravated regional economic inequality between San Juan and the rest of the island. The unfulfilled promises of industrialization in Salinas have also, however, fueled the local mobilization for alternatives.

Environmental Effects in Puerto Rico

One of Puerto Rico's most important industrial recruitment tools was the generally less stringent enforcement of environmental protection laws than that on the U.S. mainland (Concepción 1990); not surprisingly, this development strategy has exacted a high environmental price from the island.[47]

The dramatic increase in energy use since the start of Operation Bootstrap — in an island approximately 110 miles long by 40 miles wide, with a population of more than three million — gives one indication of the magnitude of environmental degradation. Between 1949 and 1979 energy use in Puerto Rico increased 1,400 percent in absolute amounts. The island's

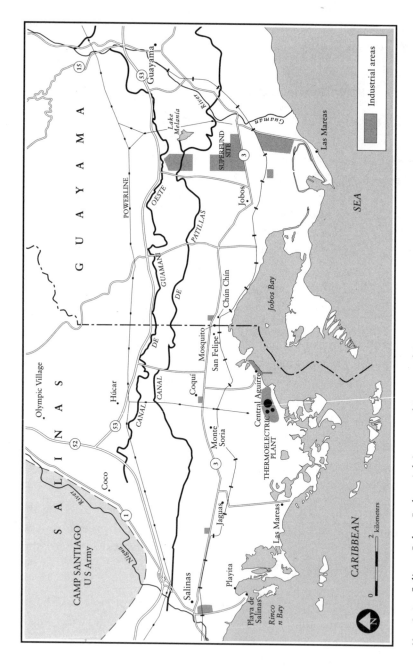

Map 3.1 Salinas-Jobos Industrial Areas and Impacted Environment

energy density, or the amount of energy used per square kilometer of active land (urban or economically productive land) increased 2,500 percent. Puerto Rico's energy density during the 1970s was four and one half times greater than that of the United States; in fact, only Holland, Belgium, and Japan had higher energy densities (Morales Cardona, Sánchez Cardona, and Caldari 1975; Morales Cardona 1979, 1990). Electric power generation and energy-intensive manufacturing are known to be highly contaminating, and the impact of such intense energy use on Puerto Rico's environment was enormous.[48]

Toxic waste disposal problems give another indication of environmental effects. Of the estimated seven thousand toxic waste dumps under United States jurisdiction some 12 percent are located in Puerto Rico. As of 1989 around a hundred U.S. toxic waste dumps had been designated as Superfund cleanup sites, of which nine were located in Puerto Rico. One hundred other Puerto Rican sites have also been considered for Superfund status, including nearly all of the island's municipal landfills. This high concentration of toxic dumps well illustrates the intensity of toxic contamination unleashed upon Puerto Rico during its heavy industrialization phase. Because most of the heavy industry in Puerto Rico was processing materials that were shipped to the United States for final assembly and use, one scientist has commented that "it's as if Puerto Rico was chosen to sacrifice its renewable natural resources (air, water, land) in order to create goods which would be transformed and consumed elsewhere" (Morales Cardona 1979, 216) (see Map 3.1).[49]

Environmental effects in Salinas: Air pollution. Salinas ranks among the island's worst municipios in terms of air pollution. The prevailing easterly trade winds bring emissions from industries located in the Jobos area of Guayama; Las Mareas, La Playa, Playita, and the pueblo are among the Salinas communities most affected. Studies have confirmed that the Aguirre units are the most polluting of Puerto Rico's thermoelectric power complexes. The plant discharges 112,452 tons of sulfur dioxide per year into the atmosphere. This is more than four times the amount of sulfur dioxide released yearly by the Phillips refinery, also a notorious polluter.[50] When combined with water vapor sulfur dioxide is converted into sulfuric acid, a corrosive and serious respiratory irritant also harmful to plants and fresh water biota. In addition, the power plant discharges nitrogen oxide, which, when combined with water vapor, produces nitric acid, a substance fatal in large concentrations; it is responsible for the rosy haze visible around Salinas on late afternoons.[51] One study placed Salinas fourth among the island's municipios in the incidence of lung cancer (the only one of the "top five" not located in the San Juan area), and indicated that environmental contamination was a determining factor (Martínez et al. 1991). Cases of other respiratory illnesses in downwind communities have also steadily increased over the last years. The visible smoke constantly emanating from the electric energy complex cannot but be a reminder of the problem.

Industrial plants located in the Jobos area also contribute to local air pollution. The worst offender is reputed to be the Phillips petroleum refinery, located at Las Mareas de Guayama. Phillips manages twelve substances identified as acute health hazards,[52] eleven identified as chronic or delayed hazards, twelve substances classified as fire hazards, and five considered chemical reactive hazards.[53] Over the years residents of nearby communities and schools have registered numerous complaints of illness allegedly caused by substances such as benzene, which is known to cause leukemia and multiple myeloma (Concepción 1990, 99). Agricultural productivity has also been affected by industrial pollution; for example, not long after the Phillips refinery opened the percentage of molasses yield from sugarcane planted downwind decreased from 13 percent to 3 percent.

SmithKline Beecham, the area's oldest pharmaceutical firm, is also associated with a long list of dangerous substances. The plant incinerates ten toxic materials as by-products of production; it also manages twenty-six acute health hazard substances, two chronic or delay health hazards, twenty-one fire hazards, and one reactive chemical hazard.[54] Reactors, centrifuges, filters, pumps, and distillation columns are employed in the production process. Environmental controls are provided by gas washers, dust collectors, ventilators, pressure chambers, and incinerators, and aqueous wastes and organic compounds are stored on-site. In what may be a tacit admission of the dangerous nature of employment, SmithKline Beecham allows voluntary resignation of employees after ten years' work, after which they may opt for a retirement compensation worth thousands of dollars.[55]

Residents of neighboring Guayama communities of Miramar and Jobos have consistently reported the appearance of skin, respiratory, and other ailments since SmithKline & Beecham (SKB) opened in 1978; such ailments often appeared to improve only when the sufferers left the area.[56] A high school located less than two miles west of both SKB and Phillips has suffered many episodes of objectionable fumes that adversely affected the health and activities of the students and staff, including hospitalization of two students during October 1990. After technical studies detected excessive levels of several toxic substances within the school, scientists from the Environmental Quality Board recommended in January 1991 that the case be investigated; they also called for environmental and health impact studies of the surrounding communities (Moreno and Vásquez 1991). The Board agreed however, to authorize emissions from SKB to continue until 1993, conditional upon specific requirements, such as that the company must ensure that no disagreeable odors that could be perceived outside of company premises would be produced. Nonetheless, a year later the school was still being evacuated at least once a month because of disagreeable odors, according to students. In an effort to improve community relations, SKB undertook to renovate a park in the village of Jobos. It is worth noting that community organizing thus far did not appear to have generated enough pressure to force the government regulating agencies to act against existing plants; nor had local activism to date significantly altered industrial practices.

Water pollution. Water pollution, both of ground water and of coastal areas, is also a serious problem.[57] Pharmaceutical plants, being the main industrial users of groundwater in Puerto Rico, locate in places with large amounts of underground fresh water. In coastal areas heavy groundwater use reduces the amount available for agricultural and residential needs and lowers the water table, causing seepage of sea water into the underground aquifers. In addition, municipal landfills that leach toxic materials, industrial waste sites, and underground storage tanks that leak have been identified as the major sources of contaminants of groundwater (Concepción 1990, 72–74). One of Puerto Rico's "Superfund" sites, the so-called Fibers public supply wells, served as alternate water supply for the pueblo of Guayama. They are located down-gradient from a number of artificial, unlined lagoons used by Fibers International during the 1960s and 1970s to discharge volatile chemical organic pollutants, solvents, heavy metals, and other poisonous industrial wastes. Four of the five public supply wells became contaminated from leaching of the wastes and had to be closed (U.S. Environmental Protection Agency 1988).

The Aguirre energy complex cools its giant turbines with large amounts of water from Jobos Bay. The superheated water (chlorinated to prevent algae buildup in the turbines) is then discharged back into the bay via a mile-long underwater pipe.[58] The Environmental Quality Board noted in 1972 that hot water discharges of the then-planned two plants into Jobos Bay would raise temperatures well above the four degrees Fahrenheit maximum established by the Department of Health in 1967, thus provoking ecological damage (Puerto Rico Environmental Quality Board 1972, 20). The fact that there are currently four units suggests that serious and perhaps irreversible ecological damage may have already occurred.

The Jobanes reserve managers say that Phillips contains its oil spills entirely within what once was Laguna Las Mareas, and immediately informs the reserve whenever a problem develops; they claim good relations and communication between themselves and Phillips (see fig. 3.3). Local fishermen tell quite a different story, however. For example, fishermen from the community of Las Mareas de Salinas complained of pollution from an oil spill just before Christmas 1990, which began washing up on the shore three weeks later and negatively affected fishing; they blamed Phillips for failing to contain the spill. Additionally, they have also discovered signs of chemical contamination in Jobos Bay. For example, in 1991 the president of La Playa's fishing association encountered pinkish gelatinous foam in his nets, and suffered burns on his hands when he attempted to remove it. He also indicated that considerable dumping of unknown wastes was taking place in Jobos Bay a mile and a half south of Central Aguirre's docks.[59]

In sum, environmental effects of industrialization in Salinas have included contamination of air, soil, fresh water, and the sea. Many residents have suffered from the negative health effects of contamination, particularly those from poor coastal communities who have not benefited from

Figure 3.3 Phillips petroleum refinery: "Thousands" of jobs no, pollution yes

the jobs created. Moreover, such environmental degradation reduces the local potential for agricultural, fishing, and tourist development that might generate the jobs that Operation Bootstrap has failed to provide.

Operation Bootstrap and Employment

Proponents of Bootstrap-type development have argued that environmental damage is a necessary evil when we face the urgent economic and social need to provide jobs. The "jobs vs. environment" argument has dubious merit, for if human and natural resources are squandered the basis for development will eventually be undermined. Allowing for the possibility that it might make short-term sense, however, let's examine the post-Bootstrap record of employment generation in Puerto Rico and Salinas.

Manufacturing, which accounted for 40 percent of Puerto Rico's gross domestic product in fiscal year 1989, is characterized as the "marrow" of the island's economy — even though half of Puerto Rico's net product leaves the island in the form of profits to non–Puerto Rican entities (Puerto Rico. Planning Board 1988). Manufacturing provides 17 percent of all jobs. Of this total so-called high technology enterprises contribute around 70% percent of manufacturing's share of the GDP and nearly 40 percent of manufacturing employment — meaning that labor-intensive industries typical of Bootstrap's early stage still provide most manufacturing jobs.

As an employer the manufacturing sector lags behind the government (23 percent), services (23 percent), and commercial (19 percent) sectors (Puerto Rico. Planning Board 1990).

The overall development strategy has not successfully addressed Puerto Rico's chronic unemployment problem. In spite of the rapid transformation of Puerto Rican society over the last forty years, and despite massive and unimpeded emigration to the United States, the official overall unemployment rate in early 1992 was 17.5 percent, higher than the rate of 15.5 percent in 1950, near the beginning of Operation Bootstrap.[60] Moreover, although the jobless rate in San Juan hovers around 10 percent, away from the metropolitan area the figure can run two or three times higher.

According to government figures Salinas's official unemployment rate in 1989 was 26.2 percent. A 1989 Puerto Rico Department of Agriculture study put Salinas's real unemployment at around 40% percent; this figure includes underemployed persons, as well as those who are not formally seeking work. When one takes into consideration that the municipio's two largest industrial employers — Central Aguirre and Salinas Manufacturing — have gone out of business since 1990, it is possible that local claims of 50 percent real unemployment are correct, at least for those neighborhoods where the sugar industry provided virtually all the jobs.

As part of a region whose economy was traditionally dominated by sugar production, Salinas has suffered from chronic high unemployment since the decline of Puerto Rico's sugar industry. The grossly inadequate educational and occupational training system away from the San Juan area has done little to change the unskilled, agriculturally oriented nature of the local labor force. Even during the height of prosperity during the 1970s Puerto Rico's petroleum-based industries did not generate sufficient or appropriate employment. The subsequent closure of the Fibers petrochemical plant and labor-intensive manufacturers in the late 1970s and early 1980s served only to further depress the local economy. The 1990 closure of Central Aguirre delivered what some local residents called a "knockout punch" to Salinas. Finally, Operation Bootstrap has exacerbated regional inequalities; for example, the income gap between San Juan and the rest of the island has increased since Operation Bootstrap was initiated (Mann 1985, 7). A brief comparison of Salinas with Puerto Rico

Table 3.1 Comparison of Economic Indicators in Salinas, Puerto Rico, and San Juan

	Salinas	Puerto Rico	San Juan
Average family yearly income ($)	4,271	5,923	7,668
Families below federal poverty line (%)	76.2[a]	58.0	43.3
Inadequate housing (%)	23.2	10.2	11.8
Years of schooling	8.6	10.3	12.2
Illiteracy (%)	16.5	10.3	7.0

Source: Planning Board 1987.
[a]Education and Employment Board 1989.

as a whole paints a grim picture, and when the comparison is with the island's capital the picture is even grimmer (table 3.1).

Social Change in Puerto Rico Since Operation Bootstrap

It might seem that well-planned economic development should be able to promote different industries — agriculture, fishing, tourism, commerce and services, manufacturing — in a mutually reinforcing and beneficial manner. The reality, that development in Salinas more often has set these economic sectors against one another, is in great part due to political power imbalances aggravated by one of the most troubling effects of Operation Bootstrap: the widening economic and social gaps between the well-to-do and the poor majority, and between San Juan and the rest of the island. These social changes deserve mention, for they not only help explain the increasing marginalization of places such as Salinas, but they also have inspired resistance and a search for alternatives.

The U.S. takeover of Puerto Rico at the turn of the twentieth century deepened and perpetuated the poverty of the masses but increased social mobility and power for some, especially for those people who served as intermediaries for the colonial government and North American capital. This trend not only continued, but accelerated under Operation Bootstrap. This second great transformation took place after World War II, as a result of the "modernization" of the island under the newly formed Partido Popular Democrático (PPD). That political party brought to power a class of professionals and United States–educated, New Deal–trained technocrats. As part of this transformation they also promoted the mass emigration of hundreds of thousands of rural poor to the urban ghettoes of the United States, the famous "safety valve" that weakened both the independence and the labor movements in Puerto Rico (Wessman 1977, 73). In Salinas the twentieth century's steady population growth was reversed almost overnight, as the municipio lost more than 7 percent of its inhabitants during the first twenty years of Operation Bootstrap, a clear signal that benefits of the program were going elsewhere. Only return migration from the United States since 1970 — another indication of vanishing opportunities, this time overseas — has managed to restore and increase Salinas's population.

The urban shantytowns of San Juan, which had begun to sprout following the U.S. invasion, filled nearly to bursting with newly unemployed rural poor who had come to the city in search of manufacturing jobs. These shantytowns were for the most part destroyed during the 1960s and 1970s, and were replaced by public housing projects in less desirable locations. Once more, people were uprooted and community ties severed (Maldonado Denis 1980, 151–52). In addition, since the 1950s Puerto Rico has seen the rise of a middle class and a small working-class elite, oriented in their lifestyle goals toward those of their North American counterparts (ibid.). The less affluent among them live in sprawling *urbanizaciones*, made up of modest one-story concrete dwellings. Upwardly mobile professionals prefer either condominium complexes, built on the sites of former shantytowns, or well-appointed, suburban, single-family housing complexes, characterized by private roads and twenty-four-hour security. People speak openly of class warfare being waged in the island's capital when referring to the city's high crime rate.

Out "on the island," away from the metropolitan area, vestiges of the old Puerto Rican way of life, such as strong neighborly ties and community spirit and a generally slower pace, still linger. Because, however, of Puerto Rico's uneven development, which has focused most of the island's economic dynamism upon San Juan, most residents of the countryside are dependent upon some form of government assistance. Residents of *la isla* (the island) experience much higher unemployment and lower incomes, even if they find work; unlike the thriving informal economy in the capital, opportunities for earning income through informal activity is largely confined to weekends, when they can sell food, drinks and crafts to touring *sanjuaneros*. The distribution of state activity and services among regions is highly unequal, and rural areas tend to receive the worst of everything, be it schools, health care, or utilities (Vidal 1985). As is true of the urban poor, many of the rural poor spend much of their lives migrating between the island and the urban ghettoes of the United States (Hernández Cruz 1982). Moreover, Puerto Ricans who spent their working years in the United States often return to the countryside to retire, and form a substantial percentage of the rural population.

In sum, the "modernization" of Puerto Rican society has served to crystallize the fundamental regional and class inequalities that have long characterized the island (Nieves Falcón 1985a, 121–23) and has deepened the poor majority's economic and social marginalization. Indeed, one of the most common themes sounded by ordinary Salinas residents is the feeling of marginalization from the mainstream. They feel that the San Juan elites have benefited most, and the average *salinense* least, from the changes occurring in Puerto Rico as a result of Operation Bootstrap; although they know things must change, they are skeptical of ideas or actions that seem like the same old story of being "done for and done to." Nevertheless, far from being passive victims, people in Salinas have resisted their exploitation in various ways at every stage. Their history is full of successes and failures, accommodation and challenge, but always "*aquí en la lucha*" (here in the struggle).

4 Resistance

Salinas's legacy of exploitation through colonialism and development tells only part of the story of present local efforts to create alternatives. It is also important to understand the influence of popular responses: accommodation, opposition, challenge — in short, resistance. One of the results of Operation Bootstrap that its planners saw as positive was greatly increased emigration to the United States. This also had some unintended consequences, however, such as increased political consciousness and the acquisition of skills by some Salinas emigrants, who later returned home and applied the lessons learned overseas. As happened throughout the world during the turbulent 1960s and 1970s, there was also significant activism among high school and university students. Other recent influences included involvement in movements — sometimes quite militant in character — that responded directly to some of Bootstrap's effects, such as labor organizing, land occupations, and environmentalism. Finally, the influence of liberation theology provided what some core activists termed a "missing link" in the evolution of their ideas and practices of community mobilization and the specific projects they have set in motion.

The Circular Migration Experience

Students of history have pointed out that specific actions have often produced unintended consequences. For example, the modern Puerto Rican migration experience[1] is a direct and partially planned outcome of the social change produced by Operation Bootstrap; however, this experience has also exerted a strong influence upon the present Salinas activism.

As a region virtually destroyed and recreated by colonialism, the Caribbean has produced migration patterns that have always been intimately related to world and regional economic conditions; since the late nine-

teenth century the direction of this human stream has been largely chan-
neled by the labor needs of U.S. capital (Richardson 1989, 209; 1992).
Puerto Rican migrations form an important subplot within the overall
Caribbean story. We have already seen the early-twentieth-century shift of
the island's rural population away from the collapsing subsistence and
mixed-crop economy, and toward the rapidly growing sugar industry,
thanks to the influx of U.S. capital. Puerto Ricans were also contracted as
agricultural laborers in Hawaii at the turn of the century, in the Dominican Republic during the 1920s, and on the U.S. mainland throughout the
twentieth century. But by far the most massive and well-documented
movement of Puerto Ricans to U.S. cities has been taking place ever since
the initiation of Operation Bootstrap.

Although the program's planners counted on the "safety valve" of massive emigration to partially resolve the island's unemployment problems,
they did not foresee that many would also return. Nonetheless, "by the
early 1970s the volume and diversity of these migration currents, the
persistence and multiplication of the structural conditions impelling them,
and the almost casual acceptance of repeated uprootings as a common-
place feature of national life made it questionable if the use of the word
"migration' was descriptive of this aspect of the Puerto Rican experience"
(History Task Force 1979, 140). The proximity of Puerto Rico to the
mainland, the ready availability of cheap airfare, and the freedom of
movement facilitated by U.S. citizenship have all contributed to the extraordinary mobility of Puerto Ricans. This mobility "permits them to
compare their experiences within contexts which though geographically
distinct are socially and economically similar. The condition of working
or unemployed Puerto Ricans in the United States is not fundamentally
different from their island counterparts" (Maldonado Denis 1982, 168–
69). This condition was certainly an unintended consequence of Puerto
Rican emigration.

Much has been written about the negative effects of circular migration,
such as cultural confusion and the economic and social problems encountered in both locations. For many, however, the experience has also reinforced a strong sense of national pride and a determination to survive and
prosper: "Being Puerto Rican in the United States, as in Puerto Rico, has
produced cultural expressions that differ in complicated ways. . . . Despite

the diversity of cultural expression, national identity and commitment are high among Puerto Ricans in the United States and are reinforced by the experience of new forms of economic, political, cultural, and racial domination encountered there" (History Task Force 1979, 158). Among Salinas activists who have lived, worked, studied, or spent part of their childhood in the United States, their experiences on the mainland served to strengthen their desire to break the cycle of dependence and powerlessness that they saw around them and to work actively for community empowerment and national pride — particularly back home in Salinas.

Student and New Left Radicalism as a Key Influence

One of the most striking hallmarks of the 1960s was the worldwide upsurge of radical student movements forming the vanguard of what became known as the "New Left." Although this phenomenon seemed to spring up virtually overnight, its roots can be traced to post–World War II developments such as the Cold War, decolonization, and the increasing economic, cultural, and political domination by the United States of most of the rest of the world. During that time the extraordinary economic growth spurred by Operation Bootstrap and the expansion of the state bureaucracy accelerated urbanization, increased the size of Puerto Rico's middle and upper working classes, and opened up more opportunities to receive a college education. The concurrent repression of the labor and independence movements would later be challenged by many of these students, inspired by events both at home and abroad. The colonial status of Puerto Rico served to intensify and personalize pro-socialist and anti-imperialist struggles.

Students and leftist intellectuals founded the University Pro-Independence Front (known as FUPI, for its initials in Spanish) in 1956 (Silén 1978, 146–47). FUPI provided the major impulse for the creation of the Movimiento Pro-Independentista (MPI) in 1959; this initially nonpartisan organization also brought together Nationalists, Communists, disaffected left-leaning members of the Puerto Rican Independence Party (PIP), and others who were galvanized by the Cuban Revolution. The MPI involved itself in a broad variety of struggles, from high school student mobilization through the Federación Estudiantil Pro-Independencia (FEPI, formed in 1963), and the struggle against threats of environmental destruction by mining corporations, tourist development, and the U.S. military, through increasingly radical opposition to the Vietnam War.[2] In 1971 the MPI became the Partido Socialista Puertorriqueño (PSP), which became deeply involved in industrial labor organizing and legal aid for squatters.[3]

The personal histories of some of the Salinas activists reveal that student activism played a formative role in their political and social development. For example, during the 1960s Danilo Cruz Miranda was active in both the Partido Independentista (PIP) and Movimiento Vanguardia (comprised of local left-oriented university students) and wrote for most of the left student and partisan publications that came and went so quickly in those years. La Playa and El Coquí native Nelson Santos, a south coast organizer for the PSP during the early 1970s, led study groups for FEPI. It was at such meetings that a junior high school student and "Brisas del Mar" public housing project resident named Tata Santiago became politically active, first helping to struggle for better school facilities and selling the PSP newspaper *Claridad,* and later continuing her community activism as an economics and law student in the United States. During the late 1980s she returned to Salinas and has been a key contributor to a number of projects. Finally, another FEPI and PSP veteran, named Héctor Vásquez, later became the director of a nonprofit cultural organization known as ARTESUR and based in El Coquí (described in chapter 5).

It should also be noted that the less positive experiences of left-oriented activism inspired these same individuals to reevaluate their ideas and strategies. For example, the increasing isolation of leftist politics from the Puerto Rican masses during the late 1970s and early 1980s, due to both state repression and internal factionalization, motivated the Salinas activists to look for more inclusive ways to do progressive work for social change — beginning at home.

Militant Unions in the Era of Heavy Industrialization

At the beginning of the 1960s the Puerto Rican labor and independence movements were moving along parallel paths. Operation Bootstrap's initiation and the suppression of independent unions were also accompanied by attempts by the AFL-CIO to organize industrial workers; by 1968 it represented approximately 40 percent of organized island workers. It was during the 1960s that both labor and independence forces encountered "Third World" anti-imperialist, revolutionary Marxism — inspired above all by Cuba — whose influence was also reflected in other contemporary movements on the island (Silén 1978, 141). Intense unionization activity among petrochemical and public utility workers (such as UTIER, the electrical and water workers' union), as well as among teachers and other public sector employees, independent of PPD-dominated structures, accompanied the phase of heavy industrialization. Additionally, the fact that Taft-Hartley regulations did not apply to public employees also helps explain their greater independence and militancy; because of these qualities they stood out in stark contrast to the mainland-affiliated private-sector unions. Strikes were bitter and often violent, since workers fought not only for economic benefits but for occupational safety and political power as well.

In the Salinas area organizers affiliated with the new Puerto Rican Socialist Party were involved in helping to form a union in the Fibers International petrochemical plant. Workers there struck for better pay and working conditions during May and June 1973; a May Day march celebrated during the strike brought thousands out in the streets of Salinas. But the most important organizing took place among public-sector employees. During the 1970s big strikes took place at the Aguirre electric energy complex, among teachers, Puerto Rico Legal Services workers, government telephone company employees, and sugar industry workers in and around Central Aguirre.

A strike in the Aguirre electric energy complex during 1975 turned tragically violent when one worker and strike organizer was murdered and another paralyzed. Occupational safety was a major issue, since union leaders charged that the units were often kept running in spite of known flaws and the sounding of alarms; they also believed that Aguirre's fire prevention system was not functioning properly.[4] Blackouts caused by fires or explosions occurred repeatedly between 1977 and 1979, especially during a four-month strike in 1978.[5] The Electric Energy Authority (AEE) charged the union with sabotage, though investigators found no such evidence. The government responded to the increasingly militant union activity during the 1970s with a policy of heavy repression. Between 1972 and 1976 the Puerto Rican National Guard was mobilized twice against strikers (Concepción 1990, 114), while undercover agents conducted a COINTELPRO-type campaign of infiltration and terrorism against union organizers and pro-independence activists.[6]

Then in 1976 the PSP committed what many felt was a crucial error when it nominated UTIER leader Luís Lausell to run for governor on its own slate. The party suffered a debilitating division over the decision to enter electoral politics, rather than continuing to emphasize syndicalist and community organizing. Many community-identified members — including several leaders from Salinas — left the party at that time, thus contributing to the general isolation of the Puerto Rican Left from the masses.

The economic recession and closure of the Fibers plant and other industries in the Salinas area during the early 1980s severely weakened the local industrial labor movement (a phenomenon also occurring at the same time throughout Puerto Rico, the United States, and Latin America). Since the late 1970s most new industries in the Salinas/Guayama area have been linked to the pharmaceutical industry. In contrast to the United States, pharmaceutical industry workers in Puerto Rico are not unionized. Although there is no legal prohibition against their unionization, prospective pharmaceutical industry employees are carefully screened, and those with a history of union activism are not hired. In addition, employees of pharmaceutical firms in Puerto Rico may feel less impulse to organize, since they are relatively well-paid for island workers — though wages are considerably lower than on the U.S. mainland. Nor are the workers unionized in Salinas's ten remaining factories — whether clothing, electronics, or fruit drink manufacturers. "Jobs are gold in Salinas," according to one resident; in a region where jobs are scarce and fast disappearing, the factories are not presently fertile ground for labor organizing.

Defending Our National Inheritance:
The Puerto Rican Environmental Movement

It would be impossible to assess the influence of the environmental movement on the present activism in Salinas without including at least a brief look at Puerto Rican environmentalism in general. This movement arose during the 1960s in response to five manifestations of Puerto Rico's political and economic development. First, nationalist opposition to the displacement of poor residents of coastal areas through expansion both by the U.S. military and by high-rise hotels took on increasingly environmentalist overtones.[7] Second, local scientists called attention to the increasingly serious problem of erosion as a result of the extraction of sand and rock for massive construction projects, which provided Puerto Rico with an infrastructure capable of handling the island's development strategy (Cadilla 1977). Third, nationalists and environmentalists joined forces to block plans to strip-mine the island's interior for copper and other minerals (García Martínez 1972; Massol 1984). Fourth, the discovery that the U.S. military had experimented with nuclear irradiation and pesticide bombing in the El Yunque tropical rain forest (Agent Orange was created here) provoked environmentalist, nationalist, and antimilitary protests. Finally, beginning in the late 1970s and early 1980s workers and communities joined with environmentalists to address the environmental havoc that resulted from the strategy of heavy industrialization (García Martínez 1984).

Given the never-ending debate on the island concerning Puerto Rico's political status as a "territorial possession" (to use Washington's euphemism for a colony) of the United States, it is understandable that activism around environmental issues would from the outset become extremely politicized (as does, indeed, every controversial issue in Puerto Rican society). In fact, many of the island's earliest and best-known environmentalists were also key members of labor, socialist, feminist, and pro-independence organizations. It could even be argued that campaigns against military expropriation, military toxic experiments, coastal privatization, and mining were initially nationalist causes, and only later became conscious environmentalist struggles. Environmentalists' fight against powerful multinational interests, and their struggle against the privatization of natural resources — commonly referred to as the "national inheritance" — has often cast a "pinkish" tint upon environmentalist rhetoric and actions, according to some critics. Thus, the old complaint by government and corporate interests that environmentalism on the island was politicized and leftist was to some extent true.

It would be an error to dismiss it as such today, however. Although all environmental campaigns have from the beginning been able to mobilize some local support, it is the problem of environmental degradation and health threats to workers and communities that has broadened the movement to include members of nearly every social and ideological sector on the island. One nonprofit organization in particular, Misión Industrial de Puerto Rico, was instrumental in bridging the gap between leftist, intellectual environmentalists and ordinary working communities. Founded in 1969 by a number of progressive local Christian denominations to mediate labor-management disputes, the organization quickly changed its focus to organize communities around occupational and environmental health. For more than twenty years Misión Industrial has functioned as an environmental watchdog and educator as well as a community informational and organizational resource. In this work they have been joined by organizations such as Servicios Científicos y Técnicos (SCT), an environmental assessment firm that often provides its services to poor communities free of charge.

Environmental groups became quite adept at utilizing the media to inform and mobilize broad sectors of the Puerto Rican public quickly; such quick and well-publicized responses sometimes forced corporations, the island and federal governments, even the U.S. military, to drop or modify plans that were barely off the drawing board. Examples include the delay of proposals during the early 1970s to establish an oil "superport" on the west coast until the sharp rise in oil prices made it unfeasible. During the 1980s activists mobilized local, national, and international support to block construction of a "Club Med" resort on the southwest coast within the unique tropical dry forest at Guánica, which has been designated an International Biosphere Reserve by the United Nations; they also continued pressuring the government until the island's Conservation Trust was able to purchase the threatened area. Active citizen campaigns during the 1990s included the successful fight against the siting of a coal-burning electric plant in Mayagüez by the North Carolina–based firm Cogentrix, which sought tax exemption under U.S. tax law section 936. Community groups waged campaigns to prevent construction of giant regional waste incinerators and toxic landfills. It should also be noted that a campaign begun during the 1960s against proposals to strip-mine the western interior mountain region for copper was still active in the 1990s. The most significant development in the Puerto Rican environmental movement during the 1980s and into the 1990s was the organizing of ongoing community groups that went beyond single-issue, local concerns to support regional and islandwide initiatives; these included regional groups, such as SURCCO (South Against Contamination), and islandwide coalitions, such as the United Environmental Front.[8]

In Salinas, since the late 1970s struggles against environmental degradation and privatization of coastal resources have been among the most important issues for local activism. People have joined together to prevent siting of a regional toxic waste landfill, an herbicides factory, and a nuclear power plant; they have also demanded that established firms assume responsibility for the damage they have already caused. There have been both successes and failures among the various campaigns, including those in the stories recounted here.

Environmentalist Initiation:
The Nuclear Power Plant

The campaign during the early 1970s against construction of a nuclear-powered unit within the Aguirre electric power complex was the first consciously "environmentalist" struggle in the Salinas area. Puerto Rican environmental activists opposed construction of the nuclear plant, which was planned to be the biggest in Latin America. A geologic fault known to have been active within the past two hundred years runs underneath the Aguirre area (Santiago Cruz 1941). A number of Salinas residents who took part in the Villa Albizu land occupation in Coquí actively participated in the campaign against the nuclear plant and would later become involved in other local and islandwide environmentalist campaigns.

Arguing that Puerto Rico needed to diversify its energy sources, the central government planned to have nuclear power provide 20 percent of the island's energy needs by 1976. In 1966 Puerto Rico began studying the possibility of building a major nuclear plant; at first the plant was to be constructed on the north coast, but the location was soon shifted to Aguirre. Although many articles in the press stressed the growing residential need for energy, the Aguirre electric power complex — which by itself could supply all of Puerto Rico's domestic needs — was from the start designed and built to supply heavy industry, particularly oil refineries and petrochemical plants.[9]

Plans called for construction of two petroleum-fired units, plus one six-hundred-thousand-kilowatt nuclear unit. The complex would return to Jobos Bay via a specially constructed canal 1,600,000 gallons per minute of overheated water; this water would be sixteen degrees higher than the bay's natural water temperature. The U.S. Atomic Energy Commission would do experiments at the Aguirre complex, which was to be named NUPLEX. The electric energy complex was expected to provide fifteen hundred construction jobs and seventy-five permanent jobs, including positions that would be filled by personnel from the AEC nuclear experimental station at Rincón, on Puerto Rico's northwest coast.[10] The nuclear unit was slated for completion by November 1971, but Mitsui Corporation, the firm contracted to build the nuclear unit for Westinghouse, quickly fell behind schedule. They managed to complete excavation and build part of the dome before growing opposition to the plant enveloped the project in controversy.

Responding to environmentalist pressure, the Environmental Quality Board (EQB) took the AEE to court to force the Authority to hold public hearings on possible effects of the project upon Jobos Bay.[11] At the hearings the president of the AEE argued that the project would improve the environment, claiming that the hot water discharges into the bay would increase the number of fish. Delaying the project would be harmful to the environment and to health, he added, because the electric power complex was needed for hospitals, waste treatment plants, and to clean up air and water, in addition to enabling economic development.

Continuing, the AEE chief claimed that environmental studies for the project had begun before 1969, before establishment of the Environmental Quality Board, thus demonstrating the AEE's genuine interest in the ecological well-being of the country. "Suddenly," he complained, "new environmental laws were being enacted which were slowing down the plant's construction. . . . Puerto Ricans should realize how important the plant was for their future."[12] An editorial published in the same newspaper that day, however, pointed out that the environmental study had been carried out by the Puerto Rico Nuclear Center, hardly an impartial group. The editorial went on to express deep concern about the possibility of nuclear accidents.

The Atomic Energy Commission eventually decided to support construction of the nuclear plant on the north coast instead, citing a geologic fault running through Aguirre as the reason; however, the nuclear unit was never built in Puerto Rico. In the end four petroleum-based units went on-line at the Aguirre complex between 1974 and 1977. As a result of this campaign a number of Salinas residents received their first exposure to environmental activism at home. But there was little questioning of the heavy industrialization strategy or the need for a big thermoelectric plant complex, nor of its environmental effects. Such questioning would not begin until the struggle against the siting of the Monsanto herbicide factory in Salinas at the close of the 1970s.

Monsanto: A Key Success Story

It has been said that the history of the Puerto Rican environmental movement can be divided into two periods: before and after Monsanto. This is because "the political mobilization against Monsanto marked the first time in Puerto Rico that a plurality of classes and ideological positions joined together in opposition for an environmental protest" (cited in Concepción 1990, 152). The Monsanto experience has been held up ever since by Salinas's activists as the quintessential "David versus Goliath" example of a poor community's ability to work together to defeat powerful outside interests. It represents a high point in popular resistance to exploitation of natural and human resources by powerful outside forces.

As early as 1970 Monsanto had been looking to build a factory in southeastern Puerto Rico, citing tax exemptions, climate, and the loyalty of Puerto Rican workers as incentives.[13] At the time Monsanto was planning to build a chemical plant for nylon products that would offer three hundred jobs. Then early in 1978 the Monsanto Corporation announced plans to build a factory in Puerto Rico to produce Roundup, a popular broad-leaf herbicide. "The location of manufacturing facilities within Puerto Rico," announced the firm, "will provide an economical avenue for the distribution of this product to worldwide markets and materially aid the Island in its quest for industrialization."[14] The company's president had warned that recently implemented U.S. environmental regulations would have an adverse impact on industrial innovation; therefore, the Monsanto Corporation looked forward to being in Puerto Rico, where the government was eager to do business, where energy and water were subsidized and land and labor were cheap, and where they boasted relaxed environmental restrictions and tax exemptions.[15]

According to the preliminary Environmental Impact Statement (EIS) filed by the company in February 1978 Monsanto sought to purchase 200 cuerdas of agricultural land planted in sugarcane to build its factory and for possible future expansion; in addition, the firm wished to buy an adjoining 253 cuerdas of wetlands for use as a buffer zone. The facility was to be located south of Highway PR 3, and immediately west of the coastal community of Las Mareas. (Monsanto chose an alternate site some nine miles east, on the former site of Guayama's Hacienda Josefa, located west of the Phillips refinery and SKF Pharmaceuticals.) The plant would cost forty million dollars to build, would produce thirty million pounds of "Roundup" annually, and would have a yearly payroll of one million dollars. Construction of the plant would generate five hundred jobs, whereas the factory would require eighty permanent, mostly skilled employees. It was estimated that the factory would discharge 192 tons of sulfur dioxide per year into the atmosphere and consume 386,000 gallons of water daily from private wells to be drilled on the site, taking advantage of Salinas's extensive underground aquifer. In addition, the plant would generate 252,000 gallons per day of liquid waste; Monsanto planned to apply for permission to discharge into the sea more than the normal limit of effluents. Some 1,100 tons of solid waste would be produced yearly, for which there was no disposal plan. The impact of noise pollution was unknown.[16]

The Monsanto factory was to mark the first stage of Fomento's plan to develop a giant chemical industries complex in the Aguirre area, expected to generate 650–800 jobs.[17] Accordingly, Fomento worked hard to smooth out the process of obtaining the necessary permits for the project. The Department of Natural Resources went on record affirming that the proposed plant would not harm the sensitive coastal environment, and Salinas's mayor and the municipal assembly initially supported the project.

The siting process proceeded virtually without a hitch until August 1978, when the Environmental Quality Board held a public hearing in Salinas on the question of the proposed plant's emissions of contaminants into the atmosphere. Local residents picketed the municipal hall, site of the hearings; inside, representatives of a coalition later known as the Anti-Monsanto Front presented well-researched papers explaining their opposition to the project.

The Anti-Monsanto Front was a broadly based coalition of organizations and individuals opposed to construction of the Monsanto herbicide factory in the Salinas/Guayama area. Participants in the Front could be divided into four groupings. In the first were Salinas residents, including the Las Mareas Pro-Health Committee,[18] the Las Mareas Fishing Association, the Salinas Archaeological Society, individual residents, and owners of summer homes in Las Mareas. In the second were environmental experts and activists, led by Misión Industrial and its scientific advisor, Neftalí García Martínez. Labor and public service groups formed the third grouping, including the Puerto Rico Legal Services Independent Union, the sugar workers union SOUS, the Employees Union of the Puerto Rico Telephone Company, CANACELE (an islandwide organization of clients of Puerto Rico Legal Services), Puerto Rico Legal Services-Guayama Office, and the Carite Small Farmers' Union. Religious organizations composed the fourth grouping, including PRISA (Puerto Rico's progressive ecumenical Protestant organization), Sisters of El Convento Jesús Mediador (located in Bayamón, near San Juan), and Sisters of Sagrado Corazón (located in Patillas, on the southeast coast).[19]

Opponents used several arguments against Monsanto. For example, the plant's heavy water would compete with domestic and agricultural activities, which had priority under the Puerto Rico Water Act of 1976; moreover, increased water withdrawal would lower the water table and increase saltwater intrusion into the aquifer. The proposed site also fell partially within the limits of a natural reserve under the Coastal Zone Management Program, but possible adverse consequences to the valuable mangrove forest ecosystem had not been discussed in the EIS for Monsanto. Additionally, sulfur dioxide emissions from the plant would aggravate air quality in the area far more than the company predicted: air quality studies used for Monsanto's EIS had been conducted before construction of the Aguirre power plant complex, the area's number one polluter. It was predicted that plant-related contamination would eventually force relocation of the nearby communities of Las Mareas and La Jagua. As for employment, the 80 permanent factory jobs would replace 320 agricultural jobs on the proposed site, thus destroying 4 jobs for every 1 created. And it was not even certain that they would be filled by locals, since the government had reportedly promised the jobs to 450 workers in Guayanilla (west of Ponce) who were left without work when Pittsburgh Plate Glass closed there that year (Concepción 1990, 148–49; Cruz Miranda 1978). At the hearings all but one of twenty-five witnesses testified against the plant; the only witness in favor of the project, a construction worker from the Dominican Republic, had to be escorted from the building by police for his safety.[20]

The Anti-Monsanto Front held press conferences, published informative bulletins, and dialogued constantly with local residents, government officials, and others. The activists accomplished their work despite strong political and social pressures. For example, Félix Burgos, though an active *popular,* was viciously "red-baited" because of his anti-Monsanto activity since a number of fellow activists were known leftists and independentistas.[21] In their publicity campaign the Front constantly stressed that in the United States public pressure had compelled the enforcement of tough environmental laws, which Monsanto had come to Puerto Rico to avoid. The anti-Monsanto activists vowed to create the same type of public pressure in Puerto Rico to force strict compliance with environmental protection laws.[22] In response to such attacks Monsanto launched a heavy public relations campaign, claiming Roundup to be less toxic to humans than table salt and pledging to conserve the mangroves.[23] The firm also sponsored a tour of its mainland facilities for ten opposing Guayama and Salinas politicians and residents, some of whom changed their minds as a result of the trip.

The Anti-Monsanto Front kept up its pressure throughout the fall of 1978, picketing the governor's residence and agencies in San Juan. The opposition broadened its regional base when the municipal assemblies of neighboring Santa Isabel and Guayama joined that of Salinas in passing resolutions opposing the Monsanto project. In January 1979 the Environmental Quality Board disapproved the Salinas site, citing an unconvincing

Environmental Impact Statement, and offered conditional approval of an alternate site in the Jobos area of Guayama, west of the Phillips petroleum refinery. On the basis of that decision the Planning Board denied Monsanto permission to develop the Salinas site.

In February 1979 Monsanto began the process of obtaining the permits necessary for the alternative site, but the firm had from the beginning considered the Jobos site the less desirable alternative because of the more limited availability of underground water (and, some opponents charged, because there was less room for expansion and no chance to build a private port). In order to meet its water use requirements Monsanto executed an agreement in April 1979 with the Puerto Rico Water Authority under which the factory would receive a large reserved allotment of irrigated water in exchange for footing the bill for enlarging the capacity of Guayama's Lake Melania, one of the south coast irrigation system reservoirs. Environmentalists opposed the agreement on the grounds that the water would be diverted from other uses for which the water supply was already inadequate (Morris 1979). The agreement also violated the Puerto Rico Water Use Act of 1976 and was contrary to laws dating back to the 1940s.

Public hearings in Guayama were set for August 1979. The Anti-Monsanto Front was prepared to fight there as well. Moreover, industries already located in the area, such as SmithKline French Pharmaceuticals, opposed the Monsanto plant on grounds that it would use up all of the available sulfur dioxide emissions in the area, thus precluding SKF's plans for future expansion.[24]

Before the Guayama hearings could take place, however, Monsanto called a press conference on July 31, 1979, in which it announced that it was canceling its plans to build a plant in Puerto Rico; instead, existing facilities in the United States would be expanded to meet export production needs.[25] Fomento officials openly blamed the environmental organization Misión Industrial for the loss of Monsanto and suggested that community groups were being manipulated by "antidevelopment" independentistas into opposing projects that were in the community's best interest.[26] For the Anti-Monsanto Front, however, the defeat of Monsanto represented a huge victory by ordinary citizens over powerful outside interests. It also sent shock waves throughout the Puerto Rican business establishment, for it signaled that community organizations could henceforth become a powerful lobbying force with which to contend.

The Anti-Monsanto Front was notable for being a coalition of community groups, professionals, labor, and religious organizations from varying ideological perspectives, thus breaking with the Puerto Rican environmental movement's traditional identification with somewhat intellectually isolated leftist and pro-independence groups. In addition, for the first time a coalition that had been created for a specific campaign attempted to remain together after the struggle was over, in order to develop more environmentally and socially appropriate alternatives for economic development. Participants of the Front formed the Jobos Bay Corporation in 1979. They proposed to develop a plan for economic development of the southern coast and highlands from Santa Isabel to Maunabo that would involve community participation and protect the environment. The proposals concentrated on agricultural diversification, manufacturing based on agricultural products, commercialization of fishing, and tourist development (Gaskins Alcott 1978). An economist was to be hired to do feasibility studies, while participants began writing a proposal for funding from the World Council of Churches.

Unfortunately, the Jobos Bay Corporation disintegrated before any of its proposals could be elaborated. There were a number of reasons for the failure of the group.[27] A split occurred at Misión Industrial; some of its workers were ousted after efforts to broaden decision-making power in the organization to include more community representatives ended in failure.[28] Additionally, a bitter strike by the Legal Services Union effectively curtailed that organization's participation in the economic initiative. Activist "burnout" following the Monsanto victory, as well as failure to prevent siting of the Airco pharmaceutical plant in Guayama shortly after, were also cited. Finally, a number of the most influential local activists were obliged to move to San Juan to seek employment. As I will discuss in chapter 5, they went to San Juan with the intention to work, study, and think about their experiences in Salinas — both successes and failures — and to reflect upon how to achieve a truly participatory community project.

The Regional Toxic Waste Landfill:
A Community United and Victorious

The Puerto Rican government had been under pressure from Washington since 1983 to establish regional toxic waste facilities on the island, as a requirement for receiving funds for cleanup of Superfund sites. A letter sent by the United States Geological Survey office in San Juan to Governor Rafael Hernández Colón in September 1989 affirmed that *Pozo Hondo* (located on the border between Salinas and Guayama, just east of El Coquí and north of highway PR 3) was a geologically suitable site for a toxic waste landfill, in spite of the area's known geologic faults, extensive underground aquifers, and the danger of wastes leaching into the sea.

In Salinas local activists, the municipal government, schools, businesses, and other sectors of the community all united against the plan. In October 1990 a representative from Misión Industrial was invited to give lectures in the junior high school about the danger posed by the proposed landfill. The Salinas Development Committee and the local paper strongly denounced the plan, and the municipal assembly unanimously approved a resolution opposing the landfill.[29] During the first half of 1991 the proposal all but disappeared from sight and sound. Finally, in July 1991 the Environmental Quality Board rejected the petition for a permit to build the toxic waste landfill at Pozo Hondo.[30]

There is little doubt that strong and united community opposition, as well as increasingly successful alliance building with other regional and islandwide groups, played a significant role in defeating some of the most environmentally risky proposed projects for Salinas. Nonetheless, one challenge activists face there is to build upon their short-term alliances, which struggle so successfully against projects and situations, in order to prepare and struggle in the long term for environmentally and socially appropriate alternatives.

Social Change and Resource Control

The previous chapter told of deepening class and regional inequality as a result of Operation Bootstrap. This inequality manifested itself in many areas, including access to land and other issues of local resource control.

In Salinas poor people sometimes responded to failed government promises by simply taking over unused land for their communities; moreover, they often fiercely opposed well-to-do outsiders who took over local resources. The following examples indicate that local efforts to claim the rights to local resources have met with mixed success.

Redeeming the Land: The Squatters' Movement

As happened elsewhere in Latin America, during the 1970s the Puerto Rican tradition of community appropriation of land for housing and sustenance became a flash point for antigovernment struggle. As the government concentrated on providing housing for heavy industry, poor people reacted to the lack of government action on residential housing by taking over unused land and building communities — in spite of court injunctions and violent forced removal. The appropriations of the squatters' movement — known variously as illegal land occupation, land invasion, spontaneous urbanization, or *rescate de terrenos* (land redemption) as Puerto Rican activists preferred to call it — took on added political significance because it came during the island's first pro-statehood administration, Puerto Rico's first non-"popular" elected government. Once again, socialist and pro-independence organizations played a key supporting role in the movement.

Within Salinas, in 1970 an organized group of residents of El Coquí grabbed twelve cuerdas of land belonging to the Corporation for Urban Renewal and Housing (known as CRUV, for its initials in Spanish) that had been promised to them by the PPD during the 1968 elections — which the populares lost. The government moved to evict the residents of the illegal community, defiantly named "Villa Albizu" in memory of the controversial Nationalist leader Pedro Albizu Campos. The newly formed Partido Socialista Puertorriqueño (PSP) provided free legal representation for Villa Albizu residents in their battle to remain on the land. The Puerto Rican courts ruled against them on July 20, 1972. Nonetheless, a compromise was eventually reached in which the land was parceled out and deeded to the occupiers. Other land occupations during the same period in Salinas included those of land near the communities of La Playa, La Plena, and El Coco; the occupiers were for the most part successful in holding on to the

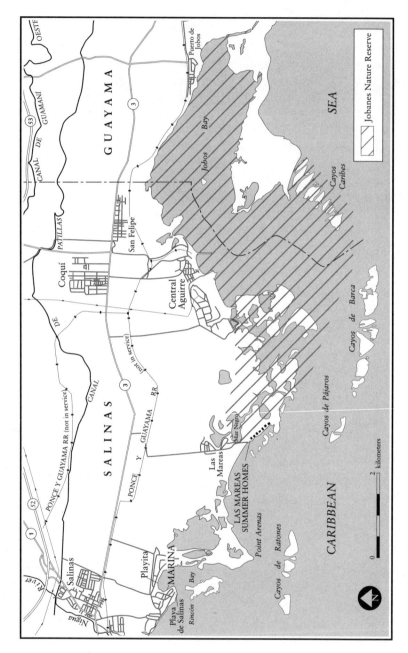

Map 4.1 Struggle for Coastal Resources

land.[31] A number of local participants joined the PSP as a result of the Villa Albizu experience, which proved to be an important influence on their early development as community activists.

Far from being a thing of the past, "land redemption" has survived its "radical" affiliation of the 1970s, and was still being practiced in Salinas in the 1990s. For example, after years of fruitless government petitions more than seventy families from El Coco took over five adjacent cuerdas of land in 1990. The next year the group offered to buy the land from its legal owner, a descendant of the traditional local landowning González family. Salinas's mayor promised to put up twenty-five thousand dollars of the municipio's funds to help buy the land if the San Juan government would provide the rest of the money.[32] As of 1992 the issue was unresolved, but the people remained on the land. Additionally, in 1994 some twenty-six families who had "redeemed" land in La Playa organized to petition the authorities to supply water and electricity to their settlement, named "Villa Cofresí," after the legendary Caribbean pirate.[33]

The "Invasion of the Rich People": Struggles for Coastal Resources

Another aspect of the struggle for land is a direct result of widening social gaps (see Map 4.1). For the past twenty years affluent, politically well-connected San Juan professionals have been purchasing land from Salinas's traditional landowners (descendants of hacendados), building summer vacation homes and a luxury marina, often dislocating local residents and destroying the fragile coastal mangrove ecosystem in the process. There have also been some attempts to sell the small islands off Salinas's coast. The appropriation of large sections of Salinas's coastline by outsiders has met with considerable resentment — and some organized opposition — from the local residents, as the following stories illustrate.

Las Mareas summer homes. As is true elsewhere in Salinas, much of the land in Las Mareas and surrounding the Mar Negro is legally the property of the González family, heirs of the municipio's largest nineteenth-century landowner. In 1971 and 1972 two parcels of land just east of Las Mareas, known as La Cuarta and La Quinta and consisting mainly of mangrove forest and wetlands, were sold to a San Juan attorney. The parcels were then subdivided into lots and sold as sites for summer homes. Such action violated Title 33 of the United States Code and the Federal Water Pollution Control Act Amendments of 1972, as well as the Puerto Rico Public Environmental Policy Act of 1970, both laws that protect wetlands. Mangroves were cut down and wetlands filled in order to build the houses and provide an access road. Moreover, the access road was built without providing drainage, thus cutting off the adjacent lagoon's access to tidewaters and negatively affecting its plant and animal life. The summer-home owners demanded and obtained basic services such as telephones, water, and electricity — even though they had not yet been provided to all of Las Mareas's residents. The new homes blocked public access to beaches and fishing spots, and the weekend visitors had been observed dumping their refuse in the surrounding forests.

In 1973 a group of local residents led by Las Mareas shop owner and fisherman Félix Burgos obtained the help of their elected representative in San Juan, who sent letters to various government agencies to urge action on behalf of the local group. An interagency committee was formed in 1975 with representation from the governor's office, the Environmental Quality Board, the Justice Department, the Planning Board, and the Department of Natural Resources, to deal with illegal construction along the coast. At that meeting the Department of Natural Resources was named chiefly responsible for reopening access to natural resources, as well as for taking legal action against the summer-home owners. Later that same year the Environmental Quality Board issued an order "to cease and desist immediately without any excuse or delay from their activities of filling and cutting of mangroves, and to abstain in the future from similar activities which could result in damage to the environment and the area's ecosystems."[34] Such activities stopped for a while, but resumed within a short time without any apparent repercussions.

During 1978 and 1979 the local activists formed an alliance with the summer-home owners to defeat the proposal to establish a Monsanto Corporation herbicides plant just west of Las Mareas. In return for the economic and political support offered by summer-home owners to the local campaign, the local activists suspended their struggle against the "rich invaders." Once the anti-Monsanto battle was over the locals resumed their fight against the summer-home owners, this time by taking them to federal court. The court action had support from the U.S. Army Corps of Engineers, who in 1977 had charged that the building, filling, and destruction of mangroves had occurred without first obtaining the Corps' permission to allow alteration of wetlands.[35] The court issued preliminary injunctions in 1978 and 1979 against the building and filling activities. In June 1981 the federal court issued a partial consent judgment in which the defendants agreed to cease and desist cutting of mangroves, filling, and construction; to replant mangroves, construct channels to restore tidal access to the lagoons; and to remove fill in certain areas. They also agreed to seek after-the-fact permits for existing structures and to seek the necessary permits from the Corps before undertaking any other alterations. The court also issued a permanent injunction on August 18, 1981. Once again, the order was only briefly and partially obeyed.

Early in 1987 fifty-seven residents of Las Mareas signed a petition asking the U.S. federal court to enforce the 1981 consent judgment; copies were sent to the U.S. Attorney's Office in San Juan, the Army Corps of Engineers and the Department of Natural Resources. The activists of Las Mareas, now organized as the Committee in Defense of Marine Resources, published a bulletin in September 1987 in which they recounted the history of the struggle against *"los invasores ricos"* (the rich invaders). The following month they wrote again to the U.S. Attorney's office demanding that the consent judgment be enforced.

After residents of Las Mareas picketed the Environmental Quality Board during September 1987, the board's director inspected the area and found that building in the area was indeed continuing, including construction of a gravel road and the installation of fire hydrants and new lines providing drinking water to the houses. No channels had been built to allow interchange of water between the sea and the lagoon, as had been ordered, and cutting of mangroves was still going on. Moreover, untreated liquid and solid waste had been illegally discharged by residents of the vacation homes. These findings were reported to the Department of Natural Resources, the agency responsible for protection of the area, as well as to the U.S. Army Corps of Engineers and the governor's office.

Meanwhile, the U.S. Army Corps of Engineers accused the Department of Natural Resources of having built and repaired the road without ever having sought the required permits. Natural Resources replied that the road had been built before the permanent injunction was issued and argued that the road was needed to access parts of the Jobanes Reserve. Nevertheless, the department filed an after-the-fact permit on January 30, 1988, and promised to work with the Corps to mitigate any environmental damage caused by the road.[36]

After Las Mareas activist Félix Burgos moved to New York in 1988 protests against the activities of the summer-home owners virtually ceased. Personal visits to the controversial site in January and March of 1991 confirmed that building, filling, forest cutting, dumping of wastes, and installation of services was still proceeding. No channels had been opened under the road between the sea and the lagoon — and the condition of that section of the lagoon and surrounding forest appeared to be deteriorating.

The luxury summer homes here are only a short walk from Las Mareas de Salinas, arguably the municipio's most economically depressed community, where nearly all of the residents had been sugarcane workers and nearly all the roads are unpaved. The official unemployment rate for Las Mareas was 40 percent in 1980, while Central Aguirre was still open.[37] The contrast between the two groups of neighbors — affluent weekend visitors and unemployed agricultural workers — could not be more stark. The only connection between the two is the occasional employment of Las Mareas residents by the visitors for domestic and other menial work.

The marina. Although title to the land around Rincón Bay has belonged for over a century to the González family, community residents have long had informal rights to the land and have built their homes, raised their families, and fished along that coast. Locals tell of several instances in which lifelong residents of La Playa were denied permission from the Regulations and Permits Authority (ARPE) to build additions to houses, construct kiosks for small businesses, and even acquire electricity and running water, ostensibly because such activity violated the ban on building in floodable and ecologically fragile areas. Meanwhile, in 1990 ARPE quickly issued permits to a wealthy San Juan architect who bought land along the bay and proceeded to build a tourist complex in La Playa; the agency also approved the building of two two-hundred-foot piers along the site. As the mangroves were cut down and piers, summer homes, and other buildings were constructed, some local residents found themselves being denied access to their long-accustomed fishing locations.[38]

Early in 1991 a Department of Natural Resources (DRN) employee charged that construction of a swimming pool, restaurant, and eighteen-room hotel in the maritime zone area had been approved without waiting for the required DRN approval. The work violated at least eight specifications required by various laws, among them the destruction of mangroves and the location of two gasoline tanks in a maritime zone (which had earlier been denied by the marina's owner in a meeting with local fishermen). The DRN issued an order to cease and desist construction. Nonetheless, sources informed the local newspaper of unspecified pressures brought to bear upon the DRN to reconsider its decision. On January 14, 1991, the municipal assembly of Salinas approved a resolution supporting construction of the marina and asking the DRN to withdraw its order. The resolution declared that the marina was designed in compliance with all regulations and that it did not threaten the sector's ecology. The statement flatly contradicted the results of the department's investigation and also was at variance with statements by local fishermen, who alleged, among other things, that the piers were built longer than the authorized two hundred feet and that the retaining wall was built of cement instead of wood, as had been specified in the original design approved by the U.S. Army Corps of Engineers. Only one member of the assembly voted against the resolution, while another qualified her endorsement on condition that the project result neither in ecological damage nor the displacement of local residents and fishermen.[39]

Some La Playa natives now refer to the newly walled street where the marina is located as "La calle de los muertos" (Street of the Dead). Although fishermen and other community residents have protested to government authorities about the illegal building and mangrove destruction, the municipal assembly and the mayor supported the marina's construction, asserting that it would help the local economy. Indeed, the marina was being depicted as a project to beautify a "slum area" and provide up to 150 jobs where no one else had cared to invest.[40] Although some local youth have found work washing pleasure yachts, most residents complain that the boat and summer-home owners dump their trash into the bay and bring very little business to the community. As of April 1992 the marina employed seventeen local residents. By 1994 the facility had doubled its hotel capacity, built a restaurant, and expanded the docking facilities. Although more jobs became available local residents spoke of the marina's revolving employment door, claiming that the owner was paternalistic and difficult to work for. As for the ongoing destruction of the once lush mangrove forest surrounding Rincón Bay, the marina's sign nailed to one diseased remnant of a tree served as an ironic reminder: Protect Our Mangroves.

Isla de Ratones: Fishermen versus MTV. Some of the potential for local loss of coastal access comes from far beyond San Juan. One example is the case of Isla de Ratones (also known as Cayo Ratones), a small islet located two miles off the Salinas coast, which comprises approximately twenty-five cuerdas of land and is a natural habitat for marine life. Considered property of the Spanish Crown until the late nineteenth century, it has been privately owned for nearly a hundred years by a succession of Gua-yama residents. For at least two centuries, however, Cayo Ratones has mainly been a fishermen's refuge during bad weather, and it is well known locally as an important site for trap fishing of lobsters, octopus, and other species. In 1988 the legal owner, reportedly frustrated over bureaucratic restrictions on developing fragile coastal lands for tourism, sold the islet to the North American music video corporation MTV for $250,000. Then, in May of that year Puerto Ricans were surprised by the announcement in New York that MTV had contracted rock star Cyndi Lauper to raffle off its "uninhabited, Caribbean, fantasy island" to one of 225 viewers who had won Caribbean cruises. Reaction to this was swift in Puerto Rico. The major dailies reported on the proposal and reaction. Vocal opposition arose from environmental organizations, the ex-secretary of the Depart-ment of Natural Resources, and various legislators.

In Salinas scores of people and groups came out strongly against the raffle and earlier sale of the islet to MTV. All of the islets were viewed as part of the fragile coastal ecosystem; like the beaches, they were consid-ered to be property of the people of Puerto Rico and thus should not be subject to sale. The local civic organization Club Abeyno fought actively, and governmental agencies such as the local health clinic and the munici-pal assembly passed resolutions in opposition. The fishing associations were especially active in this campaign. The president of the Playita Fishing Association, affirming that the island was a rich place for fishing and was vitally important for local fishermen, emphasized that the island could not be allowed to fall into private hands. Spokespersons for the Las Mareas Fishing Association warned that once one island was gone the others would also be sold; eventually, the entire coastline would be privatized, denying the people of Salinas access to their own coastal resources.[41]

MTV ignored the local opposition and in June announced that a young man from Pontiac, Michigan, had "won" the islet; the Puerto Rican dailies published a photograph of the lucky winner wearing a crown. But in Salinas people demonstrated their opinion about to whom the islet really belonged. On August 14, 1988, hundreds of fishermen from Salinas and other towns took over Isla de Ratones for a day. Joining them in support of their struggle against the raffle of the island were representatives of religious communities from Bayamón, Patillas, and Cidra, the environmental organization Misión Industrial de Puerto Rico, the mayor of Salinas, the president of the Puerto Rico Fishing Congress, and representatives of citizens' groups fighting for public access to beaches throughout the island. They held a fishing competition for children as a peaceful demonstration that the islet belonged to all of the people. The Religious Conference of Puerto Rico (an organization representing Catholic religious orders) also presented a proclamation supporting the rights of the fishermen to the islet, as well as denouncing any privatization of Puerto Rico's coast and surrounding islands. Since then, nothing has been seen or heard of MTV's "King of Fantasy Island."

In sum, the past twenty years have seen increasing privatization of the Salinas coastline, in order to serve as a vacation playground for wealthy San Juan businessmen and politicians—not to mention Fantasy Island dreamers from far away. Experiences such as the failed struggles against the Las Mareas summer homes and the marina at La Playa indicate that common citizens ordinarily do not have the political or economic clout to prevent the sale and consequent loss of valuable coastal resources to politically and economically influential outsiders. In addition, strategic alliances made in order to win one particular struggle have sometimes proved detrimental to struggles over other equally important issues. For example, during the Monsanto struggle the community activists formed a temporary alliance with the summer-home owners, but in retrospect some activists think the alliance was an error as far as the fight against the Las Mareas summer homes was concerned. Nonetheless, local residents can claim some victories in opposing this process. Organized community members have been able to exert some pressure upon government agencies to enforce laws meant to protect the coast from such development; even when this pressure proves ineffective local groups have managed to maintain some informal control. These experiences have convinced local activists that more must be done to make community control of local resources both secure and effective.

The Influence of Liberation Theology

Finally, the teachings of "liberation theology" must be considered key to the Salinas activists' approaches to community mobilization, as well as to specific projects. Liberation theology developed in Latin America during the decades following two inspirational events: the Cuban Revolution of 1959 and the liberalization of official Roman Catholic doctrine about social issues following Vatican II, which took place between 1962 and 1965.[42] By interpreting the "preferential option for the poor" as favoring the "social gospel," liberation theologians blamed poverty on inequality and oppression, rather than on the victims' sinfulness, and advocated empowering the poor as the solution; in other words, they stressed working for justice in this life, instead of waiting for the Hereafter. Liberation theology arose in Latin America at the same time that dependency theory was being formulated as a counterpoint to developmentalism (Garrett 1988, 176). Leading liberation theologians such as Peru's Gustavo Gutiérrez contended that strategies informed by the dominant development paradigm increased dependence; accordingly, activist priests and lay people organized "base communities" in order to empower ordinary people to work for locally based, participatory development that would liberate them from dependence (Brown 1990, 62).

Liberation theology also found adherents among Puerto Rico's socially conscious Catholic clergy and lay workers, as well as within Protestant groups such as PRISA, who became active in the island's labor, independence, antiwar, and environmental struggles. Groups of clergy also became involved in working for locally based solutions to the economic and social problems that poor communities faced. One group in particular has had a direct influence upon the Salinas activism.

El Convento Jesús Mediador, a convent without walls located in Bayamón, was formed during the early 1960s. It is composed of Puerto Rican nuns who wanted to form an indigenous order; also living at the convent is a Dominican priest who came to Puerto Rico from Holland in the 1940s. Their philosophy and work are situated firmly within the tradition of liberation theology; they also count among their strongest influences the work of Brazilian priest and educator Paulo Freire, particularly his concepts of popular education. The convent grounds are filled with plants, and the halls house an impressive collection of popular Puerto Rican art containing strong nationalist themes. The convent's members are dedicated to working within the local community; they are located in a poor, formerly rural area being transformed into a low-income suburb of San Juan. They sponsor workshops to teach many of the Puerto Rican traditional popular arts, including *bomba* (coastal, African-based music and dance) and *jíbaro* (mostly inland, strongly Andalusian-influenced country music and dance), community theater, carpentry, and artisanship in a wide variety of media. Catechism classes stress practical service to the community, collective and cooperative labor, and pride in popular heritage and national identity. The convent has been well known for its active support for environmental, peace, and anti-imperialist causes, the rescate de terrenos (squatters') and labor movements, and international solidarity efforts. They preach and practice an activism that emphasizes love, anti-individualism, service to the community, and self-affirmation.

While living in the San Juan area during the 1980s a number of the Salinas activists became involved as catechists and workers at the convent. They credit their experience there with changing the manner in which they approached community work and activism. The work of El Convento de Jesús Mediador provided an important "missing link" that they were seeking in how to do progressive work for social change that could reach the masses.

Although the activism presently taking place in Salinas might be characterized as typical of "new" social movements, particularly in Latin America (Slater 1985; Escobar and Àlvarez 1992), it is firmly rooted in the local geography and history. Salinas has undergone rapid and extensive changes as a result of capitalist development during the twentieth century, first as an export agricultural enclave, and then under "developmentalism" through Operation Bootstrap. Each of these phases has left its imprint on the people, the environment, and the landscape, but has also provided a background for a variety of popular responses. In Salinas a number of participants in the various campaigns described in this chapter have gone beyond resistance against the status quo, and are working to bring about positive alternatives.

5 Beyond Resistance

At the *villa pesquera* (fishing association center) the toilet could not be used until an old section of pipe from the water main could be replaced. One day a few fishermen and women and local community activists — neighbors all — spent the day taking turns breaking open the cement to get to the water main. They made a party of it, taking a collection for beer and soda, as well as for the needed new tube. It was hot, so they took their time, shared the work, offered opinions as to how best to resolve the problem, and eventually installed the new pipe. In the afternoon they rested in the shade, and eventually two women returned with a steaming pot of *arroz con pollo* for everyone. Then, several days later they collected enough money to buy cement to cover the hole. To hire a plumber would have perhaps been quicker, but also more expensive, less of a learning experience, and less fun. This is the experience of what the local activists call "building community"; it illustrates their conception of integrated development, which encompasses economic, social, educational, cultural, and spiritual aspects. It is central to an alternative vision of Salinas.

The Salinas Activists

As I discussed earlier, placing Salinas's present-day activism within its historical context requires understanding the story of popular resistance to exploitation. More recent and direct influences included involvement in movements such as those influenced by the "Third World" revolutionary Marxism and anti-imperialism of the 1960s and 1970s; of note is significant activism among high school and university students, which in Puerto Rico not only coincided with similar activism throughout the world, but also helped revitalize the island's independence movement. Especially important is the influence of liberation theology upon the Salinas activists, particularly as it affected the evolution of their ideas and practices of community mobilization and the specific projects they have set in motion. And I mentioned the experience of circular migration between Salinas and the United States — so common to the poor and working-class majority of Puerto Ricans, and indeed, to the Caribbean as a whole — as an important factor shaping their consciousness.

A number of early key activists shared a common background in left-oriented activism, including student groups such as FEPI and FUPI and political parties such as PIP and PSP. Some had lived, worked, or studied in the United States, or had served in Vietnam; while abroad they had also been politically or socially active. Some of this group have remained heavily involved in the work in Salinas, whereas others have moved away. The latter are being replaced by other salinenses; some of these individuals, among them Brisas resident Milagros Colón and Playita native "Carmín" Vega, were previously active in church, labor, and civic organizations, whereas for others the current activism is their first such experience. In fact, one of the more hopeful signs for the Salinas initiatives is that the people who have begun to assume more responsibility for the various projects bring a diversity of experiences and viewpoints, which is crucial to the eventual success of the initiatives. These include fishermen, housewives, social service providers, small-business people, teachers, students, and unemployed and retired laborers.

Although the people now involved in the various projects comprising the Salinas activism are increasingly diverse, a number of general observations can be made about them: First, nearly all were born or grew up in Salinas's poor and working-class communities. Second, many have had the experience of circular migration between Salinas, San Juan, and urban ghettoes in the United States. Third, many have been lifelong activists and leaders, whether in more traditional settings such as church, labor unions, and civic organizations, or in "new" movements such as environmentalism. Some had been active in more recent local struggles, including the successful fight against the siting of a Monsanto herbicides factory along the Salinas coast during the late 1970s. Although efforts to sustain that particular coalition beyond its NIMBY (Not-In-My-Back-Yard) issue failed at the time, the activists have incorporated that experience into their current efforts. Finally, they are convinced that the local initiatives represent the first real opportunity for Salinas's poor communities to break free of the cycle of dependence, marginality, and hopelessness.

As I mentioned earlier, a few key Salinas activists had moved to San Juan in 1979 and 1980 to work, to study, and to think about how to accomplish meaningful change in Salinas that would truly involve the people. Of this group most were university-educated and had been active in leftist organizations; however, they had become disillusioned with the intellectual elitism of the organized Left and its consequent isolation from the Puerto Rican masses. Unable to find work in Salinas (perhaps in part due to the high profile of some in the anti-Monsanto campaign and left-oriented labor and student organizing), they went back to school and worked as teachers, or in other occupations. They also became involved in a study group known as Taller Socialista (Socialist Workshop) with others who had been involved in various left-oriented organizations throughout the island. The participants sought through study and discussion to analyze the successes and failures of their various movements, as well as to look for ways to "reach the masses." At the same time a number became catechists at the Convento Jesús Mediador. Not only have they credited the experience with liberation theology with providing a missing ingredient in their approach to community work; the experience has also reinforced their commitment to returning home.

Through their experiences and study the activists concluded that in order to have any kind of mass appeal they had to change their style. First, they realized that "resistance" was not enough; viable, believable, positive alternative solutions to the various problems had to be developed from within the community. Second, they dropped ideological rhetoric, which for the most part was not accessible. They worked hard to form alliances with people from differing ideological perspectives by emphasizing putting the needs of the community first. Third, they needed both to understand what people themselves defined as their needs, and to encourage people to act on the basis of their own knowledge and experience, rather than depending on the teaching of others. Finally, they recognized that a project capable of gaining mass political support needed to be integrated in its social, cultural, spiritual, and economic aspects.

The activists began to look for ways to reintegrate themselves into their home communities. They sought ways to help the people there respond to those issues that were most pressing. Bit by bit, they initiated various projects along with the people already living there, making the trip south so often that they soon found themselves spending as much time in Salinas as in San Juan, where they lived and worked. Finally, by 1989, they had all returned to live in Salinas. In doing so they gave up their lives in the metropolitan area, which offered more economic and cultural opportunities but suffered from all the ills of a fast-paced and stressful modern city. In exchange they chose an economically limited lifestyle in Salinas that was slower-paced than that in San Juan but that gave them the opportunity to be surrounded by family, friends, and the challenge of helping a forgotten place and forgotten people to revitalize themselves. One woman in Las Mareas articulated the sadness and frustration of losing many of Salinas's most promising youngsters who, leaving in search of a better life, return only for holiday visits: "The ones that struggle to better themselves, leave to find opportunity and gain skills, but then they never come back, and we're left worse off than before. Why don't they come back home and help their own community?" The Salinas activists broke that pattern — they went back home.

Putting Ideals into Practice: Evolution of Projects

The Salinas activists have taken an integrative approach to community development by initiating autonomous yet mutually supportive cultural, social, educative, and economic projects. Some initiatives had to be abandoned or postponed, whereas others evolved into challenging and exciting projects, sometimes in surprising ways. A roughly chronological recounting here should give some picture of their experience of putting their ideals into practice.

The People's Chronicle:
Harnessing the Power of the Press

Salinas native and longtime activist Danilo Cruz Miranda had been writing for various short-lived local bulletins since the 1960s, but had long dreamed of helping to start a local newspaper committed to serving the

Figure 5.1   "The People's Chronicle"

people of Salinas. During the early 1980s Danilo, who lived in Salinas, maintained contact with other Salinas activists who had moved to San Juan. During 1986 they began working together on the newspaper, to be called *Salinas Hoy: Crónicas del Pueblo* (Salinas Today: The People's Chronicle) (see fig. 5.1).

According to Danilo, "the paper was born because Salinas lacked a means of communication in which the community could express its necessities, its concerns, and could propose alternatives to resolve its problems."[1] Another early participant thought it provided a source of information to the community and a tool for expression. The first edition, published in January 1987 and dedicated to Salinas's financially strapped baseball team, introduced the newspaper and its collaborators; it also included reports on community festivals, the assembly of the local savings and loans cooperative, Project Coquí (described later), and an article defining "popular history," as well as interviews of local residents. The first edition introduced regular columns such as *Machacando sobre verdad* (roughly translated as "insisting on the truth"), and *Paco Vecindario,* the newspaper's "bad boy." *Paco* provided a space for streetwise, sarcastic, at times offensive, but always entertaining commentary on issues that did not necessarily warrant writing an entire article. Although collaborator Tata Santiago described the column as a collective effort by all of the newspaper's contributors, some Salinas residents were convinced that it was the work of one person who preferred to remain anonymous. "Paco's" true identity thus continued to be the subject of speculation.

The May 1987 edition featured an article describing the ecological importance of the mangrove forests and denounced the illegal building activities of the summer-home owners in Las Mareas. Articles appeared describing the deterioration of public facilities such as the library, as well as suggesting community-initiated alternatives for improvement. Letters to the editor both welcomed the paper and voiced concerns about various local public infrastructure problems. An interesting letter written by the newspaper's San Juan-based printer predicted a great future as a regional newspaper for *Salinas Hoy* for the following reasons: first, the paper concentrated on one particular place, thus helping readers to identify with it. Second, it included different sections for a variety of interests, such as cooperatives, sports, popular history, local people, and politics, thus offering something for everyone. Third, the paper was infused with a contagious spirit of optimism. Finally, it portrayed communities in action and gave well-deserved recognition to local individuals and groups that were actively involved in improving the quality of life in Salinas.

Development of themes in the newspaper over time have included the reporting of local sports and popular culture; space is also provided for local poetry and community oral histories. But of special note is the extensive coverage of the various environmental, economic, and residential issues facing Salinas, as evidenced by the brief—and by no means exhaustive—following review.

In 1988 the paper publicized the struggle to prevent the sale of Isla de Ratones and the fight against the Las Mareas summer homes. Between 1988 and 1990 it gave extensive coverage to the controversial closure of the Central Aguirre sugar mill. It highlighted the unsuccessful struggle to prevent construction of the marina between 1989 and 1991, as well as the successful campaign against the siting of a regional toxic waste landfill. It gave attention to contamination of the municipal landfill by asbestos from transformers dumped by the power plant, as well as to other sources of air and water pollution, between 1989 and 1991. Then, from 1990 to 1991 the newspaper reported on the struggle of residents of La Jagua to obtain titles to the land where they live; it also detailed their fight against the plan to convert the La Rosada school into a restaurant and evict the residents, in order to develop La Jagua for summer homes. Finally, during 1994 it was a key source of information about the dangers of a proposal to build a coal-burning power plant along the eastern shore of Jobos Bay.

In its five years of existence *Salinas Hoy* has sponsored festivals, Bingo fund-raisers, family outings, a children's summer camp, and other activities. It has served as an important instrument in coordinating the organization of local residents. The all-volunteer periodical prints eleven thousand copies per month and features well-researched investigative reporting (including a few national "scoops"), citizen alerts, historical and cultural features, and local advertising. The newspaper has proved to be an effective tool for empowering ordinary citizens of Salinas to voice their concerns and join together in the search for solutions to the problems facing their community (the slogan most often expounded: For Social Problems, Community Solutions!). *Salinas Hoy* has served as an important organizing tool. Although most of the original collaborators are still actively contributing to the newspaper there is increasing participation by other Salinas residents. The editorial board has included a housewife and local church activist, students, municipal assembly members, and other concerned community residents. The paper is distributed free, but sells advertising to local businesses; in addition, the Ponce-based Airport Workers' Union (UITA) also contributes to the paper and, at times, has been given space within the newspaper in which to publish its own news.

In 1993 the newspaper changed its name to *Hoy desde Salinas* (Today from Salinas); the name change marked the beginning of an attempt to regionalize the paper. By August 1994 the newspaper collective had succeeded in recruiting collaborators in neighboring municipios, three in Guayama and two each in Patillas and Juana Díaz. This regionalizing process was considerably slowed by the final breakdown of their well-worn Mac Plus computer early in 1994, so that no newspaper editions were published between January and June. At last they resolved the situation when two of the main collaborators took out a personal loan to purchase a new Macintosh Quadra 605 and laser printer. However, in the interim they lost many advertisers; a newly active volunteer took charge of advertising sales, but progress at first was understandably slow in this economically depressed region. Moreover, local businesses were somewhat wary of committing themselves to a paper with financial difficulties and had begun advertising in the more commercially-oriented newspaper *Impacto*, out of Guayama; plus, in some cases the political background of some of *Hoy desde Salinas*'s collaborators still proved a stumbling block to sales. To make matters worse, the newspaper's printer, a company in Carolina, Puerto Rico, informed them that it would no longer print for them unless they could pay off their bill (which by that time amounted to five thousand dollars). Taking out another personal loan was out of the question; moreover, their attempts at securing a grant for the newspaper were unsuccessful, since the local foundations did not consider it to be a community project. To address the problem they formed a group called "Friends of Salinas Hoy," which began meeting in September to help raise funds so that the newspaper could continue to publish.

In addition, with the help of friends outside of the area they began searching for organizations in the United States with grant programs for projects that could incorporate the newspaper. One such idea was to get funding to train women and youth in investigative reporting, writing, and desktop publishing as a means to empower them to disseminate information within their own communities. To write proposals for the U.S.-based organizations, they needed writers with good English skills, which limited the work to two or three activists; additionally, although many of the Salinas projects were already incorporated as nonprofit organizations under Puerto Rico law, at least one would now need to be certified by federal law as well — an additional task for the overworked volunteers. By the end of 1994 three more editions of the newspaper had been published; meanwhile, the grant-writing committee continued looking for grant possibilities.

Community Organizations and Alliances

Community organizations representing both specific neighborhoods and the municipio as a whole were formed, while existing organizations, such as the fishermen's associations, were revitalized. They were significant in that they were not organized through existing structures, such as political parties, labor unions, or government agencies, but rather through direct mobilization by local activists.

Project Coquí. The village of El Coquí, located north of Highway PR 3 and almost due north of Central Aguirre, was in a marshy area that was filled in with ashes from burned bagasse (sugarcane residue) in the early part of the twentieth century. Upon the ashes was built a community of workers who came from throughout southern Puerto Rico to work in the Aguirre sugar mill and surrounding cane fields.

A community that at one time boasted a theater and dance hall, El Coquí has a long history of labor activism and other popular struggles. During the 1930s it was the local center of the Movimiento de Acción Social Independentista, the left wing of the Liberal Party headed by Luis Muñoz Marín, which later formed the nucleus of the Partido Popular Democrático (Popular Democratic Party, or PPD). Nationalist leader Pedro Albizu Campos held meetings in El Coquí during the same period, and the community had active members of the Nationalist Party until the 1950s. The PPD facilitated social programs designed to address community needs during the 1940s and 1950s and was particularly strong in El Coquí during that period.[2] During the 1970s El Coquí was the local base of operations for both the PSP and PIP; there was also a considerable amount of New Left–oriented educational and organizational work in El Coquí during that period. During the early 1970s residents of El Coquí confronted the government with a squatters' community named Villa Albizu. An International Workers' Day march held in El Coquí on May 1, 1973, attracted thousands of marchers. Residents participated in all of the militant strikes of that decade, including those against Central Aguirre, the public utilities, and the Fibers International petrochemical plant. El Coquí was also the home of Salinas's first community environmental group, the

Citizens for Conservation of Natural Resources, which actively opposed plans for a nuclear power plant in Aguirre.

In 1985 El Coquí suffered from a 44 percent unemployment rate, and the tide of migration was evident from the rise in abandoned houses. To make matters worse, the community was the site of a drug war between a local gang and an organization based in neighboring Santa Isabel that attempted to take over the trade. Of thirty-four drug-war-related deaths that year in the south, eighteen took place around El Coquí. Innocent bystanders were sometimes victims, and out of fear the residents no longer held their community festivals or used their public spaces. At the same time, activists originally from Salinas but living in San Juan were looking for a way to reinsert themselves in their home communities to do work capable of attracting mass support and participation. They saw the situation in El Coquí as an opportunity to help a community with a long history of popular struggle that was now in desperate straits.

Together with other activists living in El Coquí and the main town, the activists living in San Juan began going door-to-door and holding meetings in a local bar. They proposed popular cultural workshops for children and youths as a healthy alternative to the drug culture, as well as an all-volunteer library and tutoring to try to lower the school dropout rate; both proposals met with considerable local support. Out of an estimated population of four thousand, over a hundred El Coquí residents eventually became collaborators in the new project, which was organized in 1986 as the Coquí Institute for Cultural Development.

The various workshops were designed to impart a positive self-image and pride in the national and cultural identity of the participants. Children made "Coquí" T-shirts and sold them locally, and the *bomba/plena*[3] workshop trained the youngsters in the regional popular music and dance forms. Through the participants' efforts they succeeded in 1987 in reviving the Coquí popular festival, one of Salinas's oldest and largest street festivals, which had been discontinued; by reviving the festival the community began reclaiming its public spaces. The all-volunteer library, located in a vacant house owned by a local family, was also part of the Institute's strategy for popular cultural revival. In 1988 the institute added a theater project, the restoration of Teatro Coquí, which was dedicated to the development of popular culture in the marginalized communities of the south coast from Santa Isabel to Patillas; then in 1989 all projects were subsumed under ARTESUR, a nonprofit organization dedicated to popular cultural revival. This organization has attracted support (including funding) from the Puerto Rico Community Foundation, the Institute for Puerto Rican Culture, and the Commission for the Quincentennial Celebrations in Puerto Rico. It sponsors music and dance workshops in several Salinas and Guayama communities, and as of 1992 counted on fifteen active collaborators, forty children, and a host of occasional helpers, many of whom participated during the first days of Project Coquí.

To quote one participant, Project Coquí was a "reclaiming struggle" dedicated to raising self-esteem and to providing the building blocks for other efforts. The idea was to promote relationships between cultural, political, economic, environmental, and organizational projects, in such a way that the people involved would feel themselves to be in charge of their lives. The projects were to be nonpolitical, in the traditional partisan sense, and political rhetoric—which so often had divided people and doomed projects—was deliberately dropped. Nonetheless, it was well understood that any project reaffirming the self-worth and ability of the people to solve their own problems and create their own lives was essentially political.

Héctor Vásquez, ARTESUR's president, explained in a personal interview that he had no problem with ARTESUR's collaborating with the commission for the quincentennial celebration of Columbus' voyages to America. He emphasized that the local activities stressed a reaffirmation of popular cultural and class identity ("five hundred years of resistance"), rather than celebrating Columbus's "discovery." As of early 1992 ARTESUR had already sponsored lectures and concerts on indigenous, African, and popular history in Salinas. "We're not Puritans about accepting funds," he added. "The money comes from the government, from churches, and nonprofit organizations, as well as local donations and fundraising activities." He emphasized strongly that activism that seeks to truly involve the community must deal with cultural, social, environmental, economic, and organizational needs in an interconnected manner, and must seek to be as inclusive as possible, which precludes rigidly ideological or unnecessarily confrontational rhetoric and actions.

Since 1990 ARTESUR has organized and presented "A Plena Amista' (to full [*plena*] friendship), an annual festival dedicated to the popular coastal music and dance form known as plena. This particular cultural expression is well known for its lively rhythm and streetwise commentary on both political and personal issues. Events in this two-day celebration include a crafts fair and concerts by south coast plena bands, held in the renovated Teatro Coquí. During the fifth festival, held November 18–19, 1994, residents of Coquí and other southeastern communities were publicly recognized for their support for ARTESUR's cultural, educational, and community work.[4] ARTESUR is dedicated to the preservation and development of the south coastal region's rich cultural heritage, and is particularly aimed at involving youth. Project participants believe strongly that a popular cultural revival is key to developing an interest in community initiatives for social, economic, and political spheres. ARTESUR provides an important cultural component of the Salinas activists' overall strategy of community-based economic and social development. Nonetheless, Héctor cautioned that the organization was created "from above" (that is, by a core group of activists), and thus had some organizational weaknesses; to correct this they were actively searching for more ways to broaden the decision-making powers of the group.

Meanwhile, the Coquí community library was incorporated and expanded its programs. In 1994 it began sponsoring an adult literacy project known as MAS, which particularly aimed at the young mothers of the children who participated in the tutoring programs. The community activists hoped that by increasing the reading and writing skills of the women, their self-esteem levels would be raised and they would be encouraged to work together more on issues that they identified as of concern, such as employment, health, substance abuse, and domestic violence.

The work in El Coquí was seen from its outset as an experimental project in community organizing. The activists were looking for a way to begin work with "the masses" and break the isolation of the Puerto Rican Left.[5] Although not specifically conceived as such, Project Coquí served as a pilot, whose organizational experience was later applied in organizing community committees and other projects in Salinas.

The Salinas Development Committee. The Salinas Development Committee was created in December 1989, immediately inspired by the imminent closure of Central Aguirre and Salinas Manufacturing. The committee was Salinas's first broadly based community action group and was composed of Salinas residents from diverse ideological backgrounds. Members included community activists, merchants and professionals, the mayor, and assembly members. President of the Committee was local businessman and accountant Heriberto Conde, and Nelson Santos served as vice-president. The Salinas Development Committee was dedicated to the municipio's positive social and economic development; the operating principle is "Salinas first," and in that spirit members agreed to put aside other differences. At the outset the committee was divided into two working subcommittees: the first concentrated on investigating the government's plans for economic development projects affecting Salinas, whereas the second was dedicated to keeping the public informed. Economic proposals supported by the committee concentrated on commercial fishing, diversified agriculture, and internal tourism. By 1994, however, the committee had effectively ceased to exist, particularly after the untimely death of Sr. Conde; the Playa-Playita Community Committee (described later) took over its work as a generator of economic proposals, while the newspaper continued as a primary source of public information.

Two community committees were organized in 1990: the Brisas del Mar Pro-Children Committee and the La Playa/Playita Communal Committee, Inc. The emphases are somewhat different for the two committees.

The Brisas del Mar Pro-Children Committee was formed in 1989 by residents of the Brisas del Mar public housing project and the neighboring residential single-family housing development La Margarita. Both sit on part of the Nigua River's floodplain, on the former site of Hacienda Margarita, on flood-prone lands once planted in sugarcane. The location is just south of the Pueblo and west of Highway 701 (across the highway from most of Salinas's remaining manufacturing plants). The committee got its start when a number of residents of Brisas del Mar approached *Salinas Hoy* writer and former Brisas del Mar resident Tata Santiago to help them organize the annual Three Kings' Day celebration on January 6; Tata had just recently moved back to Salinas and was living in La Margarita. Children and youth are of special concern to the Brisas/La Margarita committee members. Accordingly, since 1990 the committee has annually sponsored a children's summer camp. During the fall of 1991 committee participants also began a daily tutoring program to help children with their schoolwork; and in 1994 they successfully petitioned the Department of Education to provide a head teacher for the tutoring program.

The committee was formed to work directly with education, recreation, and sports; it also deals with the municipal government in an organized manner to resolve problems within the community, such as the lack or deterioration of public utilities and infrastructure. In January 1995 the committee was to commence a new project called "Madres e Hijos Juntos en la Educación" (Mothers and children together in education), designed to offer young mothers a chance to earn their high school diplomas and develop general skills to help them as mothers and heads of households. The committee planned to utilize the cooperative model of popular education (inspired by Paolo Freire) that integrates formal education with daily life. This new project was seen as complementary to the ongoing tutoring and other projects for children.[6] As of March of that year, however, the project had not started, because bureaucratic foot-dragging in San Juan had delayed the release of funding that had already been approved. The committee eventually went ahead with the project without waiting for the funding; happily, the local community received the project with great enthusiasm.

The Brisas projects have already begun to bear some fruit, as manifested by some of the children and youth. One shy young boy from a large family, who could barely read, became involved in the tutoring program. For the first time he received concentrated attention from loving elders, and within a year he had won a prize in school for outstanding grades. A teenage girl struggling with heavy family responsibilities beyond those of most adolescents was encouraged to publish her writing in the local newspaper. The recognition she received inspired her to write still more, even to enter islandwide contests. She became actively involved in the Brisas projects and enrolled in college after high school graduation. Although these and other young participants face tremendous personal challenges, they have also seen that more positive life alternatives are possible, and are receiving active encouragement to try to achieve them.

Another important outcome of the work of the Brisas committee is that residents have become less timid and more questioning when dealing with government officials; this new attitude is one encouraging sign that the locals have been gaining self-confidence through their experiences of working together to solve their community's problems. Working together has become all the more important since public housing projects in Puerto Rico have recently been "privatized"; residents must therefore learn to effectively organize and to demand that the for-profit company in charge respond to residents' needs.

The La Playa/Playita Communal Committee (CCPP) was organized in 1990. It was incorporated as a nonprofit organization in 1991 according to the laws of the Commonwealth of Puerto Rico, for the following purposes: first, the committee proposed to stimulate the community's diverse social sectors to organize and participate in the construction of a more just and democratic society, following the guidelines of cooperativism and solidarity. Second, the committee was committed to the transformation of the poor communities of Salinas, as well as to any Puerto Rican community where fraternity, friendship, and solidarity exist. Third, it actively promoted the integral education of its members. Fourth, it would collaborate with other public or private entities in all programs, projects, or activities that contribute to achieving the committee's institutional mission or objectives. Finally, it promoted community economic development to counteract societal problems such as unemployment and related social ills, via creation of the educational and occupational training necessary for initiating economic enterprises.[7] The committee's active membership included local merchants, fishermen, teachers, social service workers, and youth. The committee's philosophy promoted community development through the use of its own natural and human resources; the committee explicitly recognized the capacity of each individual for the maximum development of her or his potential, directed towards the community's reconstruction. Several projects already under way reflected this philosophy. Along with the newspaper *Salinas Hoy* and ARTESUR the committee cosponsored a children's summer camp in 1991 for more than eighty children and youths from La Playa and El Coquí. It also cosponsored the La Rosada adult vocational and equivalency school in La Jagua (described later), as well as the program beginning in 1995 for young mothers in Brisas/La Margarita. By 1994 the CCPP had emerged as the primary coordinating body for writing proposals for the economic and educational projects, in effect assuming many of the duties for which the Salinas

Development Committee had been responsible; this shift did not, however, change the plan for all of the various enterprises to eventually be completely autonomous.

On July 31, 1994, the CCPP celebrated its first annual assembly. According to activist Edda Santi, "it was a day full of joys, surprises and above all, accomplishments." The gathering filled the Aguirre meeting hall with Salinas residents and with representatives of businesses and of public and private agencies that have been supporting the various projects, such as a local hardware store, the Puerto Rico Foundation, Social Services, and the Department of Agriculture's Fisheries Program. The assembly unanimously approved two resolutions: first, it called for a process of "grassroots development" and the participation of local residents to determine priorities and alternatives. Second, it rejected in the strongest terms the proposed construction of a coal-burning power plant in neighboring Guayama. The assembly also supported efforts to gain some control over government plans to revive the "Tren del Sur," the old south coastal train route, for tourism. CCPP president Nelson Santos, delivered the keynote address, emphasizing that "the mission of CCPP is the self-development of the community, using its own natural, material, and human resources, recognizing the capacity of each individual to overcome limitations and develop abilities to the maximum, in order to direct them toward the constructive work of building a people."[8]

A meeting of the CCPP on an evening in August 1994 demonstrated the organization, goals, and issues dealt with in this committee. Held in the office of the newspaper, the meeting was attended by eleven members, exceeding the seven members — half the fourteen on the committee — that were necessary for a quorum. Those absent were expected to let the others know why they did not attend. Each enterprise and project, such as the school and the worker-owned businesses, had at least two representatives on the committee; some people, active in more than one activity, were nevertheless representing only one, so as to encourage diversification of the committee membership. Nelson Santos, the committee's president, chaired the meeting, Although all members were encouraged to participate, it was clear that they respected the leadership of the president, as well as that of the committee secretary (the artistic director of the newspaper). The meeting began with a prayer, each member joining hands and standing in a circle.

First on the agenda were reports by members about various issues of concern. One fisherman complained that an outside entrepreneur who had leased three hundred cuerdas to plant corn was killing *jueyes* (land crabs, a great delicacy) and destroying mangroves near Las Mareas with his machinery, including areas within the Jobanes Nature Reserve. He also reported that the jueyes themselves were black from unreported petroleum spills by the Phillips oil refinery. In other environmental news, another member reported that the EPA was offering federal funds for environmental education; the deadline for proposals was the next October. The committee would also request that the agency monitor emissions of the Aguirre electric complex, just as they had been doing in the Cataño plants, located west of San Juan. Vigilance at that infamously polluting facility had resulted in reduced petroleum use. Unfortunately, the slack was taken up by increased burning at Aguirre, which could only aggravate the health problems that the people of Salinas already suffered. Another proposal, sponsored by the Methodist church for "minority" projects on environment and development, was also due in December.

Other announcements included the news that the Union of Airport Workers, a major supporter of the newspaper and a collaborator in various projects, was offering to sponsor a representative of the Salinas initiatives for an accounting course. It was also reported that La Rosada School (a major local project described later) would hold its teacher training for the upcoming school year for five hours each day during the following week. The fishing representative announced that the director of the commonwealth government's Fishing Affairs Office was also scheduled to visit the following week. This director was to discuss the provision of a boat for the school's fishing course, and deliver it to the Las Mareas fishing association. He would also discuss plans to support the school's program of aquaculture, including salt-water cultivation of *carrucho* (conch), as well as the navigation course.

Another member reminded everyone that the crew of *Desde Mi Pueblo* (from my town), a popular program on Puerto Rico's public television Canal 6 that visited a different municipio each week, would arrive in

Salinas the following week; they would stay in the marina, had plans to interview Nelson, and would be visiting all of the various projects. In addition, the Puerto Rico Foundation, a nonprofit organization that had funded cultural initiatives in Salinas, was scheduled to visit the economic projects in September. The first meeting of Friends of Salinas Hoy was also announced. Finally, a vote by secret ballot (counted by a visitor at the meeting) filled the committee's vacant positions of vice-president, assistant treasurer, and assistant secretary.

Nelson also gave a pep talk in which he reminded everyone that, although the CCPP had written proposals for nearly all of the various local projects, the committee was not merely a group organized to write proposals, or even to obtain material benefits. The committee's work should instead be seen as a process of group strengthening. This process also included a process of consciousness raising, where meetings were also important for discussing internal problems. According to Nelson, "It's not merely to write proposals and win even millions of dollars, if we don't understand what the millions are for. We have a mission, which is the development of a people and a community, that we're a part of. We should take care to reflect upon our attitudes, and refrain from attacking each other personally when we have disagreements, which has destroyed many groups before."

The fishing associations. As part of a federally funded program run by the Puerto Rico government, fishing associations were formed in coastal communities throughout the island during the 1970s; unfortunately, the lack of coordinated government policies in support of developing the fishing industry rendered many associations inoperative. Some, however, have survived and prospered, and in fact have commercialized their operations to some extent, particularly on the west coast (see fig. 5.2). West coast fishing cooperatives formed the Western Fishing Congress in 1982; they aimed to join forces to modernize the industry and share training and knowledge among the members, to pressure the government to adopt and support policies that the fishermen considered necessary for properly developing the industry, and to protect the coastal environment and its resources by compelling the government to enforce environmental laws against polluters. In this vein they have also worked closely with the

Figure 5.2   Making traps for fishing

Department of Natural Resources to develop management plans for the coastal areas. A congress of eastern fishermen was also created during the 1980s and operated in much the same manner.

In Salinas concerned fishermen joined forces with the recently returned activists to reorganize and revitalize the fishing associations of La Playa, Playita, and Las Mareas between 1989 and 1991. By 1992 La Playa and Playita were operating their own fishing centers; meanwhile, land was donated and an architect hired for a center in Las Mareas, which was in full operation by 1994. In general fishermen and women have been among the most active of Salinas's residents in the various campaigns against contaminating industries and coastal privatization, certainly no surprise since they would be intimately acquainted with the negative effects of these particular hazards of "development."

During the first few years of the Salinas initiatives the Don Piche Fishing Association of La Playa, Inc., at the time the best organized of the local fishing associations, played a leading role in economic and environmental projects. Its name honors the memory of a legendary local fisherman, and the Fishing Division of the Department of Agriculture chose the group in January 1991 as a model fishing cooperative. They took advantage of such recognition by lobbying hard for the funds and materials needed to modernize their operation, such as an eight-person boat to facilitate overnight fishing farther away from the coast. The association conducted a workshop from October 1990 to January 1991 to teach the art of fishing to local youth. The members also sponsored monthly family days and were instrumental in the 1991 inauguration of a (short-lived) Puerto Rican direct-sale community market. Early in 1992 the La Playa Fishing Association worked together with a specialist in community economic development to market their products; plans included building bigger freezing and processing facilities so that they could sell more lucrative cuts of fish, such as filets.

The fishing associations of La Playa, Playita, and Las Mareas cosponsored, along with the Salinas Development Committee and the Playa/ Playita Communal Committee, the new community-run La Rosada adult vocational school. The La Playa association was the first site for the community school's fishing program. Personality conflicts and philosophical disagreements over fishing and marketing practices eventually forced the school to transfer its program to Las Mareas, however.

First Economic Proposals

In the May 1987 edition of *Salinas Hoy* an article appeared describing a detailed proposal for diversified commercial agriculture in the South, utilizing a combination of family farms and cooperative marketing and technology that the Cayey-based Committee for the Rescue of Agriculture put forth. The newspaper facilitated a meeting in El Coquí that summer in which members of the committee opened a dialogue with local representatives of labor unions. An article appeared in the April 1988 edition of

Salinas Hoy supporting tourist development in Salinas; the theme was expanded upon and detailed in the June 1990 issue. Specific proposals endorsed by the Salinas Development Committee included careful development of the Point Arenas beach, the restoration of the González mansion in La Jagua for use as a hotel, and the development of Central Aguirre's historic potential.

National community market. During March 1991 La Playa's Fishing Association, the Salinas Development Committee, and *Salinas Hoy* helped organize Puerto Rico's first national community market in Ponce. Community organizations from around the island offered agricultural, artisanal, and other products for sale or barter at the market; in addition, musicians provided entertainment throughout the day. Besides offering fresh local products to the public, the markets were organized to allow community groups to begin to form networks with like-minded organizations throughout the island. The next two national markets were held in Salinas, whereas the June market took place in the mountain town of Ciales. July's market took place in Salinas during the 150th anniversary of the municipio's founding and featured only local individuals and groups. After July 1991 no more markets were organized, since they proved to be very time-consuming in every respect. Some participants expressed interest in reinstating a modified version in the near future, however.

Agriculture. In May 1991 the Salinas activists met with members of an agricultural cooperative located in Barrio Espino (located in the east-central municipio of San Lorenzo) to discuss a joint venture growing tamarind, soursop, and passion fruit trees in Salinas to help meet the cooperative's growing market demand for tropical fruit juices. According to the proposal, residents of Las Mareas, El Coquí, La Playa, and Playita were to provide the labor, and Land Authority–owned idle agricultural land in Salinas would be leased. The Barrio Espino cooperative, in turn, would be in charge of processing and marketing. The proposal fell through because the participants were unable to obtain the land. However, a similar proposal is planned as part of a course in agriculture to be offered by La Rosada School (described later).

Food products. In July 1991 local activists began developing a proposal for a worker-owned enterprise to make fish- and seafood-filled croquettes and pastries, using the local catch. Meat- and cheese-filled pastries enjoy a growing market throughout Puerto Rico, and the addition of seafood-filled pastries—as yet an uncommon offering—would be certain to be successful. The Salinas enterprise would seek to lease one of the municipio's many vacant Fomento-owned factories. The proposal was put on hold until students of La Rosada School's restaurant course were graduated in June 1992.

Tourism. Proposals by the local activists for developing Salinas's tourist industry have focused upon so-called ecotourism. In attempting to consider all aspects of economic development and environmental conservation, a definition of "ecotourism" as "tourist development that takes advantage of a region's natural and cultural resources and provides the maximum economic benefit to local residents, while helping to preserve the region ecologically, economically, and culturally" met with unanimous support from the Salinas activists.

Recommendations for ecotouristic development in Salinas have included converting Central Aguirre into a living sugar colony museum (where sugar could perhaps be grown and harvested for fuel, an old proposal never actually put into practice); locally run courses for hotel and restaurant management; promotion of small-scale, guest house–type tourist accommodations; cooperation with the Jobos Bay Estuarine Reserve (Jobanes) to take advantage of its tourist potential; restoration of the Ponce-Patillas Railroad with a view toward exploiting its tourist value; and a direct economic relationship between tourism and local fishing, agriculture, artisanship, and the cultural revival. The school would also become an important foundation for this enterprise.

Liberating Education: The Community School

A vital part of any economic strategy should be to ensure that the skills exist within the community to fill the jobs created; this aspect has tended to be conspicuously absent from top-down development strategies, such as the industrialization of the island under Operation Bootstrap. Time and time again, the lack of such educational programs in rural areas — along with the loss of jobs due to the abandonment of agriculture as well as to the decline of more locally focused, labor-intensive industries — has often resulted in the rise of local unemployment because of "development." In 1991 the Salinas activists and other residents initiated a project-oriented vocational and adult equivalency school, organized according to the principles of self-help, cooperation, and community service, as popularized by Paolo Freire, and worked together with the municipal government and the Department of Education to open it. The activists look upon the school as a key vehicle for launching the economic projects.

La Rosada School was a small, one-story public school building in La Jagua that had been abandoned since the early 1970s. Mr. Andrés Guerra Mondragón, a foreigner who had married into the González family, planned to make an Italian/Argentine restaurant in the building and claimed that the land upon which the school was located was González property. In addition, he wanted to develop ninety-two housing sites upon sixteen cuerdas of property where the fourteen families of La Jagua presently live; the people of La Jagua were longtime residents but did not have title to the land. The newspaper *Salinas Hoy* investigated the claims and discovered that the owner of the *taquería* next door to the school had documents that proved that the land underneath the school belonged to the municipio of Salinas; prompted by the newspaper, the municipal assembly declared the school as its property, and Mr. Guerra dropped his restaurant plans. Then, on January 23, 1990, the Salinas Development Committee sponsored a meeting between Mr. Guerra and residents of La Jagua. At the meeting it became known that the cost of relocating the residents would not be borne by the housing developers.[9] This fact provoked stiff opposition from local residents and the municipal assembly and was extensively reported by the newspaper. The development plan has since been put on indefinite hold.

In July 1991 the Las Mareas, Playita, and La Playa fishing associations, along with the Salinas Development Committee and the Playa/Playita Communal Committee, leased the school building from the Department of Education, and received permission from the municipio of Salinas to build a school there oriented toward adult vocational education in industries compatible with the area's resource base. The building required extensive restoration, including electrical wiring, water and sewage lines, and the construction of rooms, including restrooms. Local government and merchants donated material, and community residents voluntarily contributed both skilled and unskilled labor needed to do the job. One day a local electrician stopped off on the way from work to view the progress on restoration of the long-abandoned building. Impressed by the enthusiasm of the workers and seeing the extensive electrical work needed, he volunteered to rewire the school in his spare time. Another time a visiting student had a free day and was immediately put to work painting the newly rebuilt walls of the classrooms. People volunteered a little or a lot of time, and offered special skills or simply the willingness to work, according to what they had — and it was sufficient for the task at hand. The school's first session began in September 1991, and the school was inaugurated in a well-publicized and memorable ceremony in October 1991.

The academic component of the school's programs offers courses in ninth- and twelfth-grade equivalency and a marketing course for high school graduates. The vocational component offered three programs during the 1991–92 school year: fishing arts (including boat building, motor repair, navigation, and diving), industrial sewing, and cooking and restaurant operation. Other programs phased in during the next few years were ecotourism, aquaculture and agriculture, carpentry, and ceramics.

The students were organized to work together with instructors, and most voluntarily committed themselves to form cooperative enterprises upon completion of their courses. Instructors included schoolteachers, restaurateurs, lifelong fishermen, and former light-manufacturing employees. Salaries for the teachers were to be paid by the Job Training Partnership Act (JTPA), a federally funded program administered by the Puerto Rico Department of Education, whereas student stipends were supposed to be provided by the Right to Work Authority (ADT, for its title in Spanish), a federally-funded program administered by the Puerto Rico Department of Labor. The Fisheries Division of the Puerto Rico Department of Agriculture provided a large boat that was being restored by the fishing course students for long-distance fishing, a requirement if fishing in Salinas is to become commercially viable.

During November 1991 the Jobanes nature reserve, La Rosada School, and the fishing associations sponsored an interpretive tour of the reserve and a number of the offshore cays, to which a number of functionaries of the Department of Education were invited. As a result of that tour the Department agreed to fund a proposal for the reserve staff to train local young people to serve as ecotourism guides and boat operators. Such cooperation laid the foundation for the school's new course in ecotourism, which began in the fall of 1992.

Faced with delays by the ADT in paying stipends, the students began in January 1992 to plan strategies to make the school financially independent, through fundraising activities and by donating a percentage of their incipient businesses to the school. For example, halfway through the school year the restaurant course students began to make and sell seafood pastries to local restaurants. After graduation in June 1992 the students and school administration planned to submit a proposal to Fomento to acquire one of Salinas's abandoned factories for the seafood pastries business.

A thirty-five-cuerda parcel of land belonging to the Land Authority and located south of Highway PR 3 between the main town and La Jagua was leased to private growers for sugarcane cultivation during the 1991–92 season; that was the last season in which the parcel was to be planted in sugarcane. During January 1992 La Rosada School administrators began trying to obtain the land for the school's planned agricultural program. Once students were trained, the school, the Salinas Development Committee, and the Playa/Playita Communal Committee planned to try to lease more unused agricultural land belonging to the Land Authority for a fruit tree–growing and juice-processing project, as well as for other crops and products for which there is a market demand.

By early 1992 La Rosada School was considered to be a chief vehicle for the community-based economic development strategy. All participating organizations came under a new umbrella organization, People United in Salinas's Development, known by its Spanish acronym PUEDES (you are able). PUEDES was to be the local development effort's official representative in presenting proposals to government and private organizations for funding, as well as a key organizer of the newly developing islandwide coalition of community development groups. By 1994, however, with

CCPP taking on most proposal writing and the worker-owned businesses poised to begin operations, PUEDES referred instead to the school and its vocational programs.

A visit to La Rosada School's weeklong teacher orientation during August 1994 provided a lesson in how to develop a curriculum for "liberating education." Following the teachings of Paolo Freire, Gustavo Gutiérrez, and others particularly associated with liberation theology, the facilitator, University of Puerto Rico social psychology graduate student Lourdes Lara, discussed with the teachers five important ways in which alternative education differed from the traditional model: first, alternative education takes people's needs as the point of departure. Second, teachers and students share such needs. Third, alternative education values both teacher and student as subjects ("thinks, knows, has, can"), rather than pitting subject (teacher) against object (student). Fourth, it views life as a process of change, or constant transformation. Finally, the interdependence of the educational experience should promote the collective and the cooperative, rather than the individual and the competitive.

Students arrived the following week for their orientation, and classes began at the end of August. The 1994–95 student body was quite different from previous sessions; unlike earlier years, when the majority were adults, this time most of the newly matriculated students were between sixteen and eighteen years old. In addition, whereas previous classes were almost exclusively composed of residents of Playa, Playita, and Las Mareas, the class of 1995 included residents of Salinas Pueblo, Las Ochentas, Parcelas Vásquez — in short, from all over Salinas. The reasons for this soon became apparent. About half of the students had been sent by the government to enroll in the school to fulfill school and job training requirements. To nobody's surprise, these students showed on the average less interest in the alternative community projects being developed than those who had enrolled of their own accord. The school's administrators conceded that it was good to cooperate with state agencies; nevertheless, although it was a positive sign that the school was being recognized, they did not want to be mistaken for a government project, involved in "business as usual" instead of offering something quite different. They asked themselves whether the "draftees" could possibly be taking away spaces from more motivated students.

In addition, recognizing that it must go beyond the school walls to involve entire families and communities, CCPP in 1994 also began a new program in cooperation with the municipal government and funded by the Federal Law of Drug-Free Schools and Communities, called Emparejate.[10] The new program is directed at young high school dropouts and families at high risk for drug and alcohol abuse. The work of Emparejate is meant to further develop the three-sided "bio-psycho-social" project of the school: "bio," referring to reintegrating humans and nature; "psycho," dealing with the individual; and "social," connecting both to the community. Developing the skills of social management of members of the community, as well as raising their self-esteem and improving their ability to work in groups were key goals; methods for achieving them include education, job creation, participation in recreative and cultural activities, and recording of oral histories. There was a need for the therapy of creative labor, to enable people to provide for their needs and feel connected to their families, communities, and environment. The real challenge was, as one activist put it, "not to secure grants, nor even to create employment, but rather, how to grow as human beings," and all of the Salinas initiatives, including the school, merely provide a way to get there.

Development of Economic Proposals

It was interesting to look back in 1994 and see what had happened with the three groups — sewing, cooking, and fishing — from the class of 1992, the first at the school. First, the industrial sewing group, which during the first year appeared to be the most closely knit and committed to forming their own business, was unable to secure a locale and other needed resources. This failure exacerbated interpersonal problems that finally forced the group to disband. The school then decided to start from scratch with new program graduates; the future enterprise was tentatively to be called Coral Fashion. By contrast, the new worker-owned business Procesadora del Sur, Inc. was composed mostly of graduates of the cooking course from the first year (see fig. 5.3). They specialized in fish and seafood snacks, as well as other elaborated food products, and had submitted proposals for startup financing and a business site.

A look at the fishing program also revealed changes. At La Playa strong

Figure 5.3 Procesadora del Sur

disagreements grew between older fishermen, who prided themselves on their traditional artisanal skills, and the younger graduates of the school's program, who demanded a quicker transition to more modern methods and a more commercial enterprise. Additional personality conflicts soon turned the conflict into a split, and the school was eventually obliged to move its program to Las Mareas, which boasted a new fishing center. The participants there were very interested in diversifying their product: they wanted to popularize different species and acquire the skills for more processed offerings, such as fillets. They sought to master new technology and combine traditional techniques with modern ones. In addition, the worker-owned fishing enterprise known as Pescadería del Sur, Inc. would now be based in Las Mareas.

By the end of 1994 several worker-owned enterprises (Empresas Propiedad Tarabajadores, known as PTs) were in various stages of organization and incorporation. These included ImpreSur, Inc. — which in addition to producing *Hoy desde Salinas* offered photocopying, desktop publishing, and other office services — and the cooking and fishing enterprises.

Other businesses were in varying stages of organization. One interesting new project was Muestras del Bosque, specializing in carpentry and fine woodworking in Mosquito. It had originally been a job training project sponsored by Social Services; however, in 1994 the latter petitioned La Rosada School to take it over.

Frutas de Agua y Tierra was a planned venture featuring aquaculture (with graduates of the class of 1994) and agriculture. The agricultural component was still waiting to lease thirty cuerdas of agricultural land from the Land Authority before it could begin training. Plans were well developed to grow tropical fruit trees for juice production, a product for which there was strong demand; *acerolas* (a cherry-like fruit) were to be the first trees planted. The aquaculturists had already been trained, and Job Training Partnership Act funds had already been used to purchase tanks; all that was needed was the space to work. The CCPP had long been negotiating with the Sugar Corporation to lease land for both agriculture and aquaculture, and a proposal for funding to help launch this PT was ready to submit by the end of 1994.

Finally, Ecosur was a planned worker-owned business whose participants had graduated from the ecotourism course in 1993 and 1994. A joint effort with the Jobanes nature reserve, the school course trained them in local ecology and history, tour organizing, and related activities. The incipient business was busy negotiating with Jobanes for office space in the nature reserve's new headquarters, located in Central Aguirre near the old American Hotel. Additionally, during the first half of 1994 the school also held a five-month-long course in clay artisanship. They planned to offer this course regularly, and gear it toward both practical items and traditional artisanal products for sale to tourists.

The Salinas activists were very interested in obtaining space for some of the PTs in Aguirre, a location with no lack of plans for diverse businesses, and plenty of space. In addition, they proposed that the "Tren del Sur" be converted into a PT. As of 1994 a private company had been awarded a contract by the municipio of Salinas; however, the San Juan government was not particularly interested in the venture and wanted to sell off all of the equipment. Meetings in August 1994 were held in San Juan on the subject of economic development projects in the southeast; invited to the meeting were regional Senator Cirilo Delgado Tirado, Arroyo Representative Papo García, Mayor Baerga of Salinas, the company holding the "Tren del Sur" contract, and the government's Sugar Corporation (owners of the railroad equipment and right of way). Also invited to attend were members of the Salinas PTS Procesadora del Sur, Pescadería del Sur, Muestras del Bosque, and the aquaculture group. The CCPP planned to send representatives, but last-minute transportation problems forced them to miss the meeting.

Community Mobilization and Islandwide Alliances

Firmly believing that there is strength in numbers, the Salinas activists have attempted to extend their alliance-building and cooperative efforts beyond local boundaries. They have tried to include like-minded groups in their region and throughout the island, both for mutual assistance and to create a base for popular organizations to effectively demand social change; they have also been moderately successful in eliciting cooperation from both government and private agencies to obtain some of the resources necessary to set projects in motion. And they are involved in an ongoing process of self-examination, to ensure that their commitment to increasing community involvement and empowerment is reflected in decision making within the local organizations and initiatives.

Encuentro de Comunidades

Puerto Rico's first grassroots-organized Encuentro (Conference) of Communities and Unions took place in Salinas in May 1992. Attended by more than eighty representatives of community-based social, environmental, and economic groups, unions, and academic-based activists, the *encuentro* began a serious dialogue about the problems the respective organizations faced, such as the lack of mutual support among groups working on locally based development programs, the lack of control over resources necessary to set the programs in motion, and the lack of government support and management expertise. Participants also brainstormed about ways to join forces to effect community-based solutions on an islandwide basis, such as jointly sponsored training courses and lobbying for both public and private funds. The topics of workshops offered that day included economic development, education, recreation and culture, health, housing, and dealing with the government. Between May and October 1992 four encuentros took place. They were seen as a hopeful sign of future collaborations, from which broadly based citizens' movements for change might eventually evolve.

Other Alliance-Building Efforts

The Salinas activists have made various efforts to reach out to like-minded groups throughout the island. They have facilitated retreats for community groups, labor unions, and religious workers, as well as for socially committed academics and government representatives. By 1994, however, they realized that they were expending perhaps too much time and energy promoting islandwide alliances. "We could spend all our time traveling around the island, but neglect the work here at home," observed one activist. They still maintained contacts with groups with whom they had collaborated much in the past: these included unions such as UITA, community organizations in Cidra, Yabucoa, and Patillas, and religious activists at Convento Jesús Mediador, in Bayamón. Although they have recently cut back because of overextension, their example has inspired the formation of similar community groups in the southeast coastal region. Feeling that regional concerns were appropriate and important, the newspaper workers began recruiting regional collaborators and publicizing their neighbors' issues and organizing activities.

By 1994 other attempts at community organizing were taking place, both within Salinas and in the neighboring municipios. Within Salinas, a small sewing enterprise known as SEDICO was being initiated in Las Ochentas by a group of activists associated with the Popular Democratic Party; that particular community had long been a party stronghold.

Along the southeast coast several new groups had sprung up and were being publicized by the newspaper. One of these groups, South Against Contamination (SURCCO), denounced the signing of a contract between the AEE and AES (Applied Energy Service) allowing the latter to build and operate a coal-burning energy plant in Guayama next to Phillips petroleum refinery. This agreement apparently had been carried out secretly and without complying with existing laws requiring public hearings. Another new group, the Guayama Committee for Health and Good Environment, representing residents of the Jobos sector of Guayama, was formed to fight against the proposed coal-burning plant.

In 1994 residents of coastal Barrio Palma, in the municipio of Arroyo (just east of Guayama) organized a group called the Movement for Environmental and Ecological Defense (or MAREA, "tide" in Spanish) to generate solutions to environmental problems along the coast from Punta Guilarte, Arroyo, to the Bajo, or the Patillas shoals and sand banks. The group is composed of fishermen, university students, teachers, laborers, and others. The group began meeting with officials in an organized manner and demanded action to halt destructive developments. By the end of 1994 they had convinced authorities to limit use of "jet skis" near the *villa pesquera*. Jet skis can be described as water-snowmobiles, and are not only dangerous to their users but are destructive of habitats and wildlife. The southeast coast includes critical habitats for manatee and other endangered species, and this fact prompted authorities to try to pass a law to restrict jet skis in critical habitat areas. MAREA's goals are, first, to educate children and adults about environmental protection; second, to organize activities and research to preserve the environment and improve the quality of life in the communities; third, to promote activities that integrate humans with nature; fourth, to develop ecotourism in environmentally sensitive areas; fifth, to coordinate schools, communities, and public agencies; and sixth, to collaborate in creating economic alternatives for their area.[11]

Frustrated by the failure of government agencies to make good on promises to fund projects such as Brisas' Madres y Hijos and the PTs, people from Salinas held a fair inside the Capitolio (seat of the island legislature) during February 1995 in which they publicized their initiatives and received a significant amount of media attention. In addition, they formed groups to visit and lobby individual legislators to support community-initiated projects for economic and social development. They also invited community groups from elsewhere to participate in the day-long event. This concerted effort forced some government officials to take notice in a way rarely experienced by community organizations in Puerto Rico. The Salinas activists also realize, however, that to be most effective this type of action should eventually develop into an ongoing effort, including similar groups islandwide, as part of a process of coalition building and an effective political pressure-group strategy.

Experiences with Government and Private Agencies

The Salinas activists have written proposals and sought assistance from both government and private agencies and organizations. But from the beginning they insisted upon project autonomy and a relationship as equal partners, and they made it clear that the projects would be attempted with or without government help. They were wary of allowing anything to be funded solely by one agency or organization, which could leave them vulnerable to budget cuts, political fallout, and other problems. Instead, they have not looked for any one source to fund more than 50 percent of any project, and they have sought to obtain the balance through private donations of labor, materials and funds, and through other organizations and agencies. They were also interested in promoting mutual aid from community-based organizations in other parts of the country and have reached out to labor unions, religious organizations, and the academic community.

The local initiatives have won support from a number of government and private agencies. Supporters included the Department of Education, which has leased the La Rosada School building to the group, and the JTPA, which paid small salaries to teachers at the new community school and promised to assist with the plan to train local youth as ecotourist guides at the Jobanes reserve. The Fisheries Division of the Department of Agriculture has donated some equipment, including a large boat. Among private agencies, the nonprofit Puerto Rico Foundation awarded a grant to partially fund ARTESUR's cultural projects; in 1994 the Foundation granted twenty thousand dollars to CCPP for startup funding of the fishing and carpentry enterprises.

On November 3, 1994, representatives of *Banco Popular de Puerto Rico's* "Community Reinvestment Act" program visited CCPP (Banco Popular is the island's leading banking institution, and the largest and most powerful Puerto Rican corporation). The program aims to identify community projects that the bank can help develop. Also present were regional representatives of the Departments of Social Services and Labor and Human Resources. In particular, Social Services is interested in initiatives to strengthen the credit line of community development projects.

Members of four of the PTS — ImpreSur, Pescadería del Sur, Procesadora del Sur, and Muestras del Bosque—presented and described their respective enterprises. Teachers and students of La Rosada School also gave a presentation, which included their own agricultural and food products. The school delegation also described its support for other local projects, such as MAS ("More," El Coquí Community Library's literacy and educational project) and Madres e Hijos Juntos en la Educación (Brisas Pro-Children Committee). The guests displayed great interest in contributing to the community projects.[12] Of course, it is one matter to entertain possible funding sources, and to impress them with the activities and potential of the Salinas initiatives. It is, however, another matter to actually receive funding. During 1994 Salinas also received visitors representing the U.S. Congress, who remarked very favorably on the ongoing efforts to break away from government dependence. But, as one activist complained, "everybody wants to visit us, but nobody gives us money."

Not all outside help received has been in the form of funding. Some of the most active, enthusiastic, and significant support has come from individuals outside of Salinas, who shared the vision of community empowerment and offered important resources. These included an economic consultant with twenty years' experience in Puerto Rican community economic development. Believing that Salinas represented the location most likely to effect a locally directed economic strategy, she was helping with proposals and marketing and administration training, as well as offering general advice on how to build a successful business. Another dedicated volunteer was Lourdes Lara, a graduate student in social and community psychology at the University of Puerto Rico-Río Piedras. She began coming to Salinas as part of her field practicals in 1992 and became quite involved in the work there. Her academic plans included writing a master's thesis that would analyze the Salinas projects as a case study of urban social movements. By 1994 she was helping to write proposals and assisting with much of the bureaucracy and paperwork faced by the PTs. In addition she organized and presented the training for the teachers of La Rosada School, as well as worked on the newspaper (as did her husband) and "other things here and there," as she put it. One local remarked that "Lourdes has become a salinense in everything except where she sleeps at night," since she often commuted daily from her home in Caguas, just forty minutes north. She has proved to be a tireless and dedicated worker who has helped in numerous ways.

The Salinas Initiatives:
Accomplishments and Possibilities

On various occasions the Salinas activists discussed their involvement in a process of reflection and self-criticism over tendencies to authoritarianism within the group. Recognizing that society has taught most people to leave decision making to the experts and that it always seems simpler for a few people to make decisions, they have been consciously trying to break with that model in all of the projects, and they hope to promote true democracy and broader participation. One question often asked is "What impedes citizens from taking responsibility and decisions?" Experience has taught the activists that the answer is a perceived lack of knowledge. The commitment and challenge of all of the projects has been to help develop the knowledge and consciousness of the people on the basis of what they already know. Development was always to be considered integral, since political, economic, religious, and cultural components could not be separated. This approach has borne some fruit: although progress at times appeared to be slow, each succeeding year has seen an increasing involvement in the various projects by more local residents. In particular, the economic initiatives demonstrated that the local resistance had moved beyond mere antigovernment and antibusiness opposition. The participants had begun offering positive strategies for developing new industries that made use of the area's natural and human resources; they also encouraged participatory democracy in both the shaping of the initiatives and their economic benefits, and pursued long-range goals such as environmental and social protection and stewardship.

During the first annual assembly of the Playa-Playita Community Committee, Nelson Santos outlined the committee's achievements during its first three years of existence. He reminded the audience that the object of popular education is to develop the concept of integral health: physical, mental, environmental, and communal, in order to facilitate the creation of an empowered and capacitated personality. In the economic arena, the committee's accomplishments included helping to create worker-owned enterprises. They saw their long range goal as increasing their capacity to satisfy human needs through community work, thus abandoning dependence on the government. As of Fall 1994 CCPP was assisting four incorporated PTs to organize and search for financing: the four were Muestras del Bosque, Inc. (carpentry), Pescadería del Sur, Inc. (fishing), ImpreSur, Inc. (printing), and Procesadora del Sur, Inc. (commercial cooking).

The assembly also recognized people and agencies that had supported the work. They included the local office of the Department of Social Services, the mayor's office, local businesses, graduate students, the Department of Agriculture's Fisheries Program, and the Puerto Rico Foundation. Local representatives of unions and political parties also were on hand to congratulate the CCPP for their work.[13]

The local activists are native salinenses from poor, working- and middle-class backgrounds; many have also lived in the United States. Their ideological influences are diverse, but include student radicalism and the social gospel of liberation theology. Likewise, their activist backgrounds range from the environmental and independence movements to labor, civic, and partisan organizations. They have for the most part, however, managed to set aside their differences for the good of "Salinas first." Their projects emphasize socially and environmentally responsible use of local natural and human resources to effect the economic, social, cultural, and spiritual betterment of the poor and working majority of salinenses. Although they are willing to work together with government, private businesses, and civic organizations, they emphasize breaking the cycle of dependence and promoting community cooperation, self-reliance, and self-affirmation. In their view community empowerment and the consequent responsibility for local environmental and social health would have to be at the heart of any real "sustainable development."

A list of the activists' accomplishments thus far includes organizing the community to stop potentially damaging projects such as the regional toxic landfill of 1990–91, as well as continuing efforts to support local campaigns against other risky proposals for the region. The activists have been publishing a vibrant local newspaper and have started a community school. La Rosada School provides opportunities for participants to complete their education, which provides a tremendous boost to their self-esteem and helps expand their life options. The school also gives the students a chance to learn skills for industries that take advantage of existing local natural and human resources. The Salinas initiatives are helping to create and support worker-owned businesses, though to date those businesses are not yet fully operating and self-supporting.

The activists have helped several neighborhoods organize to request some needed services — such as recreational facilities, streetlights, other infrastructure work, and so on — to which local government has responded. They helped revitalize three local fishing associations and helped them obtain better equipment, thus increasing their income potential. They have also initiated tutoring, recreational, and cultural programs for children and youths, both during the summer and throughout the year. Such work has inspired more than one poor youngster to stay in school and aim for a better future than she or he once thought was possible. Finally, the Salinas activists have inspired similar community organizing within their region; they have also begun to participate in islandwide alliances to help build a popular movement that may one day be capable of demanding and effecting change.

Nevertheless, the alternatives that the Salinas activists propose face great obstacles — some of which originate far from Salinas, whereas others are much closer to home. Indeed, the environmental, economic, social, and political odds often appear to be stacked high against them.

6   The Obstacles

The Salinas projects would appear to have had a number of things going for them. First, the need existed and there were no actively operating alternatives; this fact alone provided a powerful motivating force for them. The low priority government and private economic planning gave Salinas was, for once, an advantage for the local initiatives, which did not have to compete with projects coming from outside. Second, the locally based initiatives and organizations were nonpartisan and have been somewhat successful in building and maintaining nonpartisan coalitions, which not only allowed for broader-based participation, but may protect the initiatives from being casualties of government power struggles. Third, Salinas's traditions of cooperation, community service, and resistance can be used as organizing tools; in fact, they form a major part of the collective cultural and regional identity that the activists have been trying to encourage. They can therefore call upon such traditions while organizing; local examples of successful community struggle that can be cited include the anti-Monsanto campaign and the establishment of La Rosada School. Fourth, the proposed projects for economic development that are based primarily upon the resources that exist in Salinas, instead of on what they lack, seem to make sense. They promote articulated economic development, primarily on the basis of Salinas's natural and human resources. Finally, the local activists are pursuing an integrated approach to community empowerment: there are economic, cultural, social, spiritual, and educational initiatives. This inclusive approach offers something for everyone and is potentially capable of mobilizing large numbers of Salinas residents from diverse backgrounds.

However promising and appropriate the Salinas initiatives may be, there nevertheless are serious obstacles to successfully putting them into practice and turning them into living, working alternatives. The obstacles are environmental, economic, social, and political. Some are manifested internally, that is, within Salinas, and even among the activists themselves. Others are external and include obstacles posed by outside capital, the state, and Puerto Rico's colonial political status, as well as by current global realities. Although some problems may need to be resolved locally and among the activists themselves, other questions require answers that must come at least in part from outside.

Bioregional Obstacles: Incongruity of Ecological and Political Systems

One particular set of obstacles is both ecological and political: the municipal boundaries cut through different ecosystems and divide up drainage basins. This arrangement means that projects taking into account political jurisdictions but not the overlapping ecosystems may turn out to be ecologically inappropriate, or even harmful. Salinas has already suffered from economic projects that do not take this ecological/political incongruity into account; one example is the capital-intensive, heavy industrialization of its eastern neighbor, Guayama. The pollution generated there most severely affects poor coastal residents on both sides of the Salinas-Guayama border, who in general do not have the skills or education to benefit much from the relatively few jobs created — another example of the dominant development strategy's failure to provide enough jobs or protect the environment.

Then again, opposition in Salinas to a proposed coal-burning plant in Guayama may not prove effective in halting the project, regardless of how strong such opposition may be; it can have a real effect only if the leaders of the fight against the plant also come from organized communities within Guayama itself. The importance of public opinion is well understood by Applied Energy Services, Inc., builders of the proposed plant. Mindful of similar proposals in Puerto Rico that were defeated by strong community and environmental campaigns, they have moved quickly to persuade Guayama's political and business leaders that the plant would be good business and environmentally safe; their efforts have included taking some leaders to see one of their currently operating plants in Connecticut. They have apparently not made similar efforts in Salinas. Understanding this dynamic, the Salinas activists have devoted as much space in the newspaper as possible to providing information about the proposal, as well as to publicizing the citizens' groups in Guayama forming to oppose the plant, such as those introduced in chapter 4.[1]

A hint of solutions to the bioregional obstacle can be found in discussions about a proposal to build a chicken-processing plant in Salinas. Although this plant is projected to generate four hundred jobs, the president of *Pollos Picú de Coamo* (Puerto Rico's largest manufacturer of chicken products) claimed that those jobs would be created at the expense of closing a similar plant in the municipio of Aibonito, thus creating jobs in one location at the expense of employment in another. His suggestions for possible solutions to this conundrum — increasing demand through a governmental commitment to promote chicken consumption in public institutions and tightening regulations that currently allow importation of inferior grades of chicken from the United States — also indicated that bioregional obstacles could have political solutions.[2] In general, bioregional obstacles to the Salinas alternatives could conceivably be addressed through growing regional cooperation to work for regionally sustainable initiatives. With sufficient and coordinated public pressure coming from several municipios which share the same ecological region, state agencies might be convinced to support more ecologically thoughtful projects. (I will discuss more fully the role of the "enabling" state in sustainable development in the concluding chapter.)

Economic, Social, and Political Obstacles

By far the most serious obstacles the Salinas alternatives face are economic, social, and political. Although some originate far from Salinas, others are much closer to home.

Internal Obstacles

So-called internal obstacles involve the difficulties of mobilizing and organizing within communities of historically powerless people and of overcoming what some writers have termed a "colonized," or dependent mentality. Coalition building is challenging at best, and often seems impossible to accomplish among people holding diverse and conflicting ideologies. The activists also face the dangers of overwork and "burnout" and must guard against the subtle danger of losing touch with their neighbors' true feelings and perceived realities.

Mobilization and the colonized mentality. Although challenges to the extremely disarticulated Bootstrap model, such as the Salinas initiatives, are certainly hopeful signs, such alternatives in general have great difficulty gaining significant support among the Puerto Rican public, which as a whole continues to look toward the Bootstrap model as the only viable option. The activists sometimes complain that the process of consciousness raising and mobilization seems to be painfully slow, and it is, with good reason. Salinas is typical of Puerto Rico in that its impoverished majority often displays attitudes of dependence and low self-esteem. This mind-set can make it difficult to maintain interest and commitment to projects that do not show immediate results — and the activists are all too aware that the economic initiatives must show tangible results in the near future.

Indeed, contemporary public and private discourse in Puerto Rico and among Puerto Ricans is often characterized by cynicism about the ability of the island and its people to make progress on environmental, social, or economic issues without significant help from the United States. Such low collective self-esteem — where the colonized have internalized the colonizer's view of them as lazy, infantile, and so on — is but one manifestation of a colonized mentality (Memmi 1991, 79–85), which government policies have played no small role in nurturing. This phenomenon is by no means restricted to Puerto Ricans; many respected writers have described the development of internalized self-hatred among people who have long been oppressed, and even its sometimes unwitting encouragement by political leaders (see for example DuBois 1969; Said 1979; Fanon 1965, 1967).

It should therefore come as no surprise that Puerto Ricans must struggle against an internalized colonizer who serves as a constant reminder of Puerto Rican inferiority, helplessness, failure, and utter dependence upon resources and know-how from "Tío (Uncle) Sam." This assessment is shared by Dr. Iris Zavala Martínez, director of San Juan's municipal mental health center and a respected scholar on related topics. Her clinical observations of "a general perception of collective lack of well-being, a massive accumulation of rage, frustration, a lack of productive strategies, feelings of impotence, powerlessness, and desperation" lead her to believe that "something more profound was invaded within our collective self, as if our historical and national psyche had been violated, forced, incubating a certain form of psychosocial trauma" (1993, 9). Key to explaining this phenomenon is a clear understanding of "the role of the still unresolved process of historical colonialism which has besieged the [Puerto Rican] national self throughout this century and that has forged the conditions of life which perpetuate individual and collective ambivalence, marginalization, and dependence" (ibid., 8).

Luís Nieves Falcón has found that, since most Puerto Ricans consider the forces that affect them to be outside their control, "there is a strong tendency to depend on external forces for the solution to problems" (1985b, 53). The dependent mentality encouraged by years of colonialism and disarticulated economic strategies reinforces the tendency to expect that only the government is capable of creating jobs, meeting local needs, and protecting the environment. When, as so often happens, the authorities seem incapable or unwilling to perform these functions, then people have long been accustomed to look to the "higher authority"—namely, Washington—for solutions, rather than taking upon themselves the responsibility for change. Other writers also point out that, rather than simply blame Puerto Rican societal problems on "cultural factors" (as has been done in the past), it makes sense to consider the effects of Puerto Rico's colonial relationship with the United States, such as the dislocations brought about by a century of capitalist- and colonialist-mandated socioeconomic transformation (Vázquez 1994).

The island's excessive reliance upon outside resources for economic development, as well as the heavy dependence upon the local and federal governments to subsidize Operation Bootstrap's failures, has exacerbated the sense of powerlessness felt by many Puerto Ricans, who have long been taught that their country has no resources, thus leaving it with no alternatives. Salinas is typical of Puerto Rico in that a high percentage of the impoverished majority experience chronic unemployment or underemployment and suffer from the social and economic problems exacerbated by circular migration. If we add to this situation the inadequate educational levels and health care, then we can predict the prevalence of such attitudes as dependence, powerlessness, and low self esteem. This mixture can erode the spirit of cooperation and impede efforts to develop less dependent alternatives; it also helps explain the difficulty that the Salinas activists, among others, are encountering in building and maintaining community support for projects that do not show immediate results. In such an environment what is most striking about "grassroots" initiatives is not that they do not enjoy more support, but that they have any support at all.

Coalition building. Broad-based coalitions are indispensable in putting together popular community initiatives — and are extremely difficult to maintain. One constantly faces the need to downplay differences, to seek common ground, and to avoid being locked into one side of any political power struggle. The Salinas activists have made remarkable strides in this regard by constantly stressing the practical problems that need to be addressed, and by trying to stress the ideals that all involved have in common, rather than by getting bogged down in their differences. For example, the activists have been able to connect with others on the basis of Christian social activism. They have learned that religious guidelines such as those of Vatican II, which emphasize the dignity of human beings and the need for empowerment and social justice, complement many of the writings of the nationalist Albizu Campos or the socialist Marx. Without completely dropping more "radical" work they have learned to emphasize the religious teachings, since many of their collaborators can identify more strongly with the latter and thus feel more comfortable about their participation. The activists have managed to do this without giving up their own ideals and have found greater acceptance than is generally the case in Puerto Rico for activists with "radical" pasts. Mindful of the Left's history of marginalization and fragmentation (some of which, though not all, can be attributed to what in retrospect seem like petty issues), the activists are determined not to let what may not be essential stand in the way of what is — the community alternatives.

The activists are not always successful, however. The leftist backgrounds of some of the core activists may not pose a stumbling block while people are getting along; but should problems arise, the personal and political attacks suddenly materialize and sometimes cast a shadow on the projects themselves. Puerto Rican–style "red baiting" is sometimes directed against collaborators who are clearly not leftists. One day, for example, a neighbor was harassing a PPD party member who has worked hard for the community alternatives. When he accused her publicly of being an independentista, her response was just as public: "if being independentista means working for the good of your community, then I'm an independentista!" Her courage was quite notable because, since independentistas have in the past lost their jobs, their health, and occasionally their lives, it would not be surprising if the fear of that label might prevent some people from actively supporting the Salinas initiatives.

The core activists have tried hard to create a climate in which people can air out their differences without resorting to resentment, back stabbing, or innuendo. But as happens everywhere, some disagreements cannot be worked out, and a parting of ways among former coalition partners is not always amicable. In one instance, the controversy among La Playa fishermen over the techniques, leadership, and general direction of their fishing business eventually led to the school's fishing arts course and Pescadería del Sur, Inc., P.T.'s being relocated to Las Mareas. This controversy caused some hard feelings that have had personal repercussions — something to be expected, for activists, supporters, and opponents are often neighbors and cannot easily avoid one another.

In the face of problems recruiting enough new activists who are willing and able to take on more responsibility, the core activists and a few others find themselves bearing the brunt of the work needed to keep the various initiatives going. For the most part they are fortunate in having supportive families and friends who, if not active themselves, are at least sympathetic to the demands that the work makes on their loved ones. But the work sometimes takes its toll. Too much of the most frustrating tasks, such as grant-proposal writing and dealing with the government bureaucracy for leases, permits, and other necessities, falls on too small a group of activists. The activists have also experienced many disappointments, in particular from outsiders who expressed interest, even made commitments, but who later did not come through. This disappointment is at least partly to blame for the occasional signs of burnout in individual activists — such as doubts about whether current efforts are worthwhile, or feelings of anger or distrust toward others who do not seem to be working equally hard in behalf of the cause.

The insider/outsider dilemma. The core activists are from Salinas and against all odds returned to give something back to their community. They see themselves as insiders, as integral community representatives, who live the daily reality of Salinas and understand their neighbors' needs, problems, and desires. But have their very experiences of leaving, getting an education, becoming politically active and intellectually sophisticated ironically also made them different from their neighbors? Such differences could also be represented in subtle ways that may not manifest themselves in everyday life but exist nevertheless. For example, their expanded education and consciousness means they could have options their neighbors do not have, in terms of employment and choice of lifestyle. It is true that they have freely chosen to forego the economic and cultural advantages of living and working in a place such as San Juan. The very fact that they had a choice could also possibly separate them from their neighbors, both in perceptions of common current experiences and the ways in which they work and relate to their communities. The activists might well ask themselves from time to time if such a dynamic could sometimes be reflected in misunderstandings of how they perceive their neighbors' needs and opinions, in what the neighbors are willing to express, or even whether their neighbors can identify with them enough to be inspired to join in the work. One supportive resident who is involved in some programs but not in the core group cited the shock expressed by some of the activists about the landslide victory of the PNP in 1992 as evidence that they did not really understand the mind-set currently prevalent among the younger public housing residents: "Hey, anyone who really hung out could have predicted what was going to happen in the elections, because they would have realized how little interest there is in progressive politics."

Sometimes the very closeness of the core activists to one another and their respective abilities can make other participants feel like outsiders and can exacerbate their feelings of inadequacy to the tasks required. One local resident, who had been involved for the first few years but then dropped out, expressed frustration over the "cliquishness" of the core group: "They have all the real power, and don't really take anything I say very seriously." Of course, it is impossible to judge such a statement without knowing all the factors that lie behind it, and there are always many sides to every situation. Yet one can easily understand how such feelings might arise, particularly if those who are attempting to get involved in an initiative that goes against most of what they have been taught are trying to break into a closely knit group of college-educated and articulate leaders who all have organizing and teaching experience. Rather than serving as role models, the leaders could be unwittingly reinforcing the feelings of inadequacy with which the new participants may be struggling, even if the "clique" of leaders consists of people who grew up next door.

According to Nelson Santos, the Salinas activists were involved in a process of reflection and self-criticism over tendencies to authoritarianism within the group. Recognizing that society has taught most people to leave decision making to the experts, and that it always seems simpler for a few people to make decisions, the activists have been consciously trying to break with that model in all of the projects, thus promoting true democracy and broader participation. One question they often ask is, "What impedes citizens from taking responsibility and decisions?" Experience has taught them that the answer is a perceived lack of knowledge. The commitment and challenge of all the projects have been to help develop the knowledge and consciousness of the people on the basis of what they already know. The activists must take great care to ensure that the mobilization work does not of itself impede the process of self-empowerment, which is essential if they are to greatly increase the numbers of people committed to the local initiatives. Although the core activists are each extremely capable and dedicated leaders, they know full well that they can not by themselves bring the various projects to the self-sustaining stage. They must take care not to be consumed by the day-to-day necessities — a tall order indeed, when a hundred crises seem to spring up at once, and only two or three people are available to deal with them as best they can! One of their top priorities must be the investment of time and energy to ensure that there will be others to take their places, in every facet of all of the projects.

External: The Question of Power

Nevertheless, even with successful efforts at self-criticism, consciousness raising, mobilization, and coalition building, there are forces from outside of Salinas that can make or break the community initiatives. These forces include the pitfalls of working with private agencies and the government, competition with powerful outside interests for Salinas's resources, and the need to build a strong islandwide popular movement that is capable of demanding change. Over this entire process looms Puerto Rico's political status, the current hemispheric move toward neocolonial economic integration, and world trends in general, none of whose future conditions and repercussions the Salinas activists can foresee, much less control. These latter extra-insular contexts are presently the subject of much speculative analysis; here, it is worthwhile to deal with the external conditions specific to Puerto Rico that pose obstacles to successful implementation of the Salinas initiatives.

Securing resources to move economic proposals. The core activists feel that their most serious problem is the difficulty of obtaining funding, either to start up projects or to maintain current commitments. For example, economic problems connected with the newspaper actually shut down that vital organ for months and in the future could permanently silence it. Because of the problems experienced in 1994 — first, with the need to replace the computer; then, with lost and reluctant advertisers; and finally, with the inability to pay off the debt owed to the printers — the activists trembled to think that they might have to face organizing against the proposed coal-burning power plant without the informative power of one of their most effective tools.

Again, the failure of government agencies to pay promised stipends on time to teachers and students of La Rosada School (which happened continuously during the school's first year of existence) erodes confidence and may lead to dropouts of both teachers and students. The failure to obtain startup capital for equipment, wages, and other necessities can put economic ventures on indefinite hold. If employment opportunities open up elsewhere — however temporary or unsatisfactory they may be — the school and other programs may be abandoned for what in the short term appears to be a "sure thing." This in fact happened during the school's first year. An announcement was made for the imminent opening of a new manufacturing plant in Aguirre in early 1992. Several La Rosada students applied for jobs and were hired, at which point they left the school program; however, the new plant never actually went into operation, and the new employees were soon laid off. It is for this reason that the core activists must spend an inordinate amount of time searching for and writing grant proposals and dealing with organizational bureaucracies outside of Salinas. Were such initial resources easier to obtain the activists would probably already have more tangible results to offer the community, which certainly would help greatly in local mobilization.

Among the new and planned PTs the sewing, cooking and woodworking groups were having problems finding a permanent site for their enterprises. In addition, as of the end of 1994 the land promised to the school for agriculture and aquaculture was still mired in government bureaucracy and disinterest. In frustration, the coordinators for four of the PTs — Pescadería del Sur, ImpreSur, Procesadora del Sur, and Muestra del Bosque — wrote an open letter to the Puerto Rican government that was published in the Christmas 1994 edition of the community newspaper:

To Whom It May Concern:

. . . We are entrepreneurs from marginalized communities with scarce economic resources, who work with dedication and enthusiasm to escape the unemployment and government dependence which afflict Salinas. Nevertheless, we lack the necessary equipment for greater, long term production.

. . . Strangers come to our municipio with (all kinds of strange) projects, such as (raising) ostriches . . . and the government gives them a half million dollars . . . and municipal endorsements. The Land Authority grants them land, permits from ARPE appear, and even lightposts are installed by the Electric Energy Authority. What do these strangers have, that they should be treated better than our own people? . . . (By contrast) our coordinating team has done everything possible to provide financing for the enterprises. We have visited the mayor, our representatives and senators, and all agencies which in one form or another could help, but they seem to have forgotten us. The Governor has said

[that] community projects for economic development will be promoted, and that the government will facilitate aid. We don't know which communities are being helped, because very little has arrived here. The government wants to create jobs, but doesn't support their creation. They want to be facilitators, but instead some agencies are obstacles.

... What will become of us, when we seek a better life and find only closed doors?

In part because of the inadequate aid forthcoming from programs based in San Juan, the activists have begun looking outside Puerto Rico for funding possibilities. Here, not surprisingly, political status complicates their efforts. The Salinas initiatives do not qualify for internationally based aid because Puerto Rico is not an independent state, but a territory belonging to the United States. At least they should be eligible for most grants offered by federal programs and United States–based nonprofit organizations. Of course, the programs that target projects in independent "Third World" countries automatically rule out Puerto Rico. Moreover, a catch-22 often applies to Puerto Rico when decision makers in nongovernmental programs meant specifically for the United States consider it, since they tend to think of Puerto Rico as foreign. This is partly because the island is not a U.S. state and is frequently considered last for federal programs as a matter of course. Proponents of statehood believe that the current political status of "ni piña ni coco" (neither pineapple nor coconut, neither one nor the other) is the primary obstacle; they argue that Puerto Rico would receive much more consideration for federal aid if it were to become a state. In view of deeply ingrained biases in United States society and government, however, the perception of "foreignness" would in all probability still count against a mostly nonwhite, Spanish-speaking, historically and culturally Latin American and Caribbean island state. In any event, the activists are finding that even a program that might not automatically reject projects in Puerto Rico will often rank them very low on its list of priorities.

Working with government and private agencies. Ironically, in spite of all the disappointments they have experienced working with government and private agencies, the Salinas activists are sometimes thought of as being too successful. Some community activists in other parts of the island have privately expressed resentment of them, in particular of their success (real or perceived) in working closely with some government agencies on projects such as the school. The complaint that "they've sold out" could also reflect some jealousy, as well as a bit of ignorance about the extent of the cooperation. The risks involved in depending upon the government, however, no matter how much or how little, should be acknowledged.

Some local political leaders, while publicly supporting the school's educational efforts and the work of the activists, privately express doubts about the viability of the economic projects. They continue to affirm their belief in the Puerto Rico development model and accordingly insist that Salinas must search for massive foreign investment in industrialization and large-scale tourism. Although one can often find individuals within the state bureaucracy who understand what is happening in Salinas, and who will use their power to provide some of the needed resources, they might also become casualties of the next election if the opposing party takes over. For this reason the Salinas activists have tried never to depend on any one external funding source for more that 50 percent of any project, a wise strategy that is sometimes difficult to achieve in practice.

Moreover, politicians may sometimes respond to local needs but are also beholden to the demands of their party leaders and of the interests they represent; in the end they will do what they believe is necessary for reelection. Local political leaders may support and help secure resources for a community initiative for poor people, even against the pet projects of the San Juan government — especially if they come from rival parties; they may present themselves as anti–San Juan and pro-Salinas, which is nearly always sure to attract some votes. However, should the state government change hands, the same pro-Salinas politicians may turn around and support the same pet project that they earlier opposed, because now it is backed by the party leadership.

In no way was this shifting better illustrated than by the energetic opposition by the mayor and municipal assembly to the proposed regional toxic waste facility in 1990–91, followed by their support for a similar proposal in 1994. Earlier we recounted the successful campaign that was mounted in 1990–91 to defeat proposals for a regional toxic waste landfill in Salinas. At that time the PPD was in power in San Juan; meanwhile, the mayor of Salinas belonged to the PNP, and the municipal assembly was mixed. A united front was achieved in Salinas against the proposal, in part because of the activists' years of work, including their efforts to educate the citizenry through the newspaper and other means. For this and other reasons local politicians perceived the project to be politically unpopular; however, part of the local government's support of the activists was no doubt explained by the mayor's being more likely to oppose projects that were favored by the rival party government in San Juan.[3] The elections of 1992 resulted in the PNP's takeover of the state, Salinas's municipal assembly, and retention of the mayor's office.

Then, in 1994 the mayor and eleven of fourteen assembly members enthusiastically approved a state-supported proposal by waste management giant Browning Ferris Industry (BFI), not only to operate the Salinas municipal landfill, but also to build a regional landfill in Salinas to accept the waste of at least nine other municipios (including San Juan), and which theoretically could accept wastes from anywhere in the island. Not only were details of the proposal — such as timing, location, and size of the new facility — not offered for public scrutiny, but they were not even fully outlined to the assembly at the time of the vote. Among BFI's requirements was the municipio's being responsible for obtaining enough acreage to handle an average of two thousand tons of solid wastes per day for at least twenty years; BFI would pay one dollar for every ton in excess of five hundred tons per day that the landfill received. In addition, BFI would pay the municipio a bonus; the size of the bonus would depend on the speed with which permits were obtained and the regional landfill opened. For example, Salinas would receive one million dollars if everything was ready before December 31, 1995; six hundred thousand dollars if everything was ready, between January 1, 1996, and June 30, 1997; three hundred thousand dollars, between July 1, 1997 and June 30, 1998; and no bonus after that date. No environmental impact statement was offered, nor was the number of jobs estimated to be created or lost ever mentioned.[4] Such a dramatic about-face in local environmental and development policy within four years (and in some cases by the same officials) can only be explained politically. The strong talk of community solidarity and environmental concerns in 1990 were absent or quite altered by 1994; meanwhile, the activists, whose input had been welcomed the first time, were left out of the loop four years later.

Competing outside interests. As I noted earlier, marginalization can sometimes create opportunities. If a place such as Salinas has lost political and economic power over time, and if its needs and assets are generally ignored by the state and outside capital, then community initiatives may be able to gain both internal and external support, simply because of a lack of alternatives. This dynamic actually worked in favor of the current initiatives during the first few years. Changes on the political horizon can radically alter the scene, however. These shifts would be even more important if circumstances aggravating Salinas's marginality were to change, such as the lack of planning coordination between San Juan and Salinas's City Hall because of partisan power struggles. For example, the 1992 PNP candidates for the offices of both governor of Puerto Rico and mayor of Salinas publicly favored attracting foreign investment to develop large-scale tourist complexes, particularly in coastal areas considered to be underdeveloped. During those elections the PNP swept into power in San Juan and throughout the island, including in Salinas: the incumbent PNP mayor was reelected and the majority of seats in the municipal assembly were filled by PNP candidates. During the first years of the current round of Salinas activism political power had been held primarily by the PPD, and many government officials with whom the activists had dealt lost their positions after 1992. In view of Salinas's coastal resources it is clear that the municipio could easily qualify for consideration for large-scale development; in the event of the proposal of such a plan, and in the absence of serious party rivalry, only organized popular pressure could keep locally based, smaller-scale tourist projects from being swept away.

One tourist-related project is the *Tren del Sur* (Southern Train). This was the train and railroad system Central Aguirre owned and operated between Ponce and Arroyo, primarily for transporting sugarcane but also for passenger service during part of its nearly century-long history. The railroad has been completely out of service for less than ten years, and the government still owns the equipment and lines (though some equipment has been illegally sold, as reported by the local newspaper on a number of occasions). Since the late 1980s there have been several proposals, both by the Salinas activists and by several government agencies, to stimulate tourism by rehabilitating the line, which runs mostly along the scenic south coast and through or near areas of tourist interest. Although the municipal government strongly favors the proposal, support in San Juan is more mixed. The activists must struggle to have their voices included in the ongoing planning for the venture, sometimes without much success. They missed one important meeting in August in San Juan because of last-minute transportation problems. Although they were able to schedule another meeting, the first meeting went on as planned without them; it was also clear that the local and state leaders were not overly concerned with missing their input. Among the activists' strongest suggestions is that a local worker-owned enterprise operate the train; the skills already exist within Salinas, for the workers on the old line were largely local. The activists fear that the whole project could simply be sold to an outside entrepreneur with little understanding or concern for the needs of the community. Although the worst case scenario may never occur, history has taught the activists that they must be extremely vigilant when it comes to local development plans that may be controlled by outside interests.

Political power: A popular movement? Finally, the local initiatives have not yet grown into regional or national popular movements, although such developments as the *encuentros* and the community organizations' publicity-and-lobbying day in San Juan represented hopeful moves in that direction. Some observers, both inside and outside of Salinas, consider this growth to be vital to pressure the government to support community initiatives instead of hindering them. Broadly based movements can also help obtain resources necessary to initiate alternative projects and convince people of the possibility of their success. Moreover, not only might strong and organized popular pressure help keep locally based, smaller-scale projects from being swept away in the face of big money and outside interests, but without it such local projects just may not be possible. Although it may not be absolutely necessary to connect the Salinas initiatives to a broader social movement, there is no doubt that such a connection would help immeasurably in ensuring that the projects being developed in Salinas would be given a chance to succeed. For example, some activists acknowledge that they may not be able to secure the resources necessary for the PTS to become fully operational until their initiatives are regionalized.

The factors necessary for (though perhaps not sufficient to) the success of the Salinas alternative have become clearer. Within Salinas itself, reeducation efforts must be expanded on all present themes: cultural, economic, social, and environmental. La Rosada's program of "people's liberation through education" must go beyond school walls to include families (as is planned with the project EMPARÉJATE), and then throughout the communities. This expansion most likely requires additional programs designed to reach sectors of the population not presently served. Programs targeting young mothers such as El Coquí's MAS and Brisas' "Madres e Hijos" are good examples, and should be joined by others. Projects should also be initiated that deal with such issues as health and recycling.

There is a great need to collect, recover, and make use of the vast storehouse of local knowledge on a broad range of subjects before it is lost. This need calls for a project involving elderly *salinenses*. One possibility could be to assign young people to conduct oral histories and write and disseminate the recovered knowledge, perhaps organized according to topic in a local information bank for future reference. This project in turn requires great expansion of the communicative and public relations capability of the various projects. More people should learn skills in all phases of newspaper work and should be encouraged to start new publications as well. Others should also be trained as liaisons with government and private entities, including grant proposal writing.

Some factors involve cooperation with groups outside Salinas's borders. First of all, proposals for projects that pollute must be stopped, delayed, or otherwise modified, so that local natural resources and health do not further deteriorate. As for alternatives, the locally based initiatives should be coordinated with similar plans in neighboring municipios, for the benefit of all. In particular, the considerable resources of Central Aguirre must somehow be harnessed to an overall development strategy that welcomes local initiatives; those resources should not simply be sold to the highest and quickest bidder.

Many of the factors necessary to the success of Salinas alternatives are quite clearly external in nature. Startup resources for projects, including facilities, equipment, startup wages, marketing and accounting expertise, must be obtained, especially for the worker-owned enterprises. Ongoing, coordinated efforts with other islandwide groups are crucial, particularly in the southeastern region. Such work must be used to convince the government to enforce laws that favor local, worker-owned businesses, instead of granting all incentives to Bootstrap-style initiatives, which emphasize outside interests to the neglect of local needs. Islandwide organizing should also pressure the state to support initiatives aimed at helping poor people to help themselves; the politically fashionable theme of reducing welfare dependency should be incorporated into such campaigns. Local activists also need access to outside information on a broad range of topics that could be relevant and useful to their local work. For example, they would benefit from regular sources of information and resource sharing with community activists and others, not only on the island but throughout the world. If allowed access to the necessary resources the Salinas initiatives stand a good chance of providing a successful model of locally focused, ecologically and socially sustainable development. These resources include not only materials such as funding, equipment, and work sites; the resources of knowledge and power are also crucial to their success.

The Salinas initiatives represent an attempt at sustainable development at the local level. Using the lessons of the experience of the Salinas activists, I will offer in the concluding chapter a working definition of sustainable development that sees the achievement of broadly based, participatory local control as a foundation for sustainability, environmental protection, and real development alternatives on a global scale. However necessary this foundation may be, it clearly is not sufficient to the task at hand, for we must also address the problem of how to obtain power. I refer to the power to control and use resources, to decide policy — in short, political power — which is absolutely necessary for putting into practice community-directed local strategies for sustainable development. Believing that there are appropriate and necessary roles for every sector — local activists, nongovernmental organizations, private businesses, committed academics, the state — in making sustainable development possible, I conclude with some suggestions about what we all can do.

7 Lessons of the Salinas Experience

Salinas is a good example of what is wrong with prevailing notions of development. Its twentieth-century development experience chronicles increased exploitation of existing resources, while at the same time those resources became progressively less relevant to many salinenses' lives. Operation Bootstrap eliminated jobs without creating enough new ones to replace them. Moreover, the new jobs often required skills that did not exist locally; yet there were no provisions to help acquire those skills and thus ensure a smooth transition from the old to the new. Among other things this change forced many residents into permanent dependence upon government assistance, while it also pushed large numbers to leave in search of work. Chronic dependence and circular migration feed feelings of powerlessness and exacerbate the social tensions that threaten to unravel the fabric of many communities trapped in the cycle of modern poverty. As if these social problems were not bad enough, the "growth and modernization" strategy has indiscriminately burned up precious natural resources and treated the environment as an unlimited waste dump, which in turn threatens the health of the very people who were supposed to benefit from "development."

No doubt some of the problems of "top-down" development strategies may be blamed on inefficient or uninformed planning; nonetheless, we should also acknowledge who generally benefits most from development programs. We see that the pattern of old Salinas — where most of the resources benefited the elite few, whereas the powerless majority subsisted on the leftovers — has not really changed with "development," but rather has intensified. Profits may have increased, but very little has been recycled back locally. Then, too, the primary beneficiaries are not for the most part themselves local and therefore need not suffer the effects of a seriously degraded environment. To those who still insist that large-scale, externally controlled strategies can reduce poverty and spread the benefits of development without significant environmental damage, the Salinas experience replies that there must be a better way.

Salinas's current activism is taking place against the backdrop of the area's twentieth-century experience of exploitation of local resources, as well as of the local people's response to it. The failure of the prevailing development strategy to provide jobs and income has marginalized Salinas both economically and socially, but it has also inspired a local search for alternatives. With a firm commitment to alliance building and inclusionary mobilization in the name of "Salinas first," the local activists are working on various economic, educational, and cultural initiatives that aim to empower the majority of salinenses to direct their own development. In other words, they are promoting what I would call the "sustainable development" of Salinas.

The current push for sustainable development in many areas of the world indicates a growing recognition of the need for an alternative to our present destructive course. The vagueness of the concept of "sustainable development," however, while allowing practically everyone to claim to support its practice, also raises questions about its usefulness. Indeed, a number of respected scholars have called for discarding the concept altogether, contending that its problems seem insurmountable. For example, Norgaard (1994) believes that sustainable development is not practical for a number of reasons, among them that it entails practicing with a structure that is made to favor the prevailing paradigm, not its alternative. In addition, to accommodate sustainable development too much information that entails much closer cooperation among many different sources of knowledge, such as the natural and social sciences—an enormously difficult proposition—is needed. Finally, use of sustainable development by powerful institutions such as the World Bank tends to further dilute the concept, which would almost surely end any chance of its becoming a real alternative (Norgaard 1994). Lakshmann Yapa's criticism goes further, arguing that terms such as "development," "sustainable development," and even "community empowerment" have already been hopelessly co-opted, and should be discarded by those who advocate real solutions to the problem of poverty.[1]

I tend to agree that, unfortunately, the concept can easily be seen as having often been reduced to a cliché that everyone can claim to support without having to agree on its implications. Why, then, write yet another book dealing with sustainable development? As Michael Burawoy argues, "our intent is not to reject bad theories but to improve good theories. We don't believe there is a final truth which once arrived at gives incontrovertible insight. Nor do we start with a *tabula rasa,* as if social science begins with us" (1991, 7). Although I do not wish to underestimate the difficulties involved in the effort I still think it worthwhile, indeed of vital importance, to try to improve a concept that at least represents an attempt to alter our present destructive course. Moreover, although I recognize the truth of Yapa's observations, I fear that avoiding such terms because of the possibility of co-optation may ultimately leave us with no vocabulary! By the (consciously redefining) use of such terms in this book I have chosen instead to try to reclaim them.

To begin with, it seems obvious that to have any practical value "sustainable development" should first be more clearly defined, beginning with the two concepts that it combines: development and sustainability.

Development: Redefine or Discard

In recent years the quickly deteriorating global economic, ecological, and social conditions have lent a sense of urgency to the need to redefine development. There is increasing recognition that "the present crisis will not be solved by pursuing the same old policies which consist of producing more of the same. The time has come for drastic reappraisals, for a critical evaluation of projects for civilization, for . . . development aimed at the satisfaction of society's real needs and pursued in harmony with nature, in a real symbiosis between the human race and the earth" (I. Sachs 1987, 6). In a well-regarded critique S. M. Lélé defined development as "a directed process of economic growth and/or change in order to satisfy basic human needs" (1991, 608, 610). This definition has three components: first, development is deliberately planned. Second, the changes produced by such planning may or may not include economic growth. Third, planned economic change should result in an increased ability to provide for people's basic needs. Leaving aside for the moment the necessity for planning development — and particularly the question of who plans — let us examine more closely the concepts of "growth" and "basic needs."

Some writers trying to redefine development have argued that the emphasis on growth, and the use of GNP to measure it, stemmed from a misunderstanding of the nature of growth. For example, Paul Ekins (1992) noted a failure to distinguish among three types of growth: first, material growth, or an increase in an economy's use of matter and energy; second, production growth, or an increase in GNP and nonmonetary production, leading to an increase in consumption; and third, environmental growth, or an increase in available material resources or services from the natural environment. Any or all of these types of growth — not only production growth — may contribute to (or take away from) economic growth, defined by Ekins as an increase in welfare or utility. As he points out, "it is quite possible for the negative feedbacks from production growth (more wastes, environmental destruction, erosion of community) to produce negative utility effects that outweigh . . . (consumption) and so for . . . (production) growth to result in a decrease in welfare" (ibid., 155). This is certainly what has happened in Salinas, despite the increased profitability of some of its economic sectors. Clearly, there must be other welfare indicators besides GNP — where nothing counts except market-oriented production.

Indeed, in development circles the older emphasis upon growth of per capita income has largely been replaced by the call for meeting "basic needs" for all, usually defined as material needs such as adequate and safe food, water, clothing, shelter, health care and education. Although the method of measuring needs or of determining their acceptable levels may be open to debate, there seems to be general agreement that successful development requires progressively more successful meeting of such needs. Many of these new attempts at redefining development, however, still tend to echo the cultural racism inherent in the traditional view, in that they assume the necessity of "expert" intervention to pull forward those who lag behind. The new strategies emphasizing "no growth," basic needs, rural and women's development, even environmental sustainability, may still run the risk of falling into the same trap of looking at "other worlds in terms of what they lack and obstruct[ing] the wealth of indigenous alternatives which could inspire" (W. Sachs 1992, 160).

Poverty, Basic Needs, and
the Purpose of Economic Activity

If the determination of welfare and the means of increasing it are, as Ekins
suggests, culturally (and perhaps even environmentally) specific, is there
any use for a universal definition of development? If the term "development" also denotes a process of unfolding, or realization, over time (Lutz
1992), and if we are willing to grant that the ultimate good for any person
would be to fully realize her or his humanity, then should not any universal definition of development go beyond purely economic concerns and
incorporate both social and philosophical dimensions? Since misunderstanding of such concepts as "poverty," "basic needs," and the "purpose
of economic activity" may pose obstacles to a workable redefinition of
development, let us look at each in turn.

In defining "poverty," pioneering development thinkers looked upon
the high consumptive capacity of the United States population as proof of
that country's wealth and development. Consequently, they considered
the poverty of many vastly different societies to be demonstrated by their
comparatively low per capita incomes: "In this way, poverty was used to
define whole peoples, not according to what they are and want to be, but
according to what they lack and what they are expected to become. Economic disdain had taken the place of colonial contempt"(W. Sachs 1992,
162).

Wolfgang Sachs argues that, among other problems, this view of poverty fails to distinguish among at least three distinct "poor" conditions:
frugality, destitution, and scarcity. Frugality is a feature of nonaccumu-
lative, noncommodified cultures, where daily necessities are obtained
mostly through subsistence production, and only partially through the
market. Though owning few possessions, most people have access to resources such as land, water, and wood; moreover, kinship and community
duties provide services that elsewhere must be paid for with cash (either
privately or by the state). Individual hoarding of surpluses is punished by
social ostracism; extra bounty is supposed to be spent on goods, services,
or even luxuries (such as a feast) for the community. Although most people are monetarily "poor," hardly anyone goes hungry.

Destitution, on the one hand, grows whenever the foundations of frugality (access to resources, ability to meet needs, community and kinship obligations, etc.) are destroyed. Sachs points out that the first state policies on poverty, in sixteenth-century Europe, were a response to the sudden appearance of homeless beggars provoked by land enclosures. Another example of sudden destitution took place when the conversion of Puerto Rico's best lands to sugarcane after the U.S. takeover rapidly produced tens of thousands of landless rural workers. Scarcity, on the other hand, derives from modernized poverty. It particularly affects urban workers and consumers dependent upon the money economy whose buying power is insufficient to meet their needs. At the same time that their capacity to meet their needs is diminished, their desires have risen through glimpses of the conspicuously consumptive lifestyles of the affluent. This commodity-based poverty, typical of most of Salinas's population today, is what has shaped the mainstream development discourse. Whereas developmentalists have viewed poverty as the problem and proposed growth as the solution, Sachs charges that "the culture of growth can only be erected on the ruins of frugality; and so destitution and commodity dependence are its price" (1992, 165). He concludes that increasing self-sufficiency is key to reducing poverty, with "growth" being handled very cautiously.

Regarding basic needs, Anisur Rahman (1992) distinguishes between two opposing views that influence the perception of them. The consumerist view of basic needs emphasizes the expansion of consumption. Even the recent shift in developmentalist goals from increasing per capita income to more successful provision of basic needs may not affect the underlying consumerist orientation because it does not ask who in the society has the capacity to take initiatives to produce needed goods and services. Likewise, the consumerist view of poverty "focuse[s] on the 'poor' not being able to consume the things desired (or biologically needed) rather than not having the opportunity of producing (or commanding) them through their creative acts" (ibid., 172). Only government aid separates most salinenses from absolute destitution, and the creation of a class permanently dependent upon welfare should not be considered a successful outcome of any development program.

By contrast, the creativist view of development focuses on the human need "to fulfill our creative potential in ever newer ways" (ibid., 174), to be able to take an active and determining part in satisfying all of our needs, whether material or not, both individually and collectively. Poverty is seen as a "lack of entitlement to develop as a creative being," rather than as simply a lack of purchasing power. Although a person may simply be given what she or he needs (as determined by the giver), this act is likely to undermine the receiver's sense of dignity and self-worth — besides not truly contributing to a lessening of poverty. By contrast, the initiatives being developed in Salinas aim to help their participants "feel themselves to be the masters of their acts," in the words of ARTESUR's director. The old saying "give a man a fish and he'll eat today, but teach him to fish and he'll eat for life" illustrates the empowering principle behind the creativist view. Satisfaction of material needs is certainly of utmost importance, and it makes no short-term sense to simply eliminate assistance programs that provide a safety net to the most needy. Nonetheless, the sense of individual and collective empowerment to satisfy needs and desires — the increased capacity for making choices and assuming responsibility — is arguably what makes life worth living for most people, irrespective of cultural differences. Strategies that offer this long-term hope — particularly if they are of local origin — can and should be supported.

Mainstream economists may object that Salinas-type projects are "uneconomic" — that is, that they are not the most efficient way to generate profit. According to "humanistic economics" (a venerable if relatively little-known economic philosophy that opposed the classical economics of thinkers such as Ricardo and Mills), however, the goal of political economy is not "an unlimited growth of wealth" (Sismondi, quoted in Sherbourne 1972, 98), but rather "striving for the welfare of all people united in society" (ibid. 1991, 21). In this tradition development would imply both material progress and ethical progress and would see increasing wealth only as a means of helping to affirm human dignity for all. Mark Lutz (1992) explains that within humanistic economics the material aspect of a universal definition of development would seek the satisfaction of basic material human needs as defined earlier (the needs being objective and universal, whereas the means of satisfying them are cultural). Development should also attempt to meet the basic psychological need for security against the threat of material deprivation. Finally, the needs of future generations must also be taken into account. Meanwhile, the ethical component of a universal definition of development calls for a cross-cultural ethics grounded on the assumption that every human being has a unique and intrinsic worth and can therefore claim respect for her or his dignity. For Lutz "meaningful progress or development implies not only the progressive meeting of the basic material requirements of all, but also conditions and institutions consistent with respect for basic human rights" (ibid., 167). Salinas's historical development experience indicates that it may be time to change our ideas about what is or is not "uneconomic."

Toward a Workable Redefinition of Development

Is growth, then, desirable for development? It can be, but only if it results in an increase in welfare, taking into account both positives and negatives from production, material, and environmental growth. What about modernization? It is past the time that we should dispense with the old assumptions informed by racism — both biological and cultural — and colonialism. Development planning must emphasize the wealth of people's knowledge and experience. Is this an argument against change of any kind? It is certainly not; different kinds of change can often be positive, as long as such change leads to increasing people's capacity to create their own solutions to problems, to meet their own needs and aspirations. Whose needs must be met? Everyone's, of course, but the success of such a strategy should be measured by the increasing ability of those with the least power in any society to meet their needs — focusing at first on basic material needs, but recognizing the importance of satisfying nonmaterial needs as well. Who decides? The people in question should become progressively more empowered to define their own needs and to identify and utilize the resources they need to satisfy them, without destroying the environment or robbing others — both living and future generations — of the same capacity.

   In sum, an understanding of "development" that is measured by the ability of the least powerful people in any society to individually and collectively meet their own needs — material, intellectual, social, spiritual — through their own creative acts, is crucial to building an effective concept of sustainable development. By the same token, in a sustainably "developing" society this ongoing process of increasing empowerment should result in the ever greater realization of human potential, as well as the continual reaffirmation of basic human dignity and of the worth of all. It should be obvious that under this definition there are no truly "developed" societies at present, and that we all have a long way to go to achieve development, the richer countries no less than the poorer ones.

Defining Social Sustainability

If we add our understanding of development along the lines discussed earlier to the necessity of maintaining ecological diversity to ensure the survival of life on the planet, it becomes clear that maintaining — even increasing — human diversity is equally necessary to ensuring our species' survival on this planet. Although the literature does include some recognition that human difference is positive, and that social diversity can provide a basis for mutual respect (see, for example, Norgaard 1992), this recognition should not be misunderstood as merely a question of "political correctness." More important, we simply cannot afford the social destruction that modernization inflicts upon societies, because the overvaluation of some cultures and the denigration of others represents a critical loss of knowledge and wisdom, and reduces our ability to adapt to changes that we cannot foresee. It is time to add humans and the communities they form to Aldo Leopold's view of the environment as "the fountain of energy flowing through a circuit of soils, water, plants, animals" (1978, 254). Leopold's eloquent statement that "obligations have no meaning without reference to conscience, and the problem we face is the extension of social conscience from people to land" (ibid., 246) needs to be turned around as well, because the problems we face today also require extending ecological conscience from land to people.

As for the how-tos of maintaining human diversity — a topic that certainly deserves more attention — I believe that some guideposts are already available to us. For example, diversity is facilitated when policies lead to an increase in individual and collective control over people's own lives and contributes to the realization of their potential, dignity, and self-worth. This increase and realization will make it easier for people to assume greater responsibility for their actions, which can only benefit the well-being of the surrounding environment. Sustainable use of "natural" and human resources should enhance the diversity, quantity, and quality of both. Finally, the continuing dualistic way of thinking that separates humans from the environment, and that forces artificial and unhelpful separations among different disciplines of knowledge does not serve the issue of sustainability well. Clearly, to successfully negotiate the challenge of ensuring our long-term survival on this planet, we are going to need a different approach to all of the knowledge, learning, and wisdom available to us.

In sum, we may say that human activities are sustainable when they tend to maintain or increase sustainability at all biotic (genetic, species, ecosystem) and social (individual and collective) levels. It is also crucial to understand that an undertaking as great and difficult as global sustainability can work only in a world where all people feel that they have some stake in it, and where they are empowered to make choices and to take responsibility to achieve it.

The Meaning of Community Power

Tempted as we might be to rest with a combination of our understanding of development and sustainability, we still need to address the importance of planning — and particularly the question of *who* plans. I have argued that local sustainable development is key to achieving sustainability on a global scale. Community *participation* in planning may not be significant as such unless it also means that the local perspectives are a deciding force; in other words, what is really needed is community *power*. Those who advocate "community participation" in planning and implementation should understand that unless the least powerful community members are increasingly able to take part, it is probably not happening to a great enough extent to provide a real alternative to the status quo.

This primarily local focus and commitment to "the initiatives of the ordinary people" (Rahman 1992, 167) is key to implementing larger-scale strategies; it is not merely an afterthought. Global sustainability is such an enormous undertaking that the very possibility of achieving it requires building from the bottom up. In other words, everybody must be involved in meeting needs, building community, preserving our planet — in effect, making sure that there is a future. There is, quite simply, no other way to ensure environmental and social justice in our global activities. Nor are there any shortcuts to what is essentially a hard and painful process over (at least) the course of our lifetime. The Salinas activists' view of the importance of a local focus was eloquently presented in an editorial in the September 1994 edition of *Hoy desde Salinas:*

> We should invest energy in the organized communities so that they will be the ones responsible for the productive process, the decisions, the execution and distribution of the benefits of this region's economic activity. A development strategy for a community-based economy would be . . . based on the skills and needs of the people, not on corporations' needs for profit. . . . We are convinced that lasting, broad-based development of the lowest levels of society is principally achieved by promoting and strengthening community organizations. We must begin to construct from the bottom up: that is, from the community. Here are people willing to work, with their experience, with their talents, with their training, but even more, with a great desire to better themselves. . . . We call on governmental and private entities to collaborate in the birth of a new economy which permits the development, decision, and control over economic processes in order to satisfy the needs of this region's population. We invite all to harmonize the satisfaction of individual necessities with the provision of social necessities, and immediate needs with future needs.

Toward a Working Definition of Sustainable Development

At this point it seems fitting to offer a working definition of "sustainable development" that keeps the story of Salinas in mind as well as careful theoretical consideration — and remains subject, of course, to constant reevaluation in light of unfolding experience:

> Sustainable development involves locally based natural and human resource utilization that is shaped, directed, carried out, and evaluated primarily by the people of the community in question and takes forms that preserve and enhance both biotic and social diversity. Its success is measured by the degree to which the least powerful people can increasingly provide for their own needs through their own creative acts,

thus helping to reaffirm their human dignity, fulfill their potential, and share in the global responsibility for preserving life.

There are four main points to this definition: first, the maintenance of human diversity is just as important as maintaining ecological diversity. Second, development is measured by increasing empowerment of the least powerful and most marginalized people and communities, not necessarily by increasing GNP or "modernization." Third, this version of development is not restricted to the so-called Third World, but rather reflects an urgent global necessity. Finally, the question of scale must be answered: local, regional, or global? I believe a local focus should be the foundation of sustainable development, not the afterthought, because an undertaking as great and difficult as global sustainability can work only in a world where all people feel that they have some stake in it, and where they are empowered to make choices and to take responsibility to achieve it. Although no local program by itself can ultimately be successful without linking up to regional concerns, we need to fully recognize the importance of the local arena for most of the world's population; quite simply, people need to feel that they have some power, some control, right where they live.

Lessons of the Salinas Experience

The Salinas case study appears to offer some valuable lessons about the practical application of sustainable development. For example, for community-based strategies to germinate and grow, they must first be profoundly rooted in the geographic reality and the historical experiences of the community in question, and the leadership must be local and generally accepted as belonging there. Additionally, recognizing that communities may include people with different political, economic, and social perspectives, community-based leaders must strive to build coalitions among all who agree to work together for the good of the community. Then again, they should promote integrated and mutually supportive projects that take into account the relatedness of virtually all community-defined needs (such as employment, education, popular culture, recreation, infrastructure, health, and so forth).

With respect to the possibilities for implementing a strategy, Salinas's experience of economic and social marginalization has ironically created openings for the locally based strategy, because of the lack of outside or top-down competition. Should such competition materialize, however, more powerful arguments in favor of the community alternatives would have to gain much broader and more active community — indeed, island-wide — support in order to help prevent them from being swept away.

There are those who would criticize the emphasis on local strategies and community empowerment as naïve and utopian. Indeed, marginalized groups without control of their local resources — particularly if they have grown accustomed to dependence — do not seem likely to develop independent, sustainable alternatives in the face of the competing interests of corporate or state power. If we say that top-down strategies have not and will never work, for a variety of reasons (the profit motive, ignorance or lack of interest in local conditions and effects, exacerbation of dependence), then how can we make the local alternatives possible? It seems clear from the Salinas story that local leaders play a role that cannot be duplicated by outsiders. Those accepted as belonging to the community, who indeed have their roots and have their future invested right there, are most likely to understand the nature of the problems and to care most about the long-term effects of proposed solutions. And, although it may be true that one's own neighbors and family are not always reliable, people are usually more likely to support projects initiated by someone whom they already know. As elsewhere, the people of Salinas have grown cynical about promises made by powerful outsiders, which all too often have resulted in disappointment.

Their life experiences — education, travel, political work, migration — have proved to be a tremendous resource since the activists returned home, for they have gained understandings that allow them to envision alternatives, as well as the ability to lobby for them in a variety of settings. The initiatives are not being developed for their sakes, however, but rather for those of their neighbors who do not have the same experience or options. Clearly, the burden of responsibility cannot continue to be disproportionately borne by a small group of dedicated activists, but must be increasingly shifted to others. So local consciousness raising and mobilization are a particular challenge and responsibility for the local activists.

Some may criticize the Salinas activists for "settling for" investing their energy in cooperative local ventures that are able to win diverse support because they do not appear to politicize their participants or challenge the existing system. It is difficult, however, to see how popular politicization and effective systemic challenge can ever occur without first cementing the building blocks of individual and community empowerment. Such initiatives in themselves "do not challenge the limits within which they operate.... Yet they do plant the idea that alternatives are possible and thereby question the legitimacy of the boundaries set by the system" (Burawoy 1991, 286). Experience is teaching the local activists the value of patience and of taking the long-term view.

Even if the present Salinas initiatives should end in failure, however, the experience of activism and the search for alternatives would still be of great value. Ignacy Sachs might easily have had people such as the Salinas activists in mind when he wrote:

> What is the value of isolated and often futile experiments with another type of development? At least three reasons can be invoked in their favor. First, for those who participate in them, they constitute a social learning process of self-reliance and other values that challenge the prevailing ethics of individual mobility and greed. Second, while co-option cannot be ruled out, attempts at organizing locally for a better life are also a struggle for a redistribution of power between the civil society (the people), the state, and organized business in favor of the people. Third, time may come when scattered local movements will merge into coalitions capable of influencing the course of political life. (1984, vi)

The personal histories of the Salinas activists confirm observations elsewhere that community leaders have usually been involved in previous movements or actions, and have carried their politicization over into their current commitments (Oliver 1983; Hirschmann 1984); similarly, today's newly mobilized Salinas residents could possibly be leading local and islandwide movements in the future.

The activists recognize that most of their fellow salinenses will likely take a wait-and-see attitude toward the initiatives: for example, when asked in 1994 for his personal prognosis of the immediate future Nelson replied that all of the projects, and in particular the economic initiatives, were in a period of transition, and he estimated that "the next few years will define the movement, if it will offer an alternative or not. We will have to prove it with results." Unless the worker-owned enterprises can create local jobs, become self-supporting, and provide needed products or services, most locals are not likely to take the projects seriously. They are all too aware that the inability to obtain the resources necessary to implement initiatives comes from a lack of power, and that it is the combination of will and power that produces results.

The central problem of power has been recognized for some time. For example, in writing about "ecodevelopment" Glaeser identified

the missing link between theory and policy in ecodevelopment: the political situation in a country, its power structure. Since ecodevelopment requires change — economic and social change, change in lifestyles and attitudes — it will only be successful in more or less open and innovative environments, not in structurally conservative societies, no matter if they are located on the "right" or "left" hand of the traditional political spectrum.

. . . Ecodevelopment projects must include the power variable from the very beginning. Who has the power to mobilize resources, to corner benefits, to stall the process? If this analysis of obstacles is not an integral part of the project, it will, in all likelihood, go the way of the Green Revolution and will be perverted. Yet as far as we know there is still no general agreement upon the way to include a "power" factor in ecodevelopment.

In this sense, the concept is utopian, since it does not tell us how to get there. The route is at least as important as the destination. (1984, 35–36)

The Salinas experience lends force to the argument that it is not enough to know which natural and human resources are required to effect a workable development strategy. Believing that the primary shapers of any development strategy will also be its chief beneficiaries, one must also devise practical ways of getting into the hands of the community the power to control and direct the use of those resources. Whether the still evolving Salinas initiatives can broaden and deepen their support, both locally and throughout Puerto Rico, depends greatly upon local, national, and international factors that the local activists can scarcely foresee, much less control.

Where Do We Go From Here?

If locally controlled initiatives for sustainable development are necessary building blocks for global sustainability but do not have sufficient power or influence to obtain resources, then where can they come from? Here is where forces outside of the targeted groups have crucial roles to play. In Salinas local businesses, professionals, and government representatives have lent their support and provided material aid on numerous occasions, for example, offering materials and expertise to renovate La Rosada School, providing for summer school activities, and hiring a tutorial supervisor for the Brisas del Mar after-school program. Meanwhile, help has also been mobilized from outside Salinas to meet specific needs. Nonprofit organizations such as the Puerto Rico Foundation have funded some projects, while an investment by Banco Popular in the worker-owned enterprises would represent an appropriate contribution by outside capital. The airport workers' union has financially supported the newspaper, and community groups throughout the island have joined forces to lobby in San Juan. Government agencies have also offered crucial support; for example, the Department of Agriculture has provided the big boat necessary for the fishing program. Finally, concerned outsiders such as students, professionals, and even some government bureaucrats have devoted their free time to helping what one San Juan consultant called "one of the island's brightest hopes for a practical economic alternative at the community level." These examples illustrate some of the roles that outsiders can and should play. It is important to note that in contrast to prevailing notions of development, the local participants are not merely supplicants, but rather have a deciding voice in determining what is needed. By the same token the outsiders are not the primary decision makers or "experts," but instead provide resources for the local initiatives. The relationship is moving away from paternalism toward equality.

All of this is necessary in order to provide any hope of building a force strong enough to push the state to support (or at least not to obstruct) community initiatives instead of always favoring big moneyed interests. I am not alone in believing that the state has a crucial role to play in making initiatives like those of Salinas possible. For example, John Friedmann has for years written about the appropriate role of the "enabling" state (1992). This role includes incorporating local and regional plans, resolving contradictions, and if necessary, playing an "equilibrating role" (Friedmann 1978, 8), that is, transferring central resources to the poorer locations to help their projects succeed, in the hope of preventing mass migration to the wealthier areas. Friedmann recognized that "states don't usually act on their own initiatives. They have to be pressured, pushed and cajoled into new policies and forms of practice. Converting social into political power, therefore, will require concerted citizen action" (1987, 18). Concerned outsiders have a role to play in helping to provide access to information and other resources to facilitate network building at local, regional, national, even global levels. This next level in bottom-up organizing is crucial to the long-term success of Salinas-type projects, for it is "lateral linkages" that enable such groups "to gain the political clout necessary to make a difference on the political scene" (Friedmann and Salguero 1986, 29).

What about academics who are concerned not only with understanding sustainable development, but with helping to see it realized? Do they have a role to play beyond documenting history and formulating theory? When we review the kinds of resources that are available to academics, we see that they can potentially accomplish a great deal in support of community initiatives and popular networking. For example, access to extensive and varied sources of information can provide community activists with knowledge that they generally do not have the opportunity to gather for themselves. This knowledge might include information about similar community efforts, both domestic and foreign, that could inspire activists and that they, in turn, could compare and adapt to their own initiatives. New ideas for fundraising or tools for education, job creation, and networking are just a few of the many kinds of informational resources that are relatively simple for academics to obtain. Moreover, their status as recognized "experts" allows considerable access to (and sometimes, influence upon) some powerful government and private circles, which could be used to argue in support of community-based initiatives. Finally, academics teach students who may be directed toward working for community-based projects as part of their studies. This experience often proves to be significant, for some students later fill positions that directly impact upon community alternatives — or they may even begin similar programs back home.

In conclusion, although I argue that local sustainable development is the foundation for global sustainability, and although community participation in a significantly determining manner is necessary, I am not saying that it alone is sufficient. I would agree that, in view of the tremendous obstacles faced by marginalized people, "there remains a valid role for outsiders . . . that of facilitator(s) — assisting the emergence of capabilities where invited to do so" (Farrington and Bebbington 1993, 108). So-called communities of affinity have appropriate and necessary roles to play in ensuring that the local foundations of global sustainability are solid. Among other things, committed outsiders — particularly those with privileged social standing such as academics — can sometimes influence policy making in various ways; these include "interacting with the state to challenge the thinking behind . . . [traditional] programs, as well as helping build capacity at the grassroots so that . . . [community members] themselves exert pressure upon the state" (Bebbington and Thiele 1993, 199). The local foundations of global sustainability are made up of territorially based communities, and in particular of their least powerful members who, after all, represent the majority of humankind. To help in any way we can is not merely "correct"; if we care about the future, it makes sense.

Certainly, it would be naïve to downplay the great difficulties involved in such an undertaking. Nonetheless, it would be equally naïve to expect that the development strategies of the past will ever become more successful at meeting the needs of most people in the future. The Salinas experience points the way toward an alternative aimed at increasing the ability of poor people to control their destiny; but this alternative also needs the help that we are able to give. There are, of course, no guarantees of success; neither does this book in any way represent the last word on the subject. Given the failures of the dominant development paradigm, however, this book closes by suggesting that it is a bit late to restrict the development debate to asking whether locally based strategies for sustainable development are feasible. Rather, and in view of growing interest worldwide, it would be far more helpful to actively explore how to make possible community-directed, ecologically and socially sustainable alternatives.

Notes

Introduction

1. Many documents used for this study are available only in Spanish. Unless otherwise noted, all translations into English are my own.

1   Searching for Alternatives

1. See, for example, Ratzel (1896), Semple (1903, 1911), Huntington (1924), and Whitbeck (1926).

2. President of the Association of American Geographers R. H. Whitbeck taught that the apparent superiority of Latin America's European colonizers and of their enterprises to those of the non-European population proved that "place makes the race and then the [colonizing] race progressively remakes the [colonized] place" (1926, 11).

3. Biological racism still lives on through "sociobiology," and has influenced at least one popular book on inherited intelligence, *The Bell Curve* (Murray and Herrnstein 1994). For other examples of sociobiological works see Wilson 1978, Lopreato 1984, and Itzkoff 1991. For critical reviews see Barker 1982 and Lerner 1992.

4. Amin portrayed the essence of cultural racism as the equal ability of backward peoples to assimilate a superior culture, i.e., "the Black child raised in France becomes French" (1989, 97).

5. This theory also raises issues of gender; see Santiago-Valles 1994 on the feminization of colonized peoples.

6. Environmental, economic, and social effects of Operation Bootstrap are discussed in this book with reference to the case study area. For more general work about this program see Dietz 1986; Pantojas García 1990; and Muñoz Vásquez and García Martínez 1993.

7. The roots of such thinking may be traced to the development during the European Romantic period of the idea of "wilderness" — areas untouched by humans — as a reaction against utilitarianism (Oelschlaeger 1991; Simmons 1993).

2   The Geographical Setting

1. The Spanish word *municipio* may be described in Puerto Rico as a cross between a U.S. county and a municipality; each municipio is named for its principal town or city.

2. One cuerda = 0.97 acre. Older works on Puerto Rico in English often use *acre* as a direct translation of *cuerda*.

3. The Cayey Range is part of the Cordillera Central, the east-west mountain range that forms the spine of Puerto Rico's mountainous interior.

4. An estuary is a coastal area where fresh water mixes with the sea.

5. See, for example, Puerto Rico Environmental Quality Board 1972.

6. There are at least two sets of characteristics distinguishing a lagoon from a lake: first, lagoons are relatively shallow (between 1 and 10 meters) with a level profile, well permeated by light, and little thermic stratification; they are always located near the sea, and have some connection to the sea, often via underground channels. Second, lagoons contain abundant aquatic vegetation and organic material and consequently are zones of high biological productivity (Olivier 1988, 69).

7. There is also a community named Las Mareas (The Tides) in Guayama, near the Phillips Petroleum Refinery. All references, however, are to Las Mareas, Salinas, unless otherwise noted.

8. Sources for community population estimates include Diez Trigo 1988, Padín Bibiloni, Torres Rodríguez, and Maysonet Negrón 1981, and personal interviews. Sources for information on location, production, and employees of manufacturers include newsletters from the Puerto Rico Industrial Development Corporation, applications to the Environmental Quality Board for Emissions Sources, various Environmental Impact Statements and commentaries, and personal interviews.

9. *San Juan El Nuevo Día,* September 20, 1989, p. 3; *Salinas Hoy: Crónicas del Pueblo,* June 1989, p. 3, and September 1989, p. 3.

10. The source for these plans is a brochure and informational bulletin for the *Albergue Olímpico de Puerto Rico* (Puerto Rico Olympic Village).

11. Only some of the displaced farmers were relocated in Salinas. As in other rural areas, many were recruited for migrant agricultural labor in the United States. Salinas's population declined precipitously during the 1950s and 1960s, although it has steadily increased during the past twenty years. The migration question is discussed further in the following chapters.

12. Tata Santiago, "Antes comunidad: Ahora desolación." *Salinas Hoy,* July/August 1989, p. 10.

13. Sources include articles in *Salinas Hoy* (October 1991, February 1992) and various undated newspaper clippings, as well as interviews.

14. U.S. Army Corps of Engineers 1989; J. Laborde, Secretary, Puerto Rico Dept. of Natural Resources, to A. J. Salem, Chief, Planning Division of the U.S. Army Corps of Engineers (Jacksonville District), November 28, 1989; Maritza Díaz Alcaide, "DRN da jaque al Ejército," *San Juan El Mundo,* October 21, 1990, p. 1; Misión Industrial de Puerto Rico and Proyecto Caribeño de Justicia y Paz 1990.

15. This is explored in greater detail in Berman Santana 1996.

3   Exploitation

1. Danilo Cruz Miranda generously allowed access to his extensive documentation and notes for a historical guidebook of Salinas (in progress). Additional sources include Santiago Cruz 1941; Rodríguez Sosa 1970.

2. The British blockade of the slave trade effectively shut down shipments of Africans to Puerto Rico after 1840, and slavery was officially abolished in 1873; however, shipments to Cuba continued virtually until the abolition of slavery in 1886.

3. As of 1899, 91 percent of all cultivated land in Puerto Rico was owner-occupied, compared to 35 percent in Cuba. Nonetheless, only 2 percent of farms comprised 72 percent of all agricultural land, indicating that the bulk of the land was owned by a chosen few (Diffie and Diffie 1931, 21–22).

4. Enrique Vivoni Farage, "Encuentro cercano con la historia de una colonia azucarera." *El Nuevo Día,* Saturday, January 28, 1989, p. 60.

5. Sources for information on Central Aguirre are Danilo Cruz; articles for "Requiem para una Central" in the Sunday magazine of *El Mundo,* March 25, 1990; Central Aguirre Sugar Company, *Central Aguirre: Su historia,* n.d.; numerous newspaper articles.

6. Maritza Díaz Alcaide, "Del esplendor a la bancarrota." *El Mundo,* March 25, 1990, Sunday magazine.

7. Félix M. Ortiz, "Hace . . . ," *Salinas Hoy,* March/April, 1992, p. 17.

8. *San Juan Star,* July 2, 1970.

9. For a moving portrait of the life of a Puerto Rican sugar worker see Mintz 1974.

10. See chapter 6 for a brief history of El Coquí.

11. The high percentage of owner operatorship in Puerto Rico—though nearly three-quarters of the agricultural land was owned by 2 percent of owner-operators of farms—was soon to drop dramatically under U.S. occupation; the resulting jump in the rural population wholly dependent upon wage labor resulted in a huge labor surplus—favorable for low-wage agricultural production of export crops such as sugar cane.

12. The *agregados* were landless laborers who lived on sugar company property and were paid with company scrip; they were basically slaves of the sugar company. See the well-known ethnography by Mintz (1974) for a description in English of the Puerto Rican *agrego* system.

13. Danilo Cruz Miranda, "Alrededor de la agricultura," in the supplement on Salinas, *San Juan El Reportero,* October 10, 1981. Cruz attributes his interest in researching the 1920s (a decade virtually ignored by Puerto Rican historians) to stories told by his grandparents of repression and great fear among the people of Salinas following the 1920 Aguirre strike.

14. In 1932 the Socialist Party entered into a widely condemned electoral alliance with the pro-sugar Republicans (there was no historic connection with the U.S. political party of the same name).

15. The Nationalist Party had been formed in 1922, after the pro-political autonomy Union (later Liberal) Party eliminated the eventual goal of independence from its platform. Albizu Campos's ascendancy to the Nationalist party presidency in 1929 signaled its increasing militancy, for Albizu advocated armed struggle "if necessary" in the fight for independence.

16. Puerto Rican labor historians disagree about the importance of the ATP. Although the Taller de Formación Política (1982b) stressed that the ATP's islandwide appeal alarmed both Washington and the colonial government in San Juan, Quintero Rivera and García maintained that the ATP "died at birth" (1982, 110) because of its connection to the "petty bourgeois"–identified Nationalist Party. In any event, the ATP did not survive the 1930s as an organization.

17. A modest percentage of marginal sugar lands was subdivided and leased to landless rural workers, while some large holdings were purchased from their (Puerto Rican) owners and operated by the government as "proportional profit" farms (Cruz Baéz 1977, 41–42). For a more detailed discussion on the land reforms see Koenig 1953; Dietz 1986. Attempts to purchase land belonging to the large North American companies only succeeded in miring the Puerto Rican government in lengthy court proceedings. The holdings of the two largest firms, South Porto Rico and Central Aguirre, were not acquired until 1970, when the sugar operations of both corporations were already losing money.

18. The CGT was affiliated with the United States Congress of Industrial Organizations (CIO), in contrast to the FLT, which had been affiliated with the American Federation of Labor (AFofL) since the beginning of the twentieth century. The Communist Party also supported the PPD, for they saw in the new party possibilities for a broadly based front against imperialism; however, the *populares* publicly rejected Communist support (*El Imparcial,* January 9, 1940, p. 27; February 1, 1940, p. 2).

19. Pantojas García (1979, 93–95) gives an interesting analysis of the coalition building of the PPD leadership.

20. In addition, responding to clear indications that the U.S. military and political establishment opposed independence for the island, the PPD leadership forced out proindependence members in 1945; this led directly to the establishment the following year of the Puerto Rican Independence Party (PIP).

21. Sources for information about Caraballo include an article that appeared in the New York Spanish-language daily *El Diario-La Prensa* on February 16, 1978 (p. 8) upon the labor leader's death.

22. By 1966 the Aguirre Corporation had recognized SOUS as the exclusive representative of the workers (Collective Agreement between SOUS and Luce & Co. 1966–68, Article 1).

23. *Constitución y Reglamiento del Sindicato de Obreros Unidos del Sur de Puerto Rico,* 1964, Preamble, p. 7 (#21); Article 7, p. 21 (#6).

24. During the record production year of 1952, 12,500,000 tons of cane were harvested, yielding 1,360,000 tons of raw sugar on 390,000 cuerdas of land. That year

85,000 workers were employed and thirty-four sugar mills were in operation. Overall agricultural income that year was $185,836,000, of which sugar earned 52.24 percent. By 1972 sugarcane cultivation had dropped to 142,436 cuerdas of land (a 60.8 percent drop). Cane production had dropped 64.8 percent to 4,400,000 tons, rendering 295,000 tons of raw sugar (a 78.3 percent decline). The sugar industry employed 11,000 workers (an 87.5 percent drop) and operated fifteen sugar mills (down 55.9 percent)—many of which were operating at less than 50 percent capacity. Overall agricultural income in 1972 reached $301,950,000, of which sugar accounted for 11 percent (Cruz Baez 1977, 5–10). The tonnage and land planted to sugar cane continued its steady and precipitous decline. Nearly every year another *central* would close, lowering the milling capacity of the island, reducing the acreage planted to cane, and driving more sugarcane workers to the unemployment lines. In 1990, 68,086 tons of raw sugar were produced, worth $16,600,000, which represented 4.7 percent of income earned by agriculture; the tonnage had declined 25.4 percent from the previous year. The decrease was in part due to the closing of Salinas's Central Aguirre, one of the island's five remaining sugar mills, which had a daily milling capacity of 5,000 tons (Puerto Rico Planning Board 1990, chap. 7:7).

25. *El Mundo,* February 1, 1976; *San Juan Star,* July 2, 1970; *El Mundo,* August 4, 1970.

26. *El Mundo,* August 21, 1970; *El Mundo,* February 1, 1976; *El Nuevo Día,* December 10, 1976.

27. *El Mundo,* November 25, 1977, p. 6-A.

28. *El Mundo,* February 1, 1976.

29. *El Nuevo Día,* November 8, 1981; *Salinas Hoy,* various articles 1988–90.

30. *Salinas Hoy,* March 1990, p. 3; *El Mundo,* March 12, 1990.

31. *Salinas Hoy,* September 1989, p. 3.

32. *El Mundo,* April 18, 1990; *Salinas Hoy,* April 1990, July 1990.

33. Maritza Díaz Alcaide, "Del esplendor a la bancarrota." *Salinas Hoy,* September 1989).

34. *El Mundo,* May 6, 1990.

35. *Salinas Hoy,* July, 1990, p. 4; *El Nuevo Día,* December 31, 1991, p. 19.

36. According to Marx (1906, 232–33) low-organic-composition industries have a relatively low investment in fixed or constant capital, such as raw and auxiliary materials, machinery, and infrastructure, whereas their relative investment is high in variable capital (labor). By contrast, high-organic-composition industries invest very heavily in fixed capital, whereas their investment in variable capital is relatively low. See García Martínez 1978 for a descriptive analysis of low- and high-organic-composition industrialization in Puerto Rico.

37. Even so, "light" manufacturers characterized by low organic composition still provide 60 percent of Puerto Rico's manufacturing employment (Puerto Rico Planning Board 1991, chap. 5:2).

38. This comes from a mimeographed pamphlet the Puerto Rico Economic Develop-

ment Board put out in 1956 listing the types of factories established in Salinas; *San Juan El Vocero,* April 6, 1976, p. 10.

39. *El Nuevo Día,* November 8, 1981.

40. For a good review of the federal tax-exemption incentives that preceded Section 936, see Hernández 1985.

41. See Pantojas García 1990 for a detailed explanation of how section 936 increased benefits to U.S. corporations. The commonwealth incentives also stipulated that the percentage charged as a "tollgate" tax could be reduced if a certain amount of profits was invested in specified economic activities in Puerto Rico. According to economist Edwin Irizarry, historically most "936" enterprises have paid closer to 2 percent than to 10 percent of their profits, and in many cases have managed to avoid paying anything at all (*San Juan Claridad,* April 19–23, 1991, p. 7).

42. Pharmaceutical firms benefit in particular from the tax credit because of relatively low shipping costs for their products (compared with most other capital-intensive industries), as well as the ability to transfer product patents and trademarks to their Puerto Rican subsidiaries. Moreover, according to a U.S. Treasury Department study, in 1983 the tax savings to pharmaceuticals amounted to $57,761 per employee in Puerto Rico (Samborn 1991).

43. "Prescription for profit," *Caribbean Business,* February 21, 1991, p. 2.

44. American Home Products' closing of its Whitehall plant in Elkhart, Indiana, and its consequent transfer of production to Guayama has generated much publicity in the U.S. Congress and media. The Oil, Chemical, and Atomic Workers Union sued both A.H.P. and the Commonwealth government in Puerto Rico, under the federal Racketeer-Influenced Corrupt Organizations (RICO) civil statute, in which wide-scale fraud was charged through transferring "runaway" plants to Puerto Rico for tax benefits ("RHC administration hit with $1 billion suit," *San Juan Star,* February 26, 1992). Meanwhile, Indiana congressional representatives led the fight to modify and restrict tax exemptions under section 936, in an effort to prevent runaway plants (Samborn 1991).

45. Information was obtained in an interview with the firm's president on April 15, 1992, as well as from an article in *Salinas Hoy* (November 1991, p. 2).

46. In 1980 24.3 percent of employed Salinas residents worked outside of the municipio, whereas 23.5 percent of Salinas' jobs were held by nonresidents (Puerto Rico. Economic Development Administration 1985).

47. For detailed descriptions and analyses of the environmental effects of industrialization in Puerto Rico see Concepción 1990, Muñoz and García Martínez 1993, and other cited works.

48. See Commoner 1976 for information about the relationship between electric energy production and pollution. For similar work using Puerto Rico as the case study, see various cited articles by Tomás Morales.

49. Puerto Rico would therefore appear to have much in common with other "national sacrifice areas"—poor and ethnic minority neighborhoods, indigenous reservations, small Pacific dependencies, poor "ex-colonial" states—that receive dispropor-

tionate amounts of industrial and toxic wastes from the richer and more powerful industrialized countries. This may help explain the great similarity of Puerto Rico's mainstream environmental movement to environmental justice organizations, rather than to the "wilderness preservation" orientation typical of mainline "First World" groups (FitzSimmons and Gottlieb 1988).

50. *Salinas Hoy,* February 1991, p. 3. According to the Environmental Quality Board Application for Emissions Source (submitted in 1989) the refinery emits 25,725.45 tons of sulfur dioxide per year into the atmosphere.

51. Such emissions are not adequately controlled because the facility's development was well underway before July 1, 1970, the effective date for the Puerto Rico Public Environmental Policy Act. (According to comments on the draft environmental impact statement published by the Puerto Rico Environmental Quality Board "the decision to build a power plant complex at the Aguirre site, on Jobos Bay, antedates the current era of environmental concern" (1972, 1).

52. Substances identified by the EPA Hazard Code as acute health hazards are highly toxic, corrosive, irritants, or sensitizers. Chronic or delay health hazards are carcinogenic or toxic to blood, kidney, liver, lungs, nervous system, reproductive system, eyes, or skin.

53. Environmental Quality Board Application for Emissions Sources, 1989.

54. Substances admittedly released into the atmosphere include TDF (trifluoroperzine), HCT (hydrochlorotiazide) and athenolol. The plant synthesizes athelonol, acetate, cimetidine, HCT, and TDF; acetone and isopropyl alcohol are recovered for reuse as well.

55. List of dangerous chemical substances prepared by SK&F Labs and sent to the Puerto Rico Environmental Quality Board on October 15, 1987, in compliance with the Federal Occupational Safety and Health Act (OSHA) and section 311 of the Superfund Amendments and Reauthorization Act (SARA) of 1986; Application to Environmental Quality Board for Emissions Source, February 22, 1991; *Salinas Hoy,* February 1991, p. 2.

56. Memorandum, Servicios Legales de Puerto Rico, Guayama, August 25, 1983; "Contaminación asesina," in *Impacto* (Guayama), August 17, 1988, p. 4; *Salinas Hoy,* February 1991, p. 2.

57. According to the U.S. Army Corps of Engineers (1980) most of the island's waters violate existing water quality standards.

58. Jobanes reserve (personal communication).

59. *Salinas Hoy,* June/July 1991, p. 2.

60. Puerto Rico Dept. of Labor, cited in *San Juan Star,* February 25, 1992, pp. B1–2.

4 Resistance

1. Many writers prefer to use the terms *emigration* or *diaspora,* because of the great differences between migrating within one's own land and moving to a country with a different language, customs, history, and ethnic makeup (see for example Maldonado

Denis 1982, 7). It should be borne in mind that as mostly nonwhite Latin Americans and Caribbeans, Puerto Ricans face racial, cultural, and linguistic barriers in the United States that are scarcely eased by their being U.S. citizens. The term *circular migration* is used here because of the prevalence of "commuter-type" movement between the island and the mainland.

2. It should be noted that although Puerto Ricans on the island do not pay federal taxes or have federal voting representation, as U.S. citizens they are subject to the draft.

3. The PSP is not related to the Socialist Party that existed in Puerto Rico in the early twentieth century.

4. *El Nuevo Día,* November 7, 1978. Lack of preventive maintenance for the units appears to have been AEE policy for some time (Misión Industrial, *Notiambiente* 1991, no. 8).

5. *El Mundo,* October 14, 1978, p. 16A; *El Nuevo Día,* November 8, 1978; *El Mundo,* October 18, 1978.

6. Some information on the counterintelligence war against Puerto Rican union leaders and independentistas is recounted in Churchill 1988. Other details, such as the planting by police intelligence agents of weapons and explosives in a labor leader's car during a 1978 strike against the AEE (*El Nuevo Día,* February 26, 1992, p. 22), were revealed as a result of the Puerto Rico Senate's investigation during the early 1990s of the 1978 Cerro Maravilla murders and subsequent government cover-up.

7. The struggle began during the 1950s, after the expropriation of lands by the U.S. military in coastal areas such as Vieques, Culebra, Ceiba, Naguabo and Aguadilla resulted in communities being denied access to coastal resources. Privatization of coastal areas for tourist development first ran into opposition during the 1960s in Vacía Talega/Piñones, just east of San Juan. Activists in Vieques were the first to bring in fishermen from throughout Puerto Rico to lend support to their protests, beginning in the 1950s but continuing intermittently up to the present. During the 1970s the Puerto Rican Socialist Party (PSP) ran an islandwide campaign known as "Beaches for the People," in which fishermen, students, and others were mobilized islandwide for campaigns in specific areas (Neftali García Martínez, personal communication 1992).

8. *Hoy desde Salinas,* October/November 1994.

9. *El Imparcial,* August 21, 1970, p. 1; *El Imparcial,* August 21, 1976; *San Juan Star,* August 3, 1974, p. 3; *El Nuevo Día,* January 3, 1976.

10. *El Imparcial,* March 17, 1972; *El Nuevo Día,* July 23, 1971; *El Imparcial,* March 11, 1972.

11. *El Imparcial,* April 6, 1972; *El Imparcial,* March 11, 1972, p. 1.

12. *El Imparcial,* May 15, 1972.

13. "Ubicarían empresa en Sudeste," *El Mundo,* November 13, 1970, pp. 1, 8.

14. Environmental Research and Applications. Summary of the preliminary environmental impact statement, prepared for the Monsanto Corporation, February 1978, p. 13.

15. *El Mundo,* October 5, 1978.

16. Not mentioned publicly was that Monsanto had plans to build a port on the Caribbean just west of Las Mareas. Estimates of land and water use, as well as the quantities of wastes to be discharged in the sea, were all larger than what the proposed plant would require, according to the environmentalist organization Misión Industrial (*El Mundo,* November 16, 1978, p. 8-A).

17. *San Juan Star,* October 27, 1978.

18. Opposition to the Monsanto plant in Las Mareas crossed party lines. The president of the Las Mareas Pro-Health Committee, Felix Burgos, also chaired the community's PPD chapter; meanwhile, the leader of the PNP chapter supported the activities of the local group against Monsanto. (Minutes of the meeting of the Las Mareas Pro-Health Committee, September 10, 1978).

19. A number of island government agencies also expressed reservations about the Monsanto project, including the Department of Agriculture, the Water Resources Authority (known as AAA), and the Environmental Quality Board. The Caribbean Office of the U.S. Soil Conservation Service also went on record as opposing the plant. Meanwhile, the then-opposition Partido Popular Democrático opposed the project and charged that the PNP-led central government's support for Monsanto represented a conflict of interest.

20. *San Juan Star,* August 30, 1978.

21. Burgos, personal communication 1991.

22. *El Mundo,* September 30, 1978.

23. *San Juan Star,* October 1, 1978.

24. Richard Fielitz, President, SK&F Labs, Inc., to Kenneth Eng, EPA Region II Chief, Air and Environmental Applications Section, June 25, 1979.

25. Soon after, Monsanto constructed an overseas plant in Ireland.

26. *El Mundo,* August 1, 1979, p. 1; *San Juan Star,* October 1, 1978, p. 40.

27. Nelson Santos provided much information on the Jobos Bay Corporation.

28. In recent years decision-making power in Misión Industrial has broadened to include significant community representation.

29. Sources for information on the campaign against the regional toxic waste landfill include articles in *Salinas Hoy* (October and December, 1990, and March and August, 1991), as well as personal observation.

30. But see chapter 5 about another proposal for a regional toxic landfill in 1994, which appears to have more political support and less public input.

31. *Clarín,* March 11, 1970; *El Militante,* August 1, 1972 (both local newsletters); interviews with Nelson Santos and Danilo Cruz Miranda.

32. *Salinas Hoy,* March 1991.

33. *Hoy desde Salinas,* July 1994.

34. Environmental Quality Board, reference #DL-75-003, case# Q.QG.72-0047, "Orden de cese y desistimiento y de no hacer."

35. *United States of America v. Guillermo Godreau et al.* Civil Suit #77-173, filed January 25, 1977.

36. Letters from the Department of Natural Resources to the Environmental Quality Board (February 18, 1988), the Planning Board (February 12, 1988), and the U.S. Army Corps of Engineers (January 30, 1988).

37. Puerto Rico Employment and Training Administration, Department of Housing. Labor Market Information Newsletter: Salinas Labor Area (1980).

38. *Salinas Hoy*, June/July 1991, p. 3. It should be recalled that by law all of Puerto Rico's coastline is public property; in practice open access is often denied in areas where luxury development is taking place.

39. *Salinas Hoy*, February 1991, p. 8.

40. Unsigned personal letter recounting the developer's experience battling local opposition to the marina, dated November 20, 1990.

41. Indeed, in 1989 ten islets near Cayo de Ratones known as "Cayos de la Barca" were put up for sale for the sum of $792,000.

42. For good analytic and historical reviews of liberation theology see Rubenstein and Roth 1988; Brown 1990.

5 Beyond Resistance

1. Interview in *Salinas Hoy*, October 1988, p. 11

2. The mass emigration of poor Puerto Ricans to the United States during the 1940s and 1950s debilitated all organizations not sponsored by or subservient to the PPD. Many Salinas residents emigrated to the United States; El Coquí was particularly affected by mass emigration. (On Puerto Rican emigration, see the History Task Force 1979.)

3. Like *bomba, plena* is a popular African-based music and dance form native to the coastal regions of Puerto Rico.

4. *Hoy desde Salinas*, December 1994, p. 10.

5. The Puerto Rican independence movement, the independent labor movement, and the Left in general have been subjected to intense and systematic repression and negative propaganda by both the United States and Puerto Rican governments since the 1940s. This repression intensified during the 1970s and has been documented in a number of books, articles and reports. See, for example, Churchill and Vander Wall 1988; Mari Bras, "Un apartheid ideológico," in *Claridad*, February 21–27, 1992.

6. *Hoy desde Salinas*, December 1994, p. 15.

7. Comité Comunal Playa y Playita, "Proyectos Unidos en el Desarrollo de Salinas." First draft of a proposal, February 1992.

8. *Hoy desde Salinas*, September 1994, pp. 8–9.

9. *Salinas Hoy*, February 1990, p. 4.

10. The verb *emparejarse* could be translated as "to become equal; to match up or pair up; to bring to the same level." *University of Chicago Spanish English, English-Spanish Dictionary*, 3d ed.

11. *Hoy desde Salinas*, October/November 1994, pp. 3, 8–9; December 1994, p. 2.

12. Ibid., December 1994, p. 4.

13. Ibid., September 1994, pp. 8–9.

6 The Obstacles

1. *Hoy desde Salinas,* July, September, October/November 1994.

2. Ibid., October/November 1994, p. 4.

3. Yet, the *popular* majority assembly also opposed the facility. At least one *popular* assembly member opposed the project because of the environmental and health risks, and did not particularly care what the party leadership thought. Perhaps not surprisingly, this person also has become heavily involved with the activism in Salinas, and lost the 1992 elections to a PNP-supported neighbor (who also was involved in the local initiatives).

4. *Hoy desde Salinas,* September 1994, p. 4.

7 Lessons of the Salinas Experience

1. Personal communication, March 1994.

Author's Note

Portions of text in chapters 1 and 6 appear also in Déborah Berman Santana, "Geographers, Colonialism, and Development Strategies: The Case of Puerto Rico," *Urban Geography* 17, no. 5 (1996): 456–74.

Bibliography

Abbad y LaSierra, Frau Iñigo
  1979 *Historia Geográfica, Civil y Natural de Puerto Rico*. Río Piedras: Ed. Universitaria.
Almond, Gabriel
  1960 *The Politics of the Developing Areas*. Princeton: Princeton University Press.
Amin, Samir
  1989 *Eurocentrism*. New York: Monthly Review Press.
Anderson, Victor
  1991 *Alternate Economic Indicators*. London: Routledge.
Antrobus, Peggy
  1989 The Empowerment of Women. In *Women and International Development Annual*, edited by R. S. Gallin, A. Aronoff, and A. Ferguson. Boulder, Colo.: Westview Press.
Baran, Paul
  1957 *The Political Economy of Growth*. New York: Monthly Review Press.
Barker, Martin
  1982 *The New Racism: Conservatives and the Ideology of the Tribe*. Frederick, Md.: Aletheia Press.
Bebbington, A., and G. Thiele
  1993 *Non-Governmental Organizations and the State in Latin America: Rethinking Roles in Sustainable Agricultural Development*. New York: Routledge.
Berman Santana, Déborah
  1996 Geographers, Colonialism, and Development Strategies: The Case of Puerto Rico. In *Urban Geography*. Forthcoming.
Blauert, Jutta, and Marta Guidi
  1992 Strategies for Autochthonous Development: Two Initiatives in Rural Oaxaca, México. In *Grassroots Environment Action: People's Participation in Sustainable Development*, edited by D. Ghai and J. M. Vivian. New York: Routledge.
Blaut, J. M.
  1992 The Theory of Cultural Racism. In *Antipode* 24(4):289–99.

Boserup, Ester

    1970   *Women's Role in Economic Development.* New York: St. Martin's Press.

Brown, Robert McAfee

    1990   *Gustavo Gutiérrez: An Introduction to Liberation Theology.* Maryknoll, N.Y.: Orbis Books.

Burawoy, Michael

    1991   *Ethnography Unbound: Power and Resistance in the Modern Metropolis.* Berkeley and Los Angeles: University of California Press.

Cadilla, José

    1977   Recursos naturales de Puerto Rico. In *Geovisión de Puerto Rico: Apuntes recientes sobre el estudio de geografía,* edited by M. T. Blanco de Galiñanes. Río Piedras: Ed. Universitaria.

Centro de Estudios Puertorriqueños

    1980   *Manos de la Obra: The Story of Operation Bootstrap* (filmscript). New York: Hunter College of the City University of New York.

Chase, Stuart

    1951   *Operation Bootstrap in Puerto Rico: Report of Progress.* Washington, D.C.: National Planning Association.

Chenery, Hollis

    1979   *Structural Change and Development Policy.* Oxford: Oxford University Press.

Churchill, Ward, and Jim Vander Wall

    1988   *Agents of Repression: The F.B.I.'s Secret War against the Black Panther Party and the American Indian Movement.* Boston: South End Press.

Commoner, Barry

    1976   *The Poverty of Power: Energy and the Economic Crisis.* New York: Knopf.

Concepción, Carmen M.

    1988   El Conflicto Ambiental y su Potencial hacia un Desarrollo Alternativa: El Caso de Puerto Rico. In *Ambiente y Desarrollo* 4(1–2):135–45.

    1990   *Environmental Policy and Industrialization: The Politics of Regulation in Puerto Rico.* Ph.D. diss., University of California, Berkeley.

Cossey, Keith M.

    1990   *Co-operative Strategies for Sustainable Communities: Community-based Development Organizations.* New Brunswick: Rural and Small Town Research and Studies Programme.

Cruz Baez, Ángel D.

    1977   *Export Agriculture under Economic Development: A Geographical Analysis of the Decline of Sugarcane Production in Puerto Rico.* Ph.D. diss., University of Wisconsin.

Cruz Miranda, Danilo

    1978   La Monsanto y su Impacto en Salinas. Unpublished manuscript.

de la Court, Thijs
> 1990   *Beyond Bruntland: Green Development in the 1990s.* New Jersey: Zed Press.

Deere, Carmen Diana, ed.
> 1990   *In the Shadow of the Sun: Caribbean Development Alternatives and U.S. Policy.* Boulder, Colo.: Westview Press.

Dietz, James
> 1986   *Economic History of Puerto Rico: Institutional Change and Capitalist Development.* Princeton, N.J.: Princeton University Press.

Diez Trigo, Sarah
> 1988   *Pueblos de Puerto Rico.* Río Piedras: La Biblioteca.

Diffie, W., and J. W. Diffie
> 1931   *Porto Rico, a Broken Pledge.* New York: Vanguard Press.

DuBois, W.E.B.
> 1969   *The Souls of Black Folk.* 1903. Reprint, New York: New American Library.

Ekins, Paul
> 1992   A Four-Capital Model of Wealth Creation. In *Real-life Economics: Understanding Wealth Creation,* edited by P. Ekins and M. Max-Neef. New York: Routledge.

Environmental Research and Applications
> 1978   *Agricultural Chemicals Plant, Aguirre, P.R.* San Juan: Preliminary Environmental Impact Statement for Monsanto Caribe, Inc.

Escobar, A., and S. Álvarez, eds.
> 1992   *The Making of Social Movements in Latin America: Identity, Strategy, and Democracy.* Boulder, Colo.: Westview Press.

Fanon, Franz
> 1965   *The Wretched of the Earth.* 1963. Reprint, New York: Grove Press.
> 1967   *Black Skins, White Masks.* New York: Grove Press.

Farrington, John, and Anthony Bebbington
> 1993   *Reluctant Partners? Non-Governmental Organizations, the State and Sustainable Agricultural Development.* New York: Routledge.

FitzSimmons, Margaret, and Robert Gottlieb
> 1988   A New Environmental Politics. In *Reshaping the U.S. Left: Popular Struggles in the 1980s,* edited by Mike Davis and Michael Sprinkler. London: Verso.

Frank, A. G.
> 1966   The Development of Underdevelopment. *Monthly Review* 18(4):17–31.

Friedmann, John
> 1978   *Basic Needs, Agropolitan Development, and Planning from Below.* Los Angeles, Calif.: Graduate School of Architecture and Urban Planning, University of California, Los Angeles.

1987　*From Social to Political Power: Collective Self-Empowerment and Social Change*. Los Angeles: Graduate School of Architecture and Urban Planning.

1992　*Empowerment: the Politics of Alternative Development*. Cambridge, Mass.: Blackwell.

Friedmann, John, and Mauricio Salguero

1986　*The Barrio Economy and Collective Self-Empowerment in Latin America: A Framework and Agenda for Research*. Los Angeles: School of Architecture and Urban Planning, University of California, Los Angeles.

García Martínez, Neftalí

1972　*Puerto Rico y la Minería*. Río Piedras: Ed. Librería Internacional.

1978　Puerto Rico Siglo XX: Lo Histórico y lo Natural en la Ideología Colonialista. *Pensamiento Crítico* 8:1–28.

1984　"Apuntes para una historia de la lucha ambiental." Manuscript.

Garrett, William R.

1988　Liberation Theology and Dependency Theory. In *The Politics of Latin American Liberation Theology: The Challenge to U.S. Foreign Policy*, edited by Richard L. Rubenstein and John K. Roth. Washington, D.C.: The Washington Institute Press.

Gaskins Alcott, Jorge (Comité Contra Monsanto)

1978　Afectados versus Actores: Hacia el Desarrollo Comunitario del Área de Jobos. Unpublished manuscript.

Gil-Bermejo García, Juana

1970　*Panorama Histórica de la Agricultura en Puerto Rico*. Sevilla: GEHA.

Glaeser, Bernhard

1984　*Ecodevelopment: Concepts, Projects, Strategies*. New York: Pergamon Press.

Goodman, D., and M. Redclift, eds.

1991　*Environment and Development in Latin America: The Politics of Sustainability*. Manchester, Eng.: Manchester University Press.

Goulet, Denis

1971　Development . . . or Liberation? *International Development Review* 13(3): 6–10.

1974　*A New Moral Order: Studies in Development Ethics and Liberation Theology*. Maryknoll, N. Y.: Orbis.

1975　*The Cruel Choice: A New Concept in the Theory of Development*. New York: Atheneum.

Grant, Linda

1993　*Sexing the Millennium: Women and the Sexual Revolution*. New York: Grove.

Gudynas, Eduardo

1990　The Search for an Ethic of Sustainable Development in Latin America. In *Ethics of Environment and Development: Global Challenge, International*

Response, edited by J. Ronald Engel and Joan Gibb Engel. Tucson: University of Arizona Press.

Haines, Lundberg, and Wahler/Division of Regional and Community Planning
1968   *The Preservation of Agricultural Land in Puerto Rico.* San Juan: Puerto Rico Planning Board.

Haire, William J.
1971   Floods in the Salinas Area, Puerto Rico. In *Hydrologic Investigations Atlas HA-447.* Washington, D.C.: U.S. Geological Service.

Hanson, Earl Parker
1962   *Puerto Rico, Ally for Progress.* Princeton, N.J.: Van Nostrand.

Healy, David
1988   *Drive to Hegemony: The United States in the Caribbean, 1898–1917.* Madison: University of Wisconsin Press.

Hernández Cruz, Juan E.
1982   *A Perspective on Migration: The Circulation of Puerto Rican Workers.* Ph.D. diss., New York University.

Hernández, José Luís
1985   ¿Qué Son las Corporaciones 936? *Pensamiento Crítico,* no. 42.

Hill, Robert
1899   *Notes on the Forest Conditions of Porto Rico.* Washington, D.C.: U.S. Government, Division of Forestry, Bulletin No. 25.

Hirschmann, Albert O.
1984   *Getting Ahead Collectively.* New York: Pergamon Press.

History Task Force, Centro de Estudios Puertorriqueños
1979   *Labor Migration under Capitalism: The Puerto Rican Experience.* New York: Monthly Review Press.

Hofstadter, R.
1955   *Social Darwinism in American Thought.* Rev. ed. Boston: Beacon Press.

Huntington, Ellsworth
1924   *Civilization and Climate.* New Haven: Yale University Press.

Hurwitt, Robert
1994   Visions: Gretchen Daily. *Mother Jones,* November/December, 21–24.

Itzkoff, Seymour
1991   *Human Intelligence and National Power: A Political Essay in Sociobiology.* New York: P. Lang.

Iverson, David, and Zane Corbett
1994   A Definition of Sustainability for Ecosystem Management. *Eco-watch,* July 7, 1994.

Jackson, Peter
1987   A 'Permanent Possession'? U.S. Attitudes toward Puerto Rico. In *Race and Racism: Essays in Social Geography,* edited by P. Jackson. London: Allen & Unwin.

Jobanes (Jobos Bay Natural Reserve)

    1989   *Boletín Oficial.* 10, no. 2 (Nov./Dec.).

Koenig, Nathan

    1953   *A Comprehensive Agricultural Program for Puerto Rico.* U.S. Dept. of Agriculture and the University of Puerto Rico.

Kruijer, Gerald

    1987   *Development through Liberation: Third World Problems and Solutions.* Basingstoke, Eng.: Macmillan.

Landsberg, Martin

    1979   Export-led Industrialization in the Third World: Manufacturing Imperialism. *Review of Radical Political Economics* 11(4):50–63.

Lélé, Sharachchandra M.

    1991   Sustainable Development: A Critical Review. *World Development* 19(6): 607–21.

Leopold Aldo

    1978   *A Sand County Almanac: With Essays on Conservation from Round River.* 1978. Reprint, New York: Ballantine Books.

Lerner, Daniel

    1958   *The Passing of Traditional Societies: Modernizing the Middle East.* New York: Free Press.

Lerner, Richard

    1992   *Final Solutions: Biology, Prejudice, and Genocide.* University Park: Pennsylvania State University Press.

Levinson, Jerome, and Juan de Onís

    1972   *The Alliance That Went Astray: A Critical Report on the Alliance for Progress.* Chicago: Quadrangle.

Lewis, W. Arthur

    1950   The *Industrialization of the British West Indies. Caribbean Economic Review* 2, no. 1 (May): 1–61.

    1955   *The Theory of Economic Growth.* London: Allen & Unwin.

López Montañez, Wilfredo, and Marianne Meyn

    1989   Modelo de Desarrollo Capitalista y Destrucción Ambiental. In *La Situación Ambiental en Centroamérica y el Caribe,* edited by Ingemar Hedstrom. San José, Costa Rica: D.E.I.

Lopreato, Joseph

    1984   *Human Nature and Biocultural Evolution.* Boston: Allen & Unwin.

Lutz, Mark

    1992   Humanistic Economics: History and Basic Principles. In *Real-Life Economics: Understanding Wealth Creation,* edited by P. Ekins and M. Max-Neef. New York: Routledge.

Maas, Bonnie
  1976   *Population Target: The Political Economy of Population Control in Latin America.* Toronto: Latin American Working Group.

Maldonado Denis, Manuel
  1980   *Puerto Rico, una Interpretación Histórico-Social.* México: Siglo XXI.
  1982   *Puerto Rico y Estados Unidos: Emigración y Colonialismo.* México: Siglo XXI.

Mann, Arthur
  1985   Economic Development, Income Distribution, and Real Income Levels: Puerto Rico, 1953–1977. *Economic Development and Cultural Change* 1(3): 485–502.

Mari Bras, Juan
  1992   Un Aparteid Ideológico. *Claridad,* February 21–27.

Martínez de La Jara, Nydia
  1975   Repartimiento de Terrenos Baldios en el Pueblo de Salinas Durante el Siglo XIX. *Anales de Investigación Histórica* 2(2):48–60.

Martínez, Isidro, Raquel Torres Llauger, Julio E. Nevárez, and Cristino Ruiz.
  1991   Incidencia de Cancer por Municipios en Puerto Rico. *Boletín de la Asociación Médico de Puerto Rico* 83(6).

Martinez-Alier, J.
  1991   Ecological Perception, Environmental Policy and Distributional Conflicts: Some Lessons from History. In *Ecological Economics: the Science and Management of Sustainability,* edited by R. Costanza. New York: Columbia University Press.

Marx, Karl
  1906   *Capital: A Critique of Political Economy.* Vol. 1. New York: Modern Library.

Massol, Alexis
  1984   El Plan 2020: Nueva Estratégia Económica para Puerto Rico. *Pensamiento Crítico* 7(40):1–14.

McClymonds, N. E., and P. E. Ward
  1966   *Hydrologic Characteristics of the Alluvial Fan near Salinas, Puerto Rico.* Washington, D.C.: U.S. Geological Survey Professional Paper 550-c: C231–C234.

Meadows, Donella
  1972   *The Limits to Growth: A Report by the Club of Rome Project on the Predicament of Mankind.* New York: Universe.

Meléndez, Arturo
  1982   *La Batalla de Vieques.* Río Piedras: Ed. Edil.

Memmi, Albert
  1991   *The Colonizer and the Colonized.* 1965. Reprint, New York: Orion.

Meyer, Judy L., and Gene S. Helfman
 1993   The Ecological Basis of Sustainability. *Ecological Applications* 3(4):569–71.
Midgely, James
 1986   *Community Participation, Social Development, and the State.* London: Methuen.
Mintz, Sidney W.
 1974   *Worker in the Cane.* New York: Norton.
 1985   *Sweetness and Power: The Place of Sugar in Modern History.* New York: Viking Penguin.
Misión Industrial de Puerto Rico, and Proyecto Caribeño de Justicia y Paz
 1991   *¡Por la Paz y la Defensa de los Recursos Naturales, Culturales y el Medio Ambiente! ¡No al Uso de Terrenos para Entrenamiento Militar!* San Juan: Special Joint Publication.   ·
Morales Cardona, Tomás
 1979   *Renewable and Nonrenewable Natural Resources of Puerto Rico.* Lecture at the Woodrow Wilson School, Princeton University, April 5, 1979.
 1990   *Deficit en el Derecho Ambiental a Finales del Siglo XX.* Presented at the First Symposium on Law and Environmental Health, Puerto Rico Lawyer's Guild, January 1990.
Morales Cardona, Tomás, Víctor Sánchez Cardona and Pier Luigi Caldari
 1975   The Struggle for Puerto Rico: How to Undevelop an Island. *Environment* 17(4):34–40.
Morales Carrión, Arturo
 1983   *Puerto Rico, a Political and Cultural History.* New York: W. W. Norton.
Moreno, Nelson, and Víctor Vásquez
 1991   *Investigación del Caso Escuela Secondaria Ramona Mendoza Santos, Bo. Puente Jobos, Guayama: Primera Etapa.* San Juan: Environmental Quality Board.
Morris, Gregg
 1979   Water Supply Implications: Proposed Monsanto Facility at Jobos, Puerto Rico. Unpublished manuscript.
Moser, Caroline O. N.
 1989   Community Participation in Urban Projects in the Third World. *Progress in Planning* 23:71–133.
Muñoz Vásquez, M., and N. García Martínez
 1993   *The Relationship between Poverty, Deteriorating Health Status, and Industrial Pollution in Puerto Rico.* Hato Rey: Centro de Información, Investigación, y Educación Social.
Murray, Charles, and Richard Herrnstein
 1994   *The Bell Curve: Intelligence and Class Structure in American Life.* New York: Free Press.

Nieves Falcón, Luís

1985a   La Pobreza en Puerto Rico: Demitología de la Vitrina. In *Del Cañaveral a la Fábrica: Cambio Social en Puerto Rico,* edited by Eduardo Rivera and Rafael L. Ramírez. Río Piedras: Ed. Huracán.

1985b   The Social Pathology of Dependence. In *Puerto Rico: the Search for a National Policy,* edited by Richard Bloomfield. Boulder, Colo.: Westview Press.

Norgaard, Richard

1992   Coevolution of Economy, Society, and Environment. In *Real Life Economics: Understanding Wealth Creation,* edited by P. Ekins and M. Max-Neef. New York: Routledge.

1994   Environmental Forum Lecture, University of California, Berkeley, November 11, 1994.

O'Connor, Martin

1989   Political Economy of Ecology of Socialism and Capitalism. *Capitalism, Nature, Socialism: A Journal of Socialist Ecology* No. 3:93–106.

Oelschlaeger, Max

1991   *The Idea of Wilderness: From Prehistory to the Age of Ecology.* New Haven: Yale University Press.

Oliver, Pamela

1983   The Mobilization of Paid and Volunteer Activists in the Neighborhood Movement. *Research in Social Conflict and Social Change* 5: 133–70.

Olivier, Santiago Raúl

1988   *Ecología y Subdesarrollo en América Latina.* México: Siglo XXI.

Padín Bibiloni, Carlos

1990   *El Uso de Terrenos en Puerto Rico: Efectos de estos Cambios en el Agua.* Paper presented at the Seventh Annual Symposium on Island Ecological Systems, Inter-American University, Río Piedras, October 26, 1990.

Padín Bibiloni, Carlos, Marianela Torres Rodríguez, and Carlos Maysonet Negrón

1981   *Plan de Uso de Terrenos para el Área de la Bahía de Jobos.* M.A. Thesis, Graduate School of Planning, University of Puerto Rico.

Palmer, J. R.

1991   *What Should Sustainability Look Like?* Address given at the World Resources Institute Conference on Sustainability in Natural Tropical Forest Management, Washington, D.C., March 21, 1991.

Pantojas García, Emilio

1979   Estrategias de Desarrollo y Contradicciones Ideológicas en Puerto Rico: 1940–1978. *Revista de Ciencias Sociales* 21(1–2):73–117.

1990   *Development Strategies as Ideology: Puerto Rico's Export-led Industrialization Experience.* Boulder, Colo.: Lynne Rienner.

Pearce, D.

   1992   Economics, Equity and Sustainable Development. In *Real-life Economics: Understanding Wealth Creation*, edited by P. Ekins and M. Max-Neef. New York: Routledge.

Peet, Richard

   1985   The Social Origins of Environmental Determinism. *Annals of the Association of American Geographers* 75(3):309–33.

Perloff, Harvey

   1950   *Puerto Rico's Economic Future*. Chicago: University of Chicago Press.

Picó, Fernando

   1988   *Historia General de Puerto Rico*. Río Piedras: Ed. Huracán.

Picó, Rafael

   1974   *Geography of Puerto Rico*. Chicago: Aldine.

Presser, Harriet

   1973   *Sterilization and Fertility in Puerto Rico*. Berkeley: Institute of International Studies, University of California.

Pringle, George G.

   1969   A Temporal-Spatial Analysis of Sugar Production and Marketing in Puerto Rico. Ph.D. diss., University of Wisconsin.

Puerto Rico. Department of Labor and Human Resources; Bureau of Statistics.

   1990   *Empleo y Desempleo en Puerto Rico: Promedio Años Fiscales 1989–90 y 1988–89*.

Puerto Rico. Department of Natural Resources (DRN)

   1978   *Plan Integral de Uso, Conservación y Desarrollo de los Recursos de Agua en Puerto Rico* (draft). Office of Planning and Analysis of Water Resources.

Puerto Rico. Department of Natural Resources, and U.S. Department of Commerce. National Oceanic and Atmospheric Administration

   1983   *Jobos Bay National Estuarine Sanctuary: Management Plan*.

Puerto Rico. Economic Development Administration (Fomento)

   1975   *Competitive Position of Manufacturing Industries* (draft). Prepared for the Development Strategies Committee, E.D.A., by Hugh Barton Associates.

   1985   *La Movilidad Laboral en Puerto Rico*. Mimeograph.

   1988   *Community Profile for Guayama Area*. Office of Economic Research.

   1991   *Situación Industrial: Municipio de Salinas*. Oficina de Estudios Económicos, Division de Economía General. Sección de Estadísticas.

Puerto Rico. Environmental Quality Board

   1972   *Comments on Draft Environmental Impact Statement for Aguirre Power Plant Complex*.

Puerto Rico. Highway Authority

   1986   *Proposed Relocalization of PR#3, Salinas-Guayama Section*. Supplement to the Environmental Impact Statement.

Puerto Rico. Office of Energy

1979   La Situación Energética de Puerto Rico en el Año Fiscal 1979. Office of the Governor.

Puerto Rico. Planning Board

1955   *Municipio de Salinas: Memoria Suplementaria al Mapa de Límites del Municipio y sus Barrios.*

1974   *Preliminary Master Plan for Land Use 1985–2020.*

1985   *Informe Social.*

1988   *Indicadores Socioeconómicos por Municipio 1987.*

1989   *Informe Económico al Gobernador 1988.*

1990   *Informe Económico al Gobernador 1989.*

1991   *Informe Económico al Gobernador 1990.*

Puerto Rico. Planning Board. Water Resources Authority.

1973   *Annual Report 1971–72.*

Quintero Rivera, A. G., and Gervasio García

1982   *Desafío y Solidaridad: Breve Historia del Movimiento Obrero Puertorriqueño.* Río Piedras: Ed. Huracán.

Rahman, Anisur

1992   People's Self-Development. In *Real-life Economics: Understanding Wealth Creation,* edited by P. Ekins and M. Max-Neef. New York: Routledge.

Ramos, Julio

1992   *Amor y Anarquía: Los Escritos de Luisa Capetillo.* Río Piedras: Ed. Huracán.

Ratzel, F.

1896   *History of Mankind.* Translated from the German by A. J. Butler. London: Macmillan.

Redclift, Michael

1992   *Sustainable Development: Exploring the Contradictions.* New York: Routledge.

Redfield, Robert

1941   *The Folk Culture of Yucatán.* Chicago: University of Chicago Press.

Richardson, Bonham

1989   Caribbean Migrations, 1838–1985. In *The Modern Caribbean,* edited by Franklin W. Knight and Colin A. Palmer. Chapel Hill: University of North Carolina Press.

1992   *The Caribbean in the Wider World, 1492–1992: A Regional Geography.* Cambridge: Cambridge University Press.

Rodríguez Sosa, Sergio

1970   Notas para una Historia de Salinas. Unpublished manuscript.

Rodríguez, Octavio

1980   *La Teoría del Subdesarrollo de la* CEPAL. México: Siglo XXI.

Rostow, Walter

 1960   *The Stages of Economic Growth: A Non-Communist Manifesto.* Cambridge: Cambridge University Press.

Rubenstein, Richard L., and John K. Roth, eds.

 1988   *The Politics of Latin American Liberation Theology: The Challenge to U.S. Foreign Policy.* Washington, D.C.: The Washington Institute Press.

Sachs, Ignacy

 1984   Developing in Harmony with Nature: Consumption Patterns, Time and Space Uses, Resource Profiles, and Technological Choices. In *Ecodevelopment: Concepts, Projects, Strategies,* edited by Bernhard Glaeser. New York: Pergamon Press.

 1987   *Development and Planning.* New York: Cambridge University Press.

Sachs, Wolfgang

 1992   Poor Not Different. In *Real-life Economics: Understanding Wealth Creation,* edited by P. Ekins and M. Max-Neef. New York: Routledge.

Said, Edward

 1979   *Orientalism.* New York: Random House.

Samborn, Randall

 1991   Plant Shutdowns: Hundreds of Closings Provoke Legal Struggle. *National Law Journal* 13, no. 47 (July 29).

Santiago Cruz, Aguedo

 1941   Salinas al Través de Cien Años. *Puerto Rico Ilustrado,* September 6.

Santiago Valles, Kelvin A.

 1994   *'Subject Peoples' and Colonial Discourses: Economic Transformation and Social Disorder in Puerto Rico, 1898–1947.* Albany: State University of New York Press.

Scott, Robert E.

 1973   *Latin American Modernization Problems.* Urbana: University of Illinois Press.

Semple, Ellen Churchill

 1903   *American History and Its Geographical Conditions.* Boston: Houghton and Mifflin.

 1911   *Influences of Geographical Environment on the Basis of Ratzel's Anthropogeography.* New York: Russell and Russell.

Sherbourne, J. C.

 1972   *John Ruskin or the Ambiguity of Affluence.* Cambridge Mass.: Harvard University Press.

Silén, Juan Ángel

 1978   *Apuntes: Para la Historia del Movimiento Obrero Puertorriqueño.* Río Piedras: Ed. Cultural.

Simmons, I. G.
  1993   *Interpreting Nature: Cultural Constructions of the Environment.* New York: Routledge.
Sismondi, J.C.L.S. de
  1991   *First Principles of Political Economy.* Translated by Richard Hyse. New Brunswick, N.J.: Transaction Books.
Slater, David, ed.
  1985   *New Social Movements and the State in Latin America.* Amsterdam: CEDLA.
Spoehr, Alexander
  1956   Cultural Differences in the Interpretation of Natural Resources. In *Man's Role in Changing the Face of the Earth,* edited by William Thomas, Jr. Chicago: University of Chicago Press.
Stokke, Olav, ed.
  1991   *Sustainable Development.* Portland: Frank Cass.
Streeten, Paul
  1981   *Development Perspectives.* New York: St. Martin's Press.
Taller de Formación Política (TFP)
  1982a   *¡Huelga en la Caña! 1933–34.* Río Piedras: Ed. Huracán.
  1982b   *La Cuestión Nacional: El Partido Nacionalista y el Movimiento Obrero Puertorriqueño.* Río Piedras: Ed. Huracán.
Todaro, Michael
  1985   *Economic Development in the Third World.* New York: Longman's.
UNIPRO Architects, Engineers and Planners
  1988   *Supplement to the Environmental Impact Statement: I.C.I. Pharmaceuticals P. R., Inc., Guayama P. R.* Project No. 87068.
United Nations
  1981   *Popular Participation as a Strategy for Promoting Community Level Action and National Development.* New York: United Nations Press.
United Nations. World Commission on Environment and Development (WCED)
  1987   *Our Common Future.* New York: Oxford University Press.
United States. Agency for International Development
  1993   Sustainable Development and the Counter-Narcotics Strategy: Transition to New Realities. In *Andean Counter-Drug Initiative, Objective IV.* Semi-Annual Report (October 1992–March 1993).
United States. Army Corps of Engineers
  1977   *Ponce Regional Water Resources Management Study Summary.* San Juan Office, Jacksonville District.
  1980   *Island-Wide Water Supply Study for Puerto Rico: Executive Study.* San Juan Area Office, Jacksonville District
  1989   *Draft Environmental Assessment, Off-Post Army Training at Sixteen Sites in Puerto Rico.* Jacksonville District.

1990 *Reconnaissance Report: Rio Nigua at Salinas, Puerto Rico.* San Juan Office, Jacksonville District.

United States. Department of Agriculture: Soil Conservation Service and University of Puerto Rico, College of Agricultural Sciences

1977 *Soil Survey of Humacao Area of Eastern Puerto Rico.* National Cooperative Soil Survey.

United States. Department of the Interior

1951 *Point Four in Action.* Washington, D.C.: Government Printing Office.

United States. Environmental Protection Agency (EPA)

1988 *Superfund National Priority Lists, Puerto Rico Sites.* Washington, D.C.: Government Printing Office.

Valle Ferrer, Norma

1990 *Luisa Capetillo: Historia de una Mujer Proscrita.* Río Piedras: Ed. Huracán.

Vázquez, Angie

1994 Análisis Teórico del Cambio Social en la Familia Contemporánea Puertorriqueña. *Hómines* 17(1–2):141–47.

Vidal, Julio

1985 Dependency, Regional Inequality and the Role of the State: Puerto Rico 1950–1982. Ph.D. diss., State University of New York-Albany.

Wessman, James W.

1977 Demographic Evolution and Agrarian Structure of a Sugar Cane Region in Puerto Rico. Ph.D. diss., University of Connecticut.

Whitbeck, R. H.

1926 Presidential Address. *Annals of the Association of American Geographers* 16(1):1–11.

Wilson, E. O.

1978 *On Human Nature.* Cambridge, Mass.: Harvard University Press.

Yapa, Lakshmann

1993 What Are Improved Seeds? An Epistemology of the Green Revolution. *Economic Geography* 69(3):254–73.

Zavala Martínez, Iris

1993 Subjectividad y Construcción Social de la Violencia en Puerto Rico. In *Análisis, Reflexión, y Acción Psicológica ante la Violencia y la Criminalidad en Puerto Rico,* edited by L. E. Maldonado and B. E. Rivera. Río Piedras: AEPPR.

Index

About the Author

A veteran of the New York City public school system, Déborah Berman Santana spent years working in a variety of minimum-wage jobs and played jazz piano professionally. She earned her doctorate in geography at the University of California, Berkeley. Currently Assistant Professor in the Department of Ethnic Studies at Mills College in Oakland, California, she has created and taught courses on development theory, environmentalism, Latin America and the Caribbean, colonialism and globalization, and California. Recent publications reflect her research interests, which include the role of racism and colonialism in shaping developmentalist and environmentalist thought, the importance of human diversity for global sustainability, and the interactions among academic research, policy-making, and activism.